HEIDEGGER AND JASPERS ON NIETZSCHE:

HEIDEGGER AND JASPERS ON NIETZSCHE:

A CRITICAL EXAMINATION OF HEIDEGGER'S AND JASPERS' INTERPRETATIONS OF NIETZSCHE

by

RICHARD LOWELL HOWEY

MARTINUS NIJHOFF / THE HAGUE / 1973

PRINTED IN THE NETHERLANDS

TABLE OF CONTENTS

ACKNOWLEDGMENTS

The author wishes to thank the following publishers and copyright holders for their permission to use quotations from the material listed below:

George Allen & Unwin: *The Complete Works of Friedrich Nietzsche*, by Friedrich Nietzsche, edited by Oscar Levy and compiled by Robert Guppy, copyright, 1964; William Barrett: "Plato's Doctrine of Truth," in *Philosophy in the Twentieth Century*, by Martin Heidegger, translated by John Barlow, copyright, 1962 by Random House Inc.; Basil Blackwell & Mott LTD: *Being and Time*, by Martin Heidegger, translated by John Macquarrie and Edward Robinson, copyright, 1962; Bobbs-Merrill Company, Inc.: *The Use and Abuse of History*, by Friedrich Nietzsche, translated by Adrian Collins, copyright, 1957; and "Discourse on Method," in *Discourse on Method, Optics, Geometry and Meteorology*, by Rene Descartes, translated by Paul J. Olscamp, copyright, 1965; Cambridge University Press: *Early Religious Poetry of Persia*, by James Hope Moulton, copyright, 1911; J. M. Dent & Sons: "Nietzsche and Schopenhauer," in *Egotism in German Philosophy*, by George Santayana, copyright, 1916; Doubleday & Co., Inc.: *Either/Or*, 2 vols., by Søren Kierkegaard, translated by Walter Lowrie, copyright, 1959; Duquesne University Press: "The Language of the Event: The Event of Language," in *Heidegger and the Path of Thinking*, by Theodore Kisiel, edited by John Sallis, copyright, 1970; Faber & Faber: *Four Quartets*, by T. S. Eliot, copyright, 1943; Farrar Straus & Giroux: "Introduction," in *Karl Jaspers' Reason and Existenz*, by William Earle, copyright, 1960; and *Reason and Existenz*, by Karl Jaspers, translated by William Earle, copyright, 1960; Verlag Anton Hain KG: *Edmund Husserl: Versuch einer systematischen Darstellung seiner Phänomenologie*, by Alwin Diemer, copyright, 1956; Carl Hanser Verlag: *Werke in drei Bänden*, by Friedrich Nietzsche, edited by Karl Schlechta, copyright, 1954; Harcourt Brace Jovanovich, Inc.: *Four Quartets*, by T. S. Eliot, copyright, 1943; and *The Great Philosophers*, by Karl Jaspers edited by Hannah Arendt, translated by Ralph Manheim, copyright, 1966; Harper & Row Publishers: *Nietzsche*, by Martin Heidegger, copyright, 1961; "Who Is Nietzsche's Zarathustra?," in *The Review of Metaphysics*, vol. XX, no. 3, by Martin Heidegger, translated by Bernard Magnus, copyright, 1967; *What Is Called Thinking?*, by Martin Heidegger, translated by Fred D. Wieck and J. Glenn Gray, copyright 1968; "Splendor of the Simple," in *On Understanding Violence Philosophically and Other Essays*, by J. Glenn Gray, copyright, 1970; Harvard University Press: "Introductory Quotation," in Wilfrid Desan's *The Tragic Finale: An Essay on the Philosophy of Jean-Paul Sartre*, by Maurice Rostand, copyright, 1960; Hogarth Press LTD: "Thoughts for the Times on War and Death," and "On the History of the Psycho-Analytic Movement," in vol. XIV of the Standard Edition of *The Complete Psychological Works of Sigmund Freud*, revised and edited by James Strachey, copyright, 1957; Holt, Rinehart & Winston, Inc.: *Nietzsche the Thinker: A Study*, by William Mackintire Salter, copyright, 1917; Johnsen Publishing Company: *Theories of Ethics*, by William H. Werkmeister, copyright, 1961; Longman Group LTD: *From Exorcism to Prophecy: The Premisses of Modern German Literature*, by Michael Hamburger, copyright, 1965; Macmillan Company: *Nietzsche as Philosopher*, by Arthur C. Danto, copyright, 1965; McGraw-Hill Book Company: From "Nietzsche," in *Biographic Clinics*, copyright, 1904, P. Blakiston's Son and Co. Used with permission of McGraw-Hill Book Company; Mrs. Ernest Newman: *The Life of Richard Wagner*, by Ernest Newman, copyright, 1946, by Alfred A. Knopf; Martinus Nijhoff: *Heidegger: Through Phenomenology to Thought*, by William J. Richardson, Preface by Martin Heidegger, copyright, 1963; Northwestern University Press: *The Anatomy of Disillusion: Martin Heidegger's Notion of Truth*, by William B. Macomber, copyright, 1967; Open Court Publishing Company: "Jaspers' Relation to Nietzsche," in *The Philosophy of Karl Jaspers*. The Library of Living Philosophers, copyright, 1957, Tudor Publishing Co. Now published by the Open Court Publishing Company; Princeton University Press: *Nietzsche: Philosopher, Psychologist, Antichrist*, by Walter Kaufmann (third revised and enlarged edition, copyright (c) 1968 by Princeton University Press); and *The Collected Works of C. G. Jung*, ed. by G. Adler, M. Fordham, and H. Read, translated by R. F.

C. Hull, vol. 7, *Two Essays in Analytical Psychology* (copyright (c) 1953 and 1966 by Bollingen Foundation), reprinted by permission of Princeton University Press; Quadrangle Books, Inc.: "Ontological Autobiography," in *Phenomenology in America*, edited by James M. Edie, copyright, 1967; Random House, Inc.: *Beyond Good and Evil: Prelude to a Philosophy of the Future*, by Friedrich Nietzsche, translated by Walter Kaufmann, copyright, 1966; *The Birth of Tragedy and the Case of Wagner*, by Friedrich Nietzsche, translated by Walter Kaufmann, copyright, 1967; *The Philosophy of Nietzsche*, by Friedrich Nietzsche, edited by Willard Huntington Wright, copyright, 1954; and *The Will to Power*, by Friedrich Nietzsche, translated by Walter Kaufmann and R. J. Hollingdale, copyright, 1967; Henry Regnery Co.: *Philosophy in the Tragic Age of the Greeks*, by Friedrich Nietzsche, translated by Marianne Cowan, copyright 1962; *Schopenhauer as Educator*, by Friedrich Nietzsche, translated by James W. Hillesheim and Malcolm R. Simpson, copyright, 1965; and *Nietzsche and Christianity*, by Karl Jaspers, translated by E. B. Ashton, copyright, 1967; Routledge and Kegan Paul: *Man and His Values*, by William Henry Werkmeister, copyright, 1967; Charles Scribner's Sons: "Phases of Nietzsche," in *Egoists: A Book of Supermen*, by James Huneker, copyright, 1910; Frederick Ungar Publishing Co.: *The Existentialist Revolt*, by Kurt Reinhardt, copyright, 1960; University of Arizona Press: Reprinted from *Nietzsche: An Introduction to the Understanding of His Philosophical Activity*, by Karl Jaspers, translated by Wallraff and Schmitz, copyright, 1965; University of Nebraska Press: *Man and His Values*, by William Henry Werkmeister, copyright, 1967; The Viking Press, Inc.: *The Portable Nietzsche*, by Friedrich Nietzsche, selected and translated, with an introduction, prefaces, and notes by Walter Kaufmann, copyright, 1967; Yale University Press: *Introduction to Metaphysics*, by Martin Heidegger, translated by Ralph Manheim, copyright, 1959.

INTRODUCTION

Every philosopher presents special problems of interpretation. With Nietzsche these problems are especially crucial. The very richness of Nietzsche's thought and expression becomes a trap for the incautious or imaginative mind. Perhaps the greatest temptation for the interpreter of Nietzsche is to attempt to "systematize" his thought into a consistent whole. Any such attempt necessarily results in distortion, for there is a fluidity in Nietzsche's thought which does not lend itself to strict categorization. This is not to deny that there are certain organic patterns in his philosophy. These patterns emerge, however, as Jaspers correctly insists, only upon careful, critical comparison of pertinent passages drawn from the entire corpus of Nietzsche's works. No single passage can be taken as a definitive statement of Nietzsche's views of any particular subject. Frequently, by presenting two or three especially relevant quotations from the author being considered, a critic can support the correctness of his interpretation. With Nietzsche, however, such a procedure is inadequate, for in many cases other passages can be found which will support an alternative, if not opposite, interpretation. Nor is this difficulty alleviated by vast compilations of relevant passages, for then one could gain just as much, and quite likely more, from re-reading Nietzsche's works themselves. Thus, a compromise must be effected. The interpreter of Nietzsche must *weigh* each remark of Nietzsche not only with regard to its actual context within the work, but with regard to the context of all of Nietzsche's other utterances on the same subject as well. Only in this way can the interpreter arrive at an understanding which truly represents Nietzsche's basic thought, and only thus will he be able to present those inconsistencies which truly belong to Nietzsche. These inconsistencies are important, for they point up certain basic diffi-culties in Nietzsche's general program of philosophizing.

Another difficulty inevitably encountered in interpreting Nietzsche is one of emotional involvement. No matter how clearsightedly one begins, there is the continual temptation either to agree ecstatically or to reject vociferously. In fact, it is almost impossible to remain indifferent to Nietzsche, to be "neutral" or "objective." Nietzsche's very manner of philosophizing demands a response; the problem is so to direct that response that it is not *merely* a personal response, but a genuine philosophical response as well.

Every interpretation of Nietzsche presupposes a particular orien-tation or disposition toward Nietzsche's thought as a whole. This disposition will condition the final conclusions and evaluations and it is therefore essential in a critical study such as the one here undertaken that we examine the fundamental dispositions with regard to their adequacy from the many perspectives and aspects of Nietzsche's thought itself. That an inadequate or distorted disposition can lead to a distortion of the basic character and structure of Nietzsche's work is beyond question. The distortion and misuse of Nietzsche's thought by Stefan George and his disciples – especially Ernst Bertram, but also Gundolf – is a case in point. And the Nazi distortions in the manner of Baeumler are so well known that they require no elucidation here. Such orientations are designed to *make use* of Nietzsche's thought rather than to *understand* it. It is different in the case of Jaspers and Heidegger. Still, even when considering the Nietzsche interpretations of Jaspers and Heidegger we shall have to examine the basic dispo-sitions of these authors toward Nietzsche's thought and we shall have to consider also the question as to whether Heidegger and Jaspers are trying to make use of Nietzsche's thought for purposes of their own. It ought to be made clear here that it is possible *both* to understand *and* to use Nietzsche's thought. However, we should maintain a healthy suspicion for any and every attempt to use Nietz-sche's thought for the justification of some position which lies es-sentially outside the context of Nietzsche's thought itself. Thus, the main purpose of the present study is to present a critical examination of the Nietzsche interpretations of Heidegger and Jaspers, and then, from that basis, to present the outline of alternative interpretation.

SPECIAL PROBLEMS IN JASPERS'
NIETZSCHE INTERPRETATION

Jaspers is most helpful regarding the problems of his method of approach to, and his basic disposition toward, Nietzsche's thought, for he devotes almost twenty pages at the beginning of his Nietzsche book to these topics. Jaspers' most basic attitude is that no single mode of approach to Nietzsche's thought is by itself adequate. An adequate interpretation for Jaspers is one which is based on an examination of the entire corpus of Nietzsche's writing, the published works, the letters, and the posthumous fragments, without giving undue emphasis to any part or aspect. "It must be realized that none of Nietzsche's forms of communication has a privileged character."[1] Regarding the posthumous material (*Nachlass*) Jaspers does not agree with either Schlechta or Heidegger. Schlechta states, "I omit the already published posthumus material, because to my knowledge no *new* central thought is to be found there."[2] On the other hand, Heidegger claims, "What Nietzsche himself published during the period of his creativity remains always a foreground .... The genuine philosophy remains behind as 'posthumous material'."[3] Jaspers again presents a very balanced view and sees in the posthumous material "a fragmentary kind of thinking which constantly brings forth something new from inexhaustible wealth."[4] However, he immediately adds the cautionary remark, "Nowhere is Nietzsche's work truly centralized; there is no *magnum opus*. On the other hand, what is essential to his thought is also discernible particularly in what seems incidental and secondary."[5]

Jaspers also objects to interpretations which attempt to subsume Nietzsche under some category, such as poet, modern pre-Socratic, or prophet. Nietzsche is to be regarded primarily and most importantly as a philosopher. Every great philosopher is a unique, individual event, and every attempt to classify and categorize his thought is at best an oversimplification.

---

[1] Karl Jaspers, *Nietzsche: An Introduction to the Understanding of His Philosophical Activity*, trans. Charles F. Wallraff and Frederick J. Schmitz (Tucson, 1966), p. 5.

[2] Friedrich Nietzsche, *Friedrich Nietzsche: Werke in drei Bänden*, ed. Karl Schlechta (Munich, 1956), III, 1433, my translation.

[3] Martin Heidegger, *Nietzsche* (2 vols.; Pfullingen, 1961), I, 17, (my translation). All translations from Heidegger are mine unless otherwise indicated.

[4] Jaspers, *Nietzsche*, p. 5.

[5] *Ibid.*, p. 5.

Genuine interpretation, however, does not subsume but penetrates; it does not claim to know with finality; but, while always taking cognizance of what has just been apprehended, it proceeds by a method of questioning and answering.[6]

This remark gives us also the important clue that Jaspers' method is to be understood as a dialectical examination of Nietzsche's thought. Such a dialectic will (ideally) proceed expositorily and critically. In following Jaspers' dialectical investigations we shall have to examine continually his expositions for adequacy and his criticisms for appropriateness and accuracy.

Jaspers insists, as does Nietzsche himself, that any interpretation must be based on a careful reading of the works, which is not merely a reading but a meditating along with Nietzsche. In a section titled "Principles of Interpretation," Jaspers asserts that there can be no final interpretation of Nietzsche's thought. He stresses the process character of genuine interpretation; he sees the methodology of interpretation primarily as a laying open of essential questions. This questioning becomes the guide to an understanding of Nietzsche's thought, even though we cannot answer these questions "once and for all."

What Nietzsche means can never be assimilated by a will to possess the truth in fixed and final form but only by a will to truth which rises from the depths and strives toward the depths, which is prepared to encounter all that is questionable, is not closed to anything, and is able to wait.[7]

Here one is reminded of a similar remark which Heidegger makes at the very end of *Introduction to Metaphysics* with regard to questioning. "To know how to question means to know how to wait, even a whole lifetime." [8] While it is quite true that we should be suspicious of interpretations which make claims of correctness with dogmatic finality, it is equally true that we should be suspicious of interpretations which leave fundamental questions up in the air without even a tentative attempt at resolution.

Jaspers, in this same section on interpretation, puts forth six theses regarding an adequate approach to Nietzsche. First of all, Jaspers argues, Nietzsche is fundamentally a philosopher of contradiction. For nearly every statement he makes a counterstatement can be found.

---

[6] *Ibid.*, p. 6.
[7] *Ibid.*, p. 9.
[8] Martin Heidegger, *Introduction to Metaphysics*, trans. Ralph Manheim (New Haven, 1959), p. 206.

In any case, it is the task of the interpreter to be forever dissatisfied until he has *also* found the contradiction, to search out contradictions in all their forms, and then, if possible, to gain direct experience of their necessity. Instead of being provoked by contradiction, one should pursue contradictoriness to its source.[9]

As appealing as this thesis is, there remains the question as to whether these contradictions are really at the heart of Nietzsche's thought and not simply superficial or apparent contradictions. Jaspers' position that *"self-contradiction* is the fundamental ingredient of Nietzsche's thought" contains several difficulties.[10] His position here suggests a sententially reductive approach which, it seems, over-emphasizes the particular at the expense of the general theses of Nietzsche. This approach seems reductive in another sense also, in the sense, namely, that it tends to impose a "logical" structure on Nietzsche's thought. Here it would seem that Nietzsche's own description of his philosophy as "perspectivism" is more appropriate and not fraught with the reductive difficulties of the notion of "logical contradiction." This becomes especially apparent when the so-called contradictions are examined in context, for one discovers then that the differences are precisely "contextual differences" and provide simply an additional or new perspective. This is, of course, not to say that there are no genuine contradictions in Nietzsche's thought. Some of these contradictions play an important role in the development of Nietzsche's philosophy. We shall have occasion later to examine this problem of contradiction in some detail.

Jaspers' second point is that any adequate interpretation must systematically examine the many repetitions. In this way one discovers all of the variations and modifications concerning any one topic and also discovers those topics which Nietzsche treats in only one passage. Again, it would seem that this point is more consonant with an interpretation based on the idea of perspectivism rather than contradiction.

Thirdly, Jaspers asserts that by looking for contradictions, through the juxtaposition of Nietzsche's ideas, one is able to arrive at the "real dialectic" of Nietzsche's thought. Jaspers sees this dialectic as a kind of "logical" analysis.

But it [the dialectical clarification] cannot be attained simply through logical insight alone; it really occurs only insofar as an expansion and illumination of the realm of possible Existenz takes place. Whoever lacks the patience to labor

---

[9] Jaspers, *Nietzsche*, p. 10.
[10] *Ibid.*, p. 10.

over logical and substantive connections and has no leeway in his soul for the abundance of possibilities cannot read Nietzsche with comprehension.[11]

Jaspers here uses the word "Existenz" in his own technical sense with a series of connotations and associations which are intimately related to the central core of his philosophy. We shall have occasion later to inquire into Jaspers' meaning of *"Existenz"* and also to raise the crucial question of the relation between a set of concepts peculiar to Jaspers and Jaspers' use of these concepts in his interpretation of Nietzsche. For the moment it is sufficient to note that Jaspers does attempt to use such concepts to elucidate Nietzsche.

Jaspers' fourth point is ambiguous. He insists that Nietzsche's philosophy can be grasped as a whole. However, as Jaspers points out:

This whole is not a concept, a world-view, or a system, it is the passion of the quest for being, together with its constant overcoming through relentless criticism, as it rises to the level of genuine truth.[12]

Yet, at the same time, he asserts that this whole is inexhaustible. If Jaspers simply means that this "passion of the quest for being" provides a psychological continuity for the development of Nietzsche's thought, this is not especially informative nor does it provide grounds for distinguishing Nietzsche from many other philosophers. On the other hand, if Jaspers is talking about a whole from the point of view of metaphysics and epistemology, then it would seem that this whole is a set of related concepts which describe a world-view, even if not a perfectly consistent one. In fact, on the very next page Jaspers presents this very view: "the idea of a *timeless systematic whole* becomes our guide as we search for the timeless position of each thought and for the architechtonic of the system itself." [13]

Fifthly, Jaspers maintains that any examination of Nietzsche's thought requires a close correlation with the events in Nietzsche's life. Nietzsche himself supports this idea when he says:

It has gradually become clear to me what every great philosophy up till now has consisted of – namely, the confession of its originator and a species of involuntary and unconscious autobiography.[14]

Jaspers devotes practically a fifth of his book directly to Nietzsche's life and in the rest of the book he demonstrates in impressive fashion

[11] *Ibid.*, p. 11.
[12] *Ibid.*, p. 11.
[13] *Ibid.*, p. 12.
[14] Friedrich Nietzsche, *Beyond Good and Evil* in *The Philosophy of Nietzsche*, ed. Willard H. Wright (New York, 1954), p. 386.

the inextricable relation between Nietzsche's life and thought. Heidegger's position on this point is somewhat different, as we shall presently discover.

Finally, Jaspers demands a study of the "systematic interrelations" of Nietzsche's thoughts. Here Jaspers' use of the term "systematic" must be understood in a limited sense, for ultimately he rejects the idea that any single absolute system can be derived from the works of Nietzsche.

In the study of Nietzsche the unity of the whole, i.e., of life and thought, of temporal development and timeless system, can only be the guiding *idea*, for Nietzsche's thinking will always elude all attempts at a well-ordered presentation. It is impossible to foresee how far one will get, objectively speaking, in an attempt to obtain a definite and well-substantiated conception of the whole .... What provides the irresistibly compelling agitation in the study of Nietzsche is precisely this ever-recurring difficulty: neither of these ways makes sense when taken separately while both, taken together, cannot be brought into complete harmony.[15]

Two other major problems still remain. Jaspers argues that any adequate interpretation necessarily involves an adequate presentation, which goes beyond criticism in that it attempts to present the dialectical movements of the subject itself. He adds:

A presentation attempts to efface its own thinking in favor of that which is presented; it must not use its subject as an occasion for any philosophizing of its own. Such thinking is a constant endeavor to yield completely to the thinking of the other person; it is thinking which seeks simply to present what someone else has thought.[16]

Here Jaspers has explicitly provided us with a powerful criterion of adequacy, and it is one which we shall apply to Jaspers himself.

The final problem pertains to the relation of the interpreter to truth. Nietzsche presents a doctrine of the essential ambiguity of truth. In one respect, truth, for Nietzsche, is dependent upon passion. Truth is not capable of being grasped by the intellect alone; it must be seized through the senses, and one must come to understand that all truth is a becoming and, therefore, only a perspective, a partial truth. Thus, according to Jaspers, the interpreter of Nietzsche must attempt to see with Nietzsche's eyes and feel with Nietzsche's passion. Any such attempt must, of course, fail in any final sense, since we are necessarily limited by our own experiences and passions. Thus, an attempt to "present" Nietzsche necessarily becomes an existential

15 Jaspers, *Nietzsche*, p. 13.
16 *Ibid.*, p. 14.

dialogue with Nietzsche, which is a self-discovery as well as a discovery of Nietzsche.

Our task is to become ourselves by appropriating Nietzsche. Instead of yielding to the temptation to take the apparent univocality of doctrines and laws as proof of their universal validity, each of us should respond to his challenge by attaining individually the highest rank of which his nature is capable. We should not subordinate ourselves to oversimplified principles and imperatives but, rather, through him find the way to the genuine simplicity of truth.[17]

This rejection of univocality raises, of course, the inevitable problem of the subjectivity of interpretation.

Jaspers' approach to Nietzsche, then, is not as straightforward and explicit as it seems on the surface. Jaspers has attempted to draw some rather fine lines while at the same time admitting a certain degree of overlapping. What makes an examination and evaluation of Jaspers' interpretation especially difficult is that he, like Nietzsche, has a tendency to regard ambiguity as a virtue. As an interpreter Jaspers has at least the responsibility to make clear the nature of Nietzsche's ambiguities. Thus, in considering Jaspers, we shall have to concern ourselves repeatedly with the question of whether his ambiguities are obfuscations or extreme subtleties.

SPECIAL PROBLEMS IN HEIDEGGER'S NIETZSCHE INTERPRETATION

Heidegger's approach to Nietzsche is radically different from Jaspers' and poses its own set of problems. Heidegger is concerned primarily with Nietzsche's metaphysics and views the rest of Nietzsche's philosophy as essentially derivative from metaphysics. To understand this approach we must first understand the historical perspective in which Heidegger places Nietzsche.

For Heidegger the entire history of metaphysics is grounded in a mistake made in the development of philosophy after Heraclitus and Parmenides. Heraclitus and Parmenides had started movements toward a genuine ontology. Later Greek philosophers, however, turned away from those earlier insights and, instead of being concerned with the meaning of Being as such, turned toward the meaning of Being understood as the totality of beings. The formalization of this mistake was primarily a result of Aristotle's metaphysics. According to Heidegger, this fundamental mistake was a part of the unfolding of the

[17] *Ibid.*, p. 23.

history of Being and had to be brought to a final development through Descartes and Kant, culminating in Hegel and, especially, Nietzsche. For Heidegger, Nietzsche is the last metaphysician and, in some ways, the greatest, for not only did he bring to fulfillment the historical unfolding of metaphysics, but he prepared as well, the ground for the possibility of a fundamental ontology. Thus, for Heidegger, Nietzsche is the great turning-point in the history of philosophy. Here we have one of the most crucial problems in Heidegger's Nietzsche interpretation: Heidegger regards Nietzsche primarily as a metaphysician and treats all other aspects of his philosophy as systematically derivative from his metaphysics. Apparently Jaspers and Heidegger agree at this point, for Jaspers' notion that the continuity of Nietzsche's philosophy is provided by his "passion of the quest for being" sounds very Heideggerian indeed. The agreement is, however, only an apparent one, for Heidegger and Jaspers assign very different meanings to the phrase in quotation marks. For Jaspers the continuity is a result of Nietzsche's passion as an existentially unique being, and it is through this passion that *he* is able to *reveal Being*. Heidegger, however, maintains that it is through Nietzsche's passion that *Being* is able to *reveal itself*. The major difference here is that Heidegger tends to give thought (as a revelation of Being) a kind of historical autonomy, which it does not possess for Jaspers. We have here a basic difference between Heidegger and Jaspers in their respective approaches to Nietzsche. Jaspers explicitly accepts the title "existentialist," whereas Heidegger explicitly rejects it. For Jaspers everything arises out of the particularity of *Existenz;* whereas for Heidegger human existence or *Dasein* is the place at which *Being* reveals *itself*. For Heidegger the existential analytic of human Dasein as presented in *Being and Time* is simply preparatory to the real issue which is ontology.

In contrast to Heidegger, Jaspers does not acknowledge the need for an ontology, that is, a fundamental discipline embracing the totality of being. The "philosophy of existence" – a title to which the philosophy of Jaspers definitely lays claim – must be satisfied with the illumination of the possibilities of individual, concrete existence in its freedom, uniqueness, and ineffability.[18]

One other observation regarding the historical development of metaphysics needs to be made here, *viz.,* that Heidegger regards his own ontology as an "overcoming" of metaphysics and yet a further stage in the historical unfolding of Being. This, then, means that Heidegger quite explicitly establishes a definite perspective from which to regard

[18] Kurt Reinhardt, *The Existentialist Revolt* (New York, 1960), p. 177.

Nietzsche's work. He sees Nietzsche as providing the seeds which ripen in Heidegger's own ontology. This means that Heidegger regards Nietzsche's doctrines in the light of his own philosophy.

The introductory sections of Heidegger's book are concerned with establishing the foundations of Nietzsche's metaphysics. Heidegger argues that the nucleus of Nietzsche's philosophy is to be found in the conception of the Will to Power.

The question as to what beings are, seeks the Being of beings. All Being is, for Nietzsche, a Becoming. This Becoming, however, has the character of the action and activity of willing. Will, however, is in its essence, Will to Power.[19]

The Will to Power, as the Being of beings, is thus the foundation of Nietzsche's metaphysics. But then Heidegger asks, "What and how is the Will to Power itself? Answer: the Eternal Recurrence of the same."[20] In other words, he sees the doctrines of Will to Power and of Eternal Recurrence as indissolubly bound up one with the other – a unity brought about through the doctrine of Transvaluation of All Values. Thus, it is clear from the beginning that Heidegger cannot claim the kind of "neutrality" which Jaspers claims, and yet both would claim a kind of "objectivity." Operative here, however, are two different senses of "objectivity." Jaspers, even though he is willing to risk the ambiguity of an existential encounter with the thought of Nietzsche, would nonetheless argue that such an encounter is not subjective, for it goes beyond the individual to the foundation of the cultural situation within which the encounter takes place. Heidegger's claim to "objectivity" must be seen as a result of the historical revelation of Being through thought. Thus, for Heidegger, interpretation becomes the hermeneutic unfolding of the history of Being. But with Heidegger, as with Jaspers, we shall have to be concerned with the legitimacy of his own concepts as used to interpret Nietzsche.

A further problem with Heidegger's interpretation is the great emphasis that he gives to the book, *The Will to Power*. Heidegger sees it as the preparation for a great system which Nietzsche planned to write; a system, which would be a unified expression of Nietzsche's most mature thought. Heidegger is careful to point out, however, that *The Will to Power* is a collection of fragments which are not related in any essential way, nor is there anything authoritative about their arrangement. Thus, an essential part of Heidegger's book is his

---

[19] Heidegger, *Nietzsche*, p. 15.
[20] *Ibid.*, p. 27.

attempt to "construct" Nietzsche's "system," drawing from all the writings of Nietzsche but using *The Will to Power* as a guiding nucleus.

In contrast to Jaspers, Heidegger limits his interpretation to a basic mode of approach which is simultaneously one of the greatest weaknesses and greatest strengths of Heidegger's interpretation. By so organizing his interpretation, Heidegger is able to present a major aspect of Nietzsche's thought in great depth, but he is not able to provide the multiplicity of perspectives which Jaspers discloses. It is interesting to note here that Heidegger, like Jaspers, also insists upon a direct encounter with the spirit and passion of Nietzsche's thought, yet each understands something quite different by this encounter. For Jaspers this encounter is a dialectical interchange; for Heidegger it is permitting Being to manifest itself in its unhiddenness. In Heidegger's work, the interpreter plays a more or less passive role in relation to the self-revelation of Being. However, *Dasein* is nonetheless "actively" involved, for if authentic thought is to be achieved, there must be an attunement between *Dasein* and that which is being thought. As we shall see later when we come to an evaluation of Heidegger's interpretation of Nietzsche, Heidegger is involved in a radical and elaborate project of attempting to "overcome" the fundamental conceptual dualisms which arise out of language itself. Thus the opposition here between activity and passivity is a dichotomizing conceptualization which Heidegger attempts to overcome. The basic difference between the two approaches may therefore be stated as follows: Jaspers' interpretation is essentially investigatory, an exploration which attempts to chart an unknown spiritual territory. In contrast, Heidegger's interpretation is not simply an investigation; it is rather an explicit attempt to demonstrate a specific thesis, *viz.*, that Nietzsche is most importantly a metaphysician and that his metaphysics represents the culmination of metaphysics and at the same time provides also the ground for a new ontology, specifically Heidegger's.

AN ALTERNATIVE INTERPRETATION: A FUNDAMENTAL DUALISM

Any critical examination of Heidegger's and Jaspers' interpretations is incomplete without an evaluation. An evaluation implies a standpoint from which to evaluate. The standpoint in this case involves the presentation and defense of a particular thesis, *viz.*, that Nietzsche's epistemology and metaphysics, on the one hand, and his philosophical anthropology and value theory, on the other, cannot be brought harmoniously into systematic relation. There are certainly real and profound sets of relations between Nietzsche's major concepts, but there is also this fundamental dualism which runs through the very core of Nietzsche's thought. It will also be argued that any attempt to impose a unity or to provide a bridge of systematic relations between these two aspects, is fundamentally mistaken. Throughout our examination of Heidegger's and Jaspers' interpretations we shall be concerned with accumulating evidence for this thesis in terms of an investigation of the major doctrines of Nietzsche.

The question that must be raised here, then, is whether Jaspers and Heidegger do attempt to relate systematically the two major aspects of Nietzsche's thought. With Heidegger, the answer is clearly affirmative, for he insists that the whole of Nietzsche's thought can be systematically derived from Nietzsche's metaphysics. In certain respects Heidegger presents a very strong case for his position, and we shall have to examine his view in some detail. With Jaspers the answer is not so immediately clear. However, we can find an important guideline for our investigations in a criticism which both Heidegger and Walter Kaufmann advance against Jaspers' Nietzsche interpretation. The main charge is that Jaspers emphasizes Nietzsche's "philosophizing" at the expense of Nietzsche's philosophy; that is, Jaspers attempts to establish a kind of synthetic unity in Nietzsche's thought by dismissing his major metaphysical constructs. In other words, such doctrines as Will to Power and Eternal Recurrence, Jaspers refuses to treat metaphysically. He considers them only insofar as they relate to the position of his own *Existenzphilosophie*. "First, Jaspers admittedly discounts Nietzsche's philosophy as opposed to his 'philosophizing'; he refuses to take seriously superman and recurrence, will to power and sublimation, or any other definite concept."[21] Heidegger advances almost precisely the same criticism:

For Baeumler the doctrine of Eternal Recurrence is not reconcilable with the political interpretation of Nietzsche; for Jaspers it is not possible to take this doctrine seriously and as an essential question, because according to him there is in philosophy no truth in the concept nor in conceptual knowledge.[22]

---

[21] Walter Kaufmann, "Jasper's Relation to Nietzsche," in *The Philosophy of Karl Jaspers*, ed. by Paul Schilpp (New York, 1957), p. 431.
[22] Heidegger, *Nietzsche*, pp. 31–32.

This is, of course, a serious charge and one which we must investigate as we proceed.

Here we encounter an important methodological consideration. Before we can undertake the presentation of an alternative interpretation, we shall have finally to take a further look at the Nietzsche interpretations of Jaspers and Heidegger in terms of their entire philosophical enterprises rather than just their Nietzsche interpretations. This expanded view will result in some interesting shifts in perspective and reveal some rather striking parallelisms. Thus, in Chapter IV we would hope to correct any significant distortions of the thought of Jaspers and Heidegger that might be obtained by relying too exclusively on their Nietzsche criticism. The results of these investigations hopefully will also underscore the importance of interpreting Nietzsche in terms of the fundamental dualism between cosmology and philosophical anthropology. The key to this alternative interpretation is the doctrine of Eternal Recurrence.

CHAPTER I

NIETZSCHE AS A MAN AND AS A PHILOSOPHER

THE RELEVANCE OF NIETZSCHE'S LIFE TO HIS THOUGHT

It is not the intention here to present or even to outline a biography of Nietzsche. This would take us too far afield from the real intention of our investigations. There is a multitude of special problems pertaining to a Nietzsche biography and most existing biographies suffer from two serious limitations: (1) most biographies of Nietzsche display a radical bias of some sort on the part of the biographer (e.g., Alfred Baeumler, Ernst Bertram, Elizabeth Förster-Nietzsche) and (2) almost every biographer of Nietzsche approaches his subject from only a few of the essential perspectives from which he can be viewed. In other words, there is at present no authoritative comprehensive biography of Nietzsche. However, for our purposes, such a biography is not essential, since our interest here is a less complex one; namely, the problem of the psychological and existential relevance of Nietzsche's life-situation to his thought in general. What we shall be concerned with demonstrating is simply that there is a set of events and concerns in Nietzsche's life that is crucial for the understanding of Nietzsche's thought. Our interest here is not simply biographical, nor is it simply philosophical; rather, we are concerned with the existential psychological relations between the two, or more accurately, the *personal* philosophy of Nietzsche as an expression of his life-world. Nietzsche himself emphasizes this aspect of the interpretation of past systems when he says, "The only thing of interest in a refuted system is the personal element. It alone is what is forever irrefutable."[1]

Almost every interpreter of Nietzsche makes a special point of the importance of Nietzsche's life for understanding his thought. However,

---

[1] Friedrich Nietzsche, *Philosophy in the Tragic Age of the Greeks*, trans. Marianne Cowan (Gateway edition; Chicago, Henry Regnery Company, 1962), p. 25.

too much emphasis can be given to this relation. While the events in Nietzsche's life certainly have considerable significance for, and influence upon, his thought, Nietzsche should not be thought of as a singular case in this respect. The same argument could be advanced for Plato, Descartes, Aquinas, Berkeley, and almost every other great thinker. With Nietzsche, however, biography has a special prominence for at least two major reasons. First of all, we know more about Nietzsche's life than we do about the lives of most other great philosophers. This is partly due to the fact that Nietzsche was an inveterate letter writer, and in these letters he often provides a direct connection between some set of events and the ideas with which he was preoccupied at the moment. In addition to these letters, there is the mass of fragments which he left behind, as well as numerous reminiscences by people who were acquainted with Nietzsche. There are even lists of books in Nietzsche's library which provide some clue to influences on his thought. Also there were a number of rather dramatic events and situations in Nietzsche's life which were undoubtedly of great psychological significance; e.g., his friendship and break with Wagner, his relationships with his sister and Lou Andreas Salomé, his epiphany in the mountains (Eternal Recurrence), and, of course, his mental breakdown. The second reason revolves around these events which had such extraordinary effects on Nietzsche's thought. In fact, we might even say that these events resulted in a set of psychological fixations in Nietzsche. By "fixation" we do not mean any sort of pathological obsession in a psychiatric sense, rather what is meant here is an extreme concern and pre-occupation with certain ideas which are absolutely crucial to an understanding of Nietzsche and his philosophy.

It is a tribute to Nietzsche's depth of insight as a psychologist that he himself was, to an astonishing degree, aware of these fixations and further understood that they conditioned the character of his philosophizing in an essential manner. Freud paid an immense compliment to the power of Nietzsche's intuitive psychology.

In later years I have denied myself the very great pleasure of reading the works of Nietzsche, with the deliberate object of not being hampered in working out the impressions received in psycho-analysis by any sort of anticipatory ideas. I had therefore to be prepared – and I am so, gladly – to forgo all claims to priority in the many instances in which laborious psychoanalytic investigation can merely confirm the truths which the philosopher recognized by intuition.[2]

[2] Sigmund Freud, *On the History of the Psycho-analytic Movement*, Vol. XIV (1914–1916) of *The Complete Psychological Works of Sigmund Freud*, trans. and ed. James Strachey (London, 1957), pp. 15–16.

Jung, likewise, found in Nietzsche a wealth of psychological insight.

For my part, I had the great advantage over both Freud and Adler of not having grown up within the narrow confines of a psychology of the neuroses; rather, I approached from the side of psychiatry, well prepared for modern psychology by Nietzsche.[3]

It is precisely this extraordinary ability to analyze his own personality in depth that leads Nietzsche to his penetrating insights into the psychological and value structures of modern society as manifested in his own life-world. Zarathustra's struggles to overcome himself (and thereby his "culture") are a concrete and vital expression of Nietzsche's attempts at self-overcoming. Self-overcoming must be understood in relation to the life-world of the self (and in its most immediate and objective character – as "culture") and so it is not a conflict reducible to an egocentric subjectivism. In other words, a self-overcoming must, within the context of Nietzsche's thought, be understood as a dialectic. These fixations we have mentioned form important poles in the dialectic of Nietzsche's self-overcoming. We shall examine these fixations under six groupings.

Friendship

Nietzsche had an almost overwhelming need for friendship, but his own sensitivity and the rigorous demands which he made created a set of conditions which it was virtually impossible for any human being to fulfill. This is, of course, not to say that Nietzsche had no friends in the ordinary sense of that word. However, "friend" for Nietzsche meant something more like "spiritual companion." Three persons filled this role for a time, but eventually Nietzsche suffered disillusionment with all three: Richard Wagner, Erwin Rhode, and Lou Andreas Salomé. Wagner was perhaps the greatest human disappointment in Nietzsche's life, primarily because, at first, Wagner seemed to Nietzsche the fulfillment of his dream for a friend who was at once spiritual companion, mentor, and disciple. The breach which finally resulted between them was largely due to reciprocal misunderstanding and to Nietzsche's spiritually aristocratic passion for honesty. Nietzsche's appropriation of Wagner's notions of the Apollonian and the Dionysian led to Nietzsche's own extension and synthesis of these ideas to produce an aesthetic to which Nietzsche expected Wagner to remain true. This aesthetic, which Nietzsche formulates in *The birth of*

---

[3] Carl Gustav Jung, *Two Essays on Analytical Psychology*, Vol. VII of *The Collected Works of C. G. Jung*, trans. R. F. C. Hull (New York, 1953), pp. 115–16.

Tragedy, centers around the Apollonian-Dionysian synthesis which Nietzsche saw as the highest expression of the Will to Power.[4]

Nietzsche felt that within the context of genuine friendship Wagner should have been able to accept honest criticism. At first, Nietzsche was overwhelmed by the forceful personality of Wagner and Nietzsche's early attitude verged on hero-worship, and also Nietzsche did not immediately realize that Wagner was incapable of accepting criticism. Thus gradually Wagner became "human, all-too-human" in Nietzsche's eyes. Furthermore, the aesthetic which Nietzsche wished to impose on Wagner's work was alien to it and Nietzsche's rejection of Wagner's art as "philistine" was the result of the application of this alien standard. Nonetheless, Nietzsche continued to regard Wagner as a great genius of the age and his criticisms of Wagner were simultaneously criticisms of the historical and cultural situation which produced Wagner. The opening of Bayreuth was the beginning of the end, for Nietzsche saw Wagner as having yielded to the cultural philistines. Nietzsche expressed what he felt were honest, if extreme, criticisms, after having, for some considerable time, withheld his most severe remarks out of a concern for the continuance of their friendship. However, a certain spirit and tone of reservation is already clearly apparent even in Nietzsche's monograph *Richard Wagner in Bayreuth*. The final break came in Italy when Wagner told Nietzsche of his plans for *Parsifal*. Nietzsche, with his anti-Christianity, saw this as a betrayal of the aesthetic which he attributed to Wagner and accused Wagner of hypocrisy. There were moments later when Nietzsche felt very keenly that he should have supressed his criticisms of Wagner as is reflected when Zarathustra says, "It is nobler to declare oneself wrong than to insist on being right – especially when one is right. Only one must be rich enough for that."[5] Be this as it may, Nietzsche's compulsion toward honesty took precedence at the time and it should be noted that Nietzsche made his demands as rigorously on himself as he did upon others, as we shall later see.

It is evident that the relationship between Wagner and Nietzsche is of immense complexity. However, we can find a number of important psychological clues which give us an insight into both Nietzsche's personality and his thought. Nietzsche's concept of "friend" is essentially that of the "higher man," whom Zarathustra seeks; the

---

[4] This view runs through the entire body of Nietzsche's work up to and including *The Will to Power*.

[5] Friedrich Nietzsche, *Thus Spoke Zarathustra* in *The Portable Nietzsche*, trans. Walter Kaufmann (New York, 1967), p. 180.

man who is on his way to becoming the Superman. Thus, it is important to realize that this concept of the Superman arises out of Nietzsche's own particular psychology. Also, what Georg Brandes speaks of as Nietzsche's "aristocratic radicalism" is a result of Nietzsche's psychological constitution. Nietzsche sensed in himself and a few others the tremendous potentialities of the individual human being. This recognition was in large part the result of Nietzsche's intuitive psychological investigations into the structure of his own personality. This recognition led to a vast complex of ideas. Nietzsche's vision of the potentialities of the human being became in his early work an important aspect of his aesthetic. In fact, this ideal conception of man is profoundly Greek and it views the individual as a potential work of art which is self-created. The disparity between this ideal and the real, ordinary man was a source of great pain and disillusionment for Nietzsche. Moreover, this disparity is the source of Nietzsche's contempt for ordinary men or the "herd." This contempt is at the root of Nietzsche's humanism. For Nietzsche, the contempt that arises from the disparity between the real and the ideal is the psychologically motivating fact, a manifestation of the Will to Power, that can lead man to overcome himself and set out on the path toward the Superman. There is a profound parallel between the Greek conception of the "pursuit of excellence" and the Nietzschean conception of the pursuit of the Superman, but there is also a profound difference. This difference lies in Nietzsche's rejection of Greek rationalism, since for Nietzsche the shaping spirit of man as a potential work of art is not simply the intellect, but instinct as well. Man is not simply spirit, but animal as well, and while for the Greeks man's fulfillment was the transcendence of his animality through reason, for Nietzsche any transcendence must be a synthesis which integrates man's animality with his spirituality. A rejection of instinct leads, from Nietzsche's point of view, to spiritual degeneration.

The same basic problem also arises in Nietzsche's relationships with Rhode and Lou Salomé. Rhode, a contemporary and fellow student, shared Nietzsche's early interests and evidently manifested a similar passion for rebellion against the established values of the period. Rhode, however, in contradistinction to Nietzsche, remained primarily a philologist and sought personal security within the contexts of his family life and his academic pursuits. Again Nietzsche saw here a subtle kind of betrayal, for he despised a security which, in his eyes, could be attained only at the sacrifice of oneself and one's most immediate values. Nietzsche and Rhode continued to be friends, but the warmth and vitality of their early relationship was lost. In a sense Rhode's "betrayal" was as great as Wagner's, because Rhode had not remained true to the youthful visions and passions which remained as a powerful motivating force throughout Nietzsche's life. Throughout Nietzsche's work there is this aspect of the visionary and Nietzsche could only regard Rhode's growing conservatism as a sacrilege against the most fundamentally spiritual foundations of man's existence as an attempt to "overcome" and "go beyond" himself.

Nietzsche's strong sense of disappointment with other human beings is also sharply illustrated in his brief friendship with Lou Salomé. Nietzsche's side of this relationship might, without exaggeration, be termed an infatuation. But from all indications, this passionate involvement was not reciprocal and she seemed much more interested in Paul Rée. Nietzsche probably projected much more into the relationship than was actually present. At first, he believed Lou Salomé to be the ideal disciple, and although Nietzsche rarely gave anyone credit for understanding him, he believed that she genuinely understood his philosophy. In fact, he goes so far as to say, in a letter to Overbeck, "*Lou* is by far the most *intelligent* human being I have met." [6] However, Nietzsche's disenchantment came quickly, partly as a result of a campaign against Lou which Nietzsche's sister undertook. His reaction was for a time so extreme that only six months later he wrote to Malvida von Meysenbug; "Above all, what I have *now* come to know, unfortunately, *much too late!* – is that these two persons, Rée and Lou are not worthy of licking my boot soles." [7] Later, however, Nietzsche modified this attitude toward Lou, for he felt that he had come under the malicious influence of his sister. Nonetheless, this strong tendency to extremism is an important topic which we shall have occasion to examine more closely a bit later.

Nietzsche's relationships with women were, on the whole, ambivalent and frequently painful. The most important woman in his life was, of course, his sister, Elizabeth Förster-Nietzsche. Nietzsche felt a very deep bond with his sister, but also expressed much hostility toward her. Even though she was a great defender of her brother's works, she could never be a satisfactory disciple, for the simple reason that she appropriated ideas from him which she blended and distorted with

[6] Nietzsche letter to Franz Overbeck in Schlechta, *Nietzsche: Werke*, III, 1203, my translation.
[7] Nietzsche letter to Malwida von Meysenbug in Schlechta, *Nietzsche: Werke*, III, 210, my translation.

ideas of her own. (She is, in fact, largely responsible for the myths that grew up around Nietzsche in the early part of this century). For example, Elizabeth's anti-Semitism disgusted Nietzsche, as is evident from this passage in one of his letters to her.

> You have committed one of the greatest stupidities – for yourself and for me! Your association with an anti-Semitic chief expresses a foreignness to my whole way of life which fills me again and again with ire or melancholy .... It is a matter of honor with me to be absolutely clean and unequivocal in relation to anti-Semitism, namely, *opposed* to it, as I am in my writings. I have recently been persecuted with letters and *Anti-Semitic Correspondence Sheets*. My disgust with this party (which would like the benefit of my name only too well!) is as pronounced as possible, but the relation to Förster, as well as the after effects of my former publisher, the anti-Semitic Schmeitzner, always brings the adherent of this disagreeable party back to the idea that I must belong to them after all .... It arouses mistrust against my character, as if publicly I condemned something which I favored secretly – and that I am unable to do anything against it that the name of Zarathustra is used in every *Anti-Semitic Correspondence Sheet*, has almost made me sick several times.[8]

Nonetheless, she tried to use Nietzsche's philosophy of power as a foundation for her anti-Semitic views. Thus, Elizabeth could never be a disciple in Nietzsche's sense nor could Peter Gast (pseudonym for Heinrich Köselitz), who blindly accepted and revered everything that Nietzsche uttered. Von Gersdorff, Overbeck, Gast, Lou, Elizabeth, and Paul Rée were hardly candidates for that group of "higher men" which Nietzsche sought after and longed for. Nietzsche understood only too well that propensity for distortion and abuse which disciples practice on the ideas of their mentors, but he understood equally well the disastrous results of uncritical obeisance. The "higher men" whom Nietzsche sought had to be at once pupil and master, friend and critic. Throughout his life he was bitterly disappointed that he found no such friend and disciple among his contemporaries. Out of his solitude he sought out the "higher men" of the past, the "super-historical individuals" who, like Nietzsche, had stood alone and isolated beyond their age. Nietzsche thus sought comfort in his isolation through a spiritual kinship with such "super-historical individuals" as Goethe and Spinoza.

The conditions and demands entailed by Nietzsche's conception of friendship result in part from Nietzsche's isolation which at the same time exempted him from most of the usual social and familial responsibilities. The lack of these obligations permitted him to live in a situation

---

[8] Nietzsche letter to his sister in *The Portable Nietzsche*, trans. Walter Kaufmann (New York, 1967), pp. 456–57.

relatively free from the practical pressures of day-to-day social life and it was precisely this situation that permitted him to make such extreme demands upon himself in the realm of the spirit.

With Nietzsche man stands alone, as he himself did, neurotic, financially dependent, godless, and worldless. This is no ideal for a real man who has a family to support and taxes to pay. Nothing can argue the reality of the world out of existence, there is no miraculous way round it.[9]

Thus the spiritual intensity of Nietzsche's views is a direct result of his life-situation and Nietzsche made relatively little allowance for the radically different life-situations of others. His conception of spiritual interaction with other human beings presupposed a life-situation similar to his own in terms of relative freedom from responsibility and in this respect Nietzsche was a dogmatist. The priority which he gives to spiritual interaction between human beings has many profound and extensive ramifications with regard to a theory of social interaction, and, on an even more basic level, creates the demand for a radical restructuring of values, a transvaluation. Here we encounter the other major aspect involved in Nietzsche's conception of friendship. In order to interact with another on a spiritual plane, one must first have achieved the level of striving toward Selfhood or, to use Nietzsche's phrase, a "returning home" to the Self. Before one can interact meaningfully with another, he must first attain an understanding of who he is and where he is metaphysically. The ultimate achievement of spiritual companionship, then, arises out of the most profound solitude and isolation which are necessary conditions for the attainment of Self and the relation of Self to the Other. This is one of the "contradictions" in Nietzsche that Jaspers is fond of pointing out. Properly understood Nietzsche's position here is not a contradiction or, if it is, it is *merely* a *logical* contradiction, for Nietzsche's contentions that solitude and isolation are pre-conditions for Selfhood and that Selfhood is a pre-condition for entering into a spiritual community, certainly do not result in a *psychological* or *existential* contradiction. Here one is strongly reminded of the parallel in Hesse's *Journey to the East* which is a metaphysical rather than a physical journey. The double theme of solitude and loneliness plays a central role in Nietzsche's conception of the essential nature of philosophy and it is these topics which we must now examine.

---

[9] Jung, *Two Essays on Analytical Psychology*, VII, p. 235.

Solitude, Loneliness, and Philosophy

Nietzsche had the extraordinary ability to transform negative factors in his environment and personal make-up into factors of at least partial positive import. Nietzsche recognized the danger of his desire for disciples and recognized further that this desire arose out of his loneliness. Of even greater consequence, however, is his understanding that the indulgence of this desire constituted a spiritual weakness which contained within it an immense destructive force, for its ultimate object was the satisfaction of vanity. The eloquent speech which Zarathustra gives at the end of the first book contains a double message, in fact, a double warning. The warning to the disciples is obvious enough.

> Now I go alone, my disciples. You too go now, alone. Thus I want it. Verily, I counsel you: go away from me and resist Zarathustra! And even better: be ashamed of him! Perhaps he deceived you.
> The man of knowledge must not only love his enemies, he must also be able to hate his friends.
> One repays a teacher badly if one always remains nothing but a pupil. And why do you not want to pluck at my wreath?
> You revere me; but what if your reverence tumbles one day? Beware lest a statue slay you.[10]

However, less obviously Zarathustra's speech contains a warning for himself.

> You say you believe in Zarathustra? But what matters Zarathustra? You are my believers – but what matter all believers? You had not yet sought your-selves: and you found me. Thus do all believers; therefore all faith amounts to so little.[11]

Zarathustra's warning of the disciples against himself is also a warning to himself against disciples or "believers." Here and elsewhere *Thus Spoke Zarathustra* can serve as a guide to the central core of Nietz-sche's thought, for it is in this book that most of Nietzsche's early major ideas achieve fruition and the works which follow it are, in a very important sense, explications and elaborations of the major themes, both explicit and implicit, in *Thus Spoke Zarathustra*. In this sense one can speak of this book as the axis of Nietzsche's phi-losophy. What is interesting here is not only Nietzsche's recognition of the danger of potential appeal to his vanity, but the further aware-ness that this danger arose from his spiritual isolation. This struggle, which is a painful reality for many, was greatly heightened in Nietz-

---

[10] Nietzsche, *Thus Spoke Zarathustra*, p. 190.
[11] *Ibid.*, p. 190.

sche's case due to his almost overwhelming need for sympathetic concern and encouragement with regard to his work. Here we encounter another of those existential oppositions which are central to Nietzsche's life-situation. The very intensity of Nietzsche's self-absorbtion and self-concern made it virtually impossible for him to manifest a reciprocal concern for the life-situation of another human being. The resulting isolation is a consequence of the dialectical relation between solitude and loneliness relative to the essential meaning of philosophy for Nietzsche. For Nietzsche all *genuine* philosophy arises out of the life-situation of the individual philosopher.

Gradually it has become clear to me what every great philosophy so far has been: namely, the personal confession of its author and a kind of involuntary and unconscious memoir; also that the moral (or immoral) intentions in every philosophy constituted the real germ of life from which the whole plant had grown.[12]

Thus, philosophy is dependent upon the existential uniqueness of the thinker and finds significant expression only in those who have plumbed the most ecstatic heights and the most terrifying depths of their own identity. It is for this reason that Nietzsche can say of Kant that he remained at the level of critic and never attained the heights and depths of philosophy. The continuous process of the discovery of Self is, then, a necessary aspect of genuine philosophizing and a pre-requisite for such discovery is solitude. Only by being alone with oneself can one aspire to philosophy. Here the word "solitude" is ambiguous, for certainly Kant's work too required a kind of solitude. We must understand the phrase, "being alone with *oneself*," in its most literal sense. Kant's solitude usually had an "external" content, whereas the solitude of which Nietzsche speaks has as its content aspects of the life-situation of Nietzsche himself. This, of course, does not mean that Nietzsche's philosophy is "merely subjective." Nietzsche, like Kierkegaard, realized that the criteria of truth arise from the life-situation of the individual and, furthermore, that "objectivity" frequently means nothing more than "collective subjectivity."

A solitude, which has as its primary characteristic a self-directedness, becomes a prime requisite for genuine philosophy. This self-understanding creates a recognition of the need of relationship to the Other as a fulfillment of one's own being. For Nietzsche, such interrelationship is immensely complicated by the demand that one never sacrifice

---

[12] Friedrich Nietzsche, *Beyond Good and Evil*, trans. Walter Kaufmann (New York, 1966), p. 13.

the interests of the Self to the Other, for to do so would, in Nietzsche's eyes, produce a mutual degradation. Nietzsche insists that significant relationships with other human beings are possible only by uncompromisingly becoming what one is. One can never sacrifice his own interests to the Other, for such an act, far from being altruistic, is a betrayal both of himself and of the Other. The result of such demands is isolation and loneliness, unless one is able to find some other human being who lives with the same self-intensity and can thus provide a spiritual companionship. As we have discovered, Nietzsche was never able to find such an individual. Solitude was for him not only necessary, but highly positive, for its product was a "joyful wisdom"; but at the same time there was the immense need to share the fruits of this solitude. Loneliness haunted Nietzsche; in fact, it is extremely likely that the oppression of his loneliness was ultimately far more painful than all of his physical torments. It should now be clear that, for Nietzsche, the realization of the Self meant becoming a philosopher in his sense of that word. Thus, it is not surprising that Nietzsche found no "friend" among his contemporaries who could palliate his loneliness, for such a "friend" (who would of necessity also be a great spiritual enemy) would have had to have been a philosopher equal to Nietzsche in rank. Out of his loneliness and his great need for communion and self-expression, Nietzsche turned to writing. It is perhaps fortunate for us that he did not find his spiritual companion; had he done so we might not have his writings. For philosophy, Nietzsche contends, solitude is essential, for philosophy is a "voluntary living amid ice and mountain heights."[13] Perhaps loneliness was essential as well. What is certain is that this loneliness plays a crucial role in Nietzsche's extremism.

Sickness and Health

In addition to the mental anguish which Nietzsche suffered, he was afflicted with migraine, insomnia, and serious stomach ailments. It is also known that Nietzsche had considerable difficulty with his eyes and at times could barely use them for reading or writing and thus had to dictate his thought, usually to von Gersdorff or Peter Gast. One commentator has gone so far as to suggest that Nietzsche's migraine, insomnia, dyspepsia, hypertension, and even his mental breakdown were the result of severe eyestrain.[14] Here we are not particularly

---

[13] Nietzsche quoted in Heidegger, *Introduction to Metaphysics*, pp. 12-13.
[14] George M. Gould, *Biographic Clinics*, II (Philadelphia, 1904).

interested in speculating about the causes, but rather we shall concern ourselves with the effects of these illnesses on Nietzsche and his attitudes toward them.

Nietzsche's most frequent complaints in his letters concern his insomnia and his migraine attacks and it is well known that he rather indiscriminately used all kinds of medicines in an effort to get relief. It has been suggested by some commentators that there is a correlation between Nietzsche's use of drugs and the ecstatic states during the writing of *Thus Spoke Zarathustra* and moments such as his epiphany of Eternal Recurrence on the mountain. There is, however, little concrete evidence for such a conjecture and any rejection of ideas ostensibly propounded under such influences is simply a case of the genetic fallacy.

A more important question is the question of Nietzsche's sanity prior to his breakdown at the end of 1888. Extremists have wished to dismiss the whole of Nietzsche's writings as the ravings of a madman. On the other hand, Nietzsche's apologists have constructed elaborate and tenuous arguments trying to establish that he was unquestionably sane and lucid up to the very moment of his complete breakdown. In fact, both kinds of arguments are irrelevant for two reasons. First of all, this is again an example of the genetic fallacy; Nietzsche's ideas must be evaluated in terms of their value and quality *as ideas*. It is quite possible that a "madman" can be the creator of highly significant and insightful thoughts. Lucidity is not the exclusive property of normality, nor even of sanity. The second difficulty is the ambiguity of the word "insanity." "Insanity" is not a technical term and has been applied to everything from psychoses resulting from physiological damage, to any form of behavior or expression not consonant with the views of the particular critic. If by "sane" we mean "rationally meaningful and coherent," then certainly even Nietzsche's last writings were "sane" if somewhat extreme. What can be said is that Nietzsche was certainly medically insane after the end of 1888, but on no reasonable grounds can one dismiss any of Nietzsche's works as "mere ravings of a madman." It is an extremely instructive exercise to compare one of Nietzsche's last works, *The Anti-Christ*, for example, with *The Diaries of Vaslav Nijinsky*. The tone of Nietzsche's book is sometimes shrill and harsh, but it is nonetheless lucid and coherent, whereas the Nijinsky *Diaries* are clearly a product of insanity, at once touching and terrifying. What we must remember is that none of

Nietzsche's writings, no matter how extreme or caustic, can simply be dismissed as products of insanity.

The most significant aspect of Nietzsche's illnesses derives from his attitude towards them. For Nietzsche his illnesses became concrete manifestations of the metaphysical principle of the world-obstacle. Every individual encounters his own limitations and in addition importunities inflicted by his environment; obstacles to the realization of one's Self and one's freedom. The important thing is not the negativity of these obstacles, but rather their positive aspect as something to be overcome, something to test one's strength against. The overcoming of such obstacles is an intrinsic part of the process of self-realization. These obstacles are a direct challenge to the individual's Will to Power, and here again Nietzsche is merciless in his demands; he will not countenance self-indulgent rationalization. As Zarathustra says, "Life is hard to bear; but do not act so tenderly." [15] His position here is one of an all-consuming Will to Strength. This doctrine is a call to nobility, a challenge to pit one's strength against the world-obstacle and if one cannot overcome, then at least one fails magnificently. It is true that sometimes Nietzsche in his letters complains bitterly of his afflictions in a fashion "human, all-too-human," but he nevertheless continues to wrestle with them and attempts to overcome them up to the very moment of his breakdown. Nietzsche may have faltered, but he never succumbed.

Out of this basic doctrine Nietzsche developed a whole philosophy of strength and health, spiritual as well as physical. Just as there are diseases of the body, so there are diseases of the spirit. Indeed, Nietzsche's writings on ethics might be regarded as textbooks on moral pathology. There are diseases of the spirit that are *especially* virulent and even the strongest men fall prey to them. It is *highly* significant that in the process of Zarathustra's struggle to achieve Selfhood, he describes himself as a convalescent. Even the great individual, who is on the path to the Superman, suffers from the diseases of his culture and must undergo a radical "cure" in order to overcome himself and become what as yet he is only potentially. Thus, the doctrine of strength and its Will to Power lead inexorably to the doctrine of the Superman.

It is also here that we discover the roots of Nietzsche's conception of the freedom of the individual and the psychological ramifications of that conception. The entire notion of man's potential nobility and

[15] Nietzsche, *Thus Spoke Zarathustra*, p. 153.

superiority as the Superman rest upon the possibility for the individual to combat and overcome not only his inherent weaknesses, but also the weaknesses that have been conditioned into him by his culture. This, of course, presupposes that man is not at the mercy of his environment, that he has the freedom to create himself through and in spite of his environment. Here again we encounter a strong parallel between Nietzsche's concept of man and the Greek concept of man as a potential self-created work of art. The first stage in this self-creation is the discovery of the disease, so that a cure might be effected. It is the disease which we must now consider.

Christianity and the Anti-Christ

To Nietzsche the most dangerous and the most terrible disease of contemporary European man was Christianity. We must be careful here to distinguish between Nietzsche's attitude toward the historical person of Jesus and his attitude toward Jesus as the Christ and his influence on world history. Nietzsche found things to admire in the person of Jesus, particularly his anarchism, his kindness, and his hatred of hypocrisy; but he rejected the essentially passive and negative attitude of Jesus toward earthly life. Nietzsche regarded this as an inversion of the Will to Power, such that it turned inward against itself. Ultimately he is an antagonist of Jesus, but he respects the honesty embodied in the acting out of his life-situation. For Nietzsche, the ultimate "sin" of Jesus was his permitting himself to be overcome by pity, thus becoming the progenitor of the "noble lie" which promised the meek the dominion of the earth and a privileged position in the life beyond death. Zarathustra's remark about God also applies here to Jesus as an historical person: "He offended the taste of my ears and eyes; I do not want to say anything worse about him now that he is dead."[16] Zarathustra also warns against pity.

One ought to hold on to one's heart; for if one lets it go, one soon loses control of the head too. Alas, where in the world has there been more folly than among the pitying? And what in the world has caused more suffering than the folly of the pitying? Woe to all who love without having a height that is above their pity!

Thus spoke the devil to me once: "God too has his hell: that is his love of man." And most recently I heard him say this: "God is dead; God died of his pity for man."

Thus be warned of pity: from there a heavy cloud will yet come to man.[17]

[16] Nietzsche, *Thus Spoke Zarathustra*, p. 373.
[17] *Ibid.*, p. 202.

Pity, for Nietzsche, was the greatest danger to the individual's own Will to Power.

The Christ of Christianity – essentially the creation of Paul – is quite a different matter, for in Christianity, Nietzsche argues, even that which is good in the model of Jesus is perverted and used by the weak to gain dominance over those who are superior to them. It is the latter point which Nietzsche also objects to in democracy, in socialism, and in liberalism; all three of which he sees as essentially derivative from the historical development of Christianity. This perversion Nietzsche calls the "Will to Equality."

Thus I speak to you in a parable – you who make souls whirl, you preachers of *equality*. To me you are tarantulas, and secretly vengeful. But I shall bring your secrets to light; therefore I laugh in your faces with my laughter of the heights. Therefore I tear at your webs, that your rage may lure you out of your lieholes and your revenge may leap out from behind your word justice. For *that man be delivered from revenge*, that is for me the bridge to the highest hope, and a rainbow after long storms.[18]

To Zarathustra justice speaks a different truth.

I do not wish to be mixed up and confused with these preachers of equality. For, to *me* justice speaks thus: "Men are not equal." Nor shall they become equal! What would my love of the overman be if I spoke otherwise?[19]

The prophets of equality, both religious and social, Nietzsche regards as motivated primarily by revenge. The egalitarian passion is the drive to destroy the superior, to reduce all things to the level of uniform, and therefore innocuous, mediocrity. The virtues of Christianity allow the punishment of the transgressor by claiming concern for a higher good, the salvation of the transgressor's soul. In reality the motive is not the promotion of a higher good, but, on the contrary, an indulgence in man's basest passion – revenge, the desire to demean and destroy that which is superior. This, of course, Nietzsche regards as a perversion of the Will to Power, a perversion we have experienced in the fascism of Nazi Germany, in the People's Democracies of Communism, and in the pseudo-egalitarianism of American capitalism.

In liberalism, in socialism, in democracy – however anti-Christian the poses they may strike – Nietzsche sees essentially the result of enervated Christianity. In them Christianity lives on, and in comfortable mendacities of Christian origin, maintains a secular existence. Philosophy, morality, modern humanism and its egalitarian ideals in particular, are also Christian ideals in disguise. That the weak as such, the impotent of any kind, must be aided; that the mere fact

---

[18] *Ibid.*, p. 211.
[19] *Ibid.*, p. 213.

of being biologically human justifies a claim to all which is attainable only by men of excellence; that every simpleton and lowbrow should be given a chance to learn what is fit only for an original thinker; that absolute primacy goes to man's mere existence and not to his substance, not to his enthusiasm, not to whatever is genuine and spontaneous in him; that we let it appear as though everyone were capable of everything; that we do not acknowledge the rigor of given facts; that we do not accept decisions; that, in fact, we use spirituality and ideality as mere means of self-preservation, to gain power in a struggle for existence which is actually going on all the time, and that this makes all things untrue – this, to Nietzsche, is the result of the primal distortion which he lays to late Antiquity, to Judaism, and to Christianity.[20]

These remarks should indicate that Nietzsche by no means intended the doctrine of the Will to Power to be used as a foundation for and justification of political and economic machinations. The Will to Power and the doctrine of the Superman are primarily metaphysical doctrines directed at the highest spiritual development of the potentialities of the *individual* human being and apply to politics only in the sense of "great politics," which notion too Nietzsche derives primarily from the Greeks. There is, of course, implicit in this position a theory of social interaction and we shall as we proceed, be concerned with expounding it and its ramifications. What is important here, however, is the recognition that the *metaphysical* doctrine of the Will to Power does not inherently involve a value disposition, that is, it is by its nature neither good nor bad—its individual manifestations may be either.

Nietzsche's anti-Christianity is essentially religious as Nietzsche himself realized when he lets the old pope say to Zarathustra:

"What is this I hear?" said the old pope at this point pricking up his ears. "O Zarathustra, with such disbelief you are more pious than you believe. Some god in you must have converted you to your godlessness. Is it not your piety itself that no longer lets you believe in a god? And your overgreat honesty will yet lead you beyond good and evil too.[21]

Nietzsche's upbringing as a pastor's son was deeply religious and his gradual disappointment and disillusionment with Christianity came as a result of the deeply imbedded strata of hypocrisy both in Christian dogma and practice.

Against Christianity, Nietzsche repeats the largely justified charge which has been raised in the Far East ever since the Thirteenth century: that Christians do not practice what they preach, no matter what their holy books say. As

---

[20] Karl Jaspers, *Nietzsche and Christianity*, trans. E. B. Ashton (Chicago, 1967), p. 39.
[21] Nietzsche, *Thus Spoke Zarathustra*, p. 374.

Nietzsche puts it: "A Buddhist acts differently from a non-Buddhist; a Christian acts like everybody else and practices a Christianity of moods and rituals."[22]

For Nietzsche, Christianity was not religious enough and many of his criticisms |precisely parallel criticisms of the profoundly Christian Kierkegaard. In fact, many of the virtues which Nietzsche praises can be found in the primordial substance of the Christian attitude. Howe-ver, Nietzsche's reaction to nineteenth century Christianity is as profound as it is extreme.

The two deadly themes of revenge and pity along with their myriad variations provide the psychological underpinnings for historical Christianity and are, in Nietzsche's eyes, positively Machiavellian. Christianity exploits man's basest desires, first of all, by its appeal to that most dangerous of illusions – equality; and secondly, through its distortion of the individual Will to Power by teaching the Christian that he is one of God's Elect. The dialectical interplay of humility and *hybris* in Christianity would be an extremely fruitful area of study for the psychologist of religion. Nietzsche's analyses of the motivations underlying the world-view of historical Christianity reveal his great powers of penetration as a psychologist, for even Zarathustra had to wrestle with the immense forces of revenge and pity. Nietzsche was basically an extremely kind-hearted human being and suffering almost invariably moved him deeply. He was keenly aware of the fatal temptation of pity or compassion in his own person.[23] For Nietzsche, the emotion of pity concealed a double danger. If one yields to pity, one endangers his own Will to Power by making sacrifices which are destructive to his own becoming as an individual. Also pity degrades the potential nobility and strength of the Other and thereby threatens the Will to Power of the Other, for this emotion engenders an attitude which regards its object as weak and helpless. Even worse it provides the foundation for a kind of false superiority. Here we need to reflect for a moment on Nietzsche's meaning of superiority, in order to avoid certain egregious, but nonetheless frequent, types of confusion. It should be obvious that when Nietzsche speaks of superiority, he does not mean economic, social, political, religious, or racial superiority. His conception of superiority centers on the life-situation of the individual and its spiritual quality more than anything else; that is, the individual must always strive to be superior to what he is at the

---

[22] Jaspers, *Nietzsche and Christianity*, p. 47.
[23] Nietzsche uses the word "*Mitleid*" for pity or compassion and puns on it: "*mit leiden*." As a result he argues that "*mit leiden*" (com-passion) merely increases "*leiden*" or suffering.

moment. His superiority can never be the arrogance of self-satisfaction. The individual must be his own severest critic recognizing both his strengths and his weaknesses, which means he must avoid modesty and pseudo-humility as stringently as arrogance.

In spite of Nietzsche's harsh condemnations of Christianity there is, as we have seen, a strong religious motivation behind his philosophy. But what do we mean here by "religious?" Mircea Eliade in his excellent little book, *The Sacred and the Profane*, describes two primordial impulses which he believes characterize the essence of religion.[24] The first is an impulse toward the absolute, toward permanence, and the second is the attempt to create a system of explanation which organizes one's experience into a comprehensive coherent whole. This second impulse Eliade describes as the attempt to produce *kosmos* out of Chaos. A highly graphic presentation of the first impulse is to be found in Zarathustra's roundelay.

O man, take care!
What does the deep midnight declare?
"I was asleep –
From a deep dream I woke and swear:
The world is deep,
Deeper than the day had been aware.
Deep is its woe;
Joy – deeper yet than agony:
Woe implores: Go!
But all joy wants eternity –
Wants deep, wants deep eternity."[25]

This longing for eternity is also the existential foundation for Nietzsche's doctrine of Eternal Recurrence.

The second impulse basic to religion, the movement from Chaos to *kosmos*, is found in Nietzsche's philosophy taken as a whole. That he did not succeed in presenting a unified *kosmos*, we shall try to demonstrate in the chapters which follow. The important thing here is to understand Nietzsche's philosophy as such an attempt at *kosmos*. Epistemologically Nietzsche, with his doctrine of perspectivism, is a Heraclitean, but ontologically, he does not have the foundational underpinning of *Logos* which we find in Heraclitus. Nietzsche's quest for such a foundation led him again and again to the doctrine of Eternal Recurrence. But the appearance of this doctrine is far more than simply the result of an ontological-epistemological exercise.

[24] Mircea Eliade, *The Sacred and the Profane* (New York: 1961).
[25] Nietzsche, *Thus Spoke Zarathustra*, p. 436.

This longing for permanence and eternity reveals an existential-psychological limitation of the human life-situation, namely the impossibility of ever grasping and accepting our own death. Freud, in his essay, "Thoughts on War and Death," puts it very succinctly.

Our own death is indeed unimaginable, and whenever we make the attempt to imagine it we can perceive that we really survive as spectators. Hence the psychoanalytic school could venture on the assertion that at bottom no one believes in his own death, or to put the same thing in another way, in the unconscious everyone of us is convinced of his own immortality.[26]

But Eternal Recurrence was not, even for Nietzsche, a completely satisfactory solution to the problems of permanence and Being. There is a deeply rooted ambivalence in Nietzsche's attitude toward his own doctrine.

Transvaluation and Humanism

Nietzsche's philosophy has often been criticized and rejected as nihilism. Such a judgment misses the whole point of his philosophy. Nietzsche's declaration that God is dead simply makes explicit a nihilism which had already penetrated and permeated the very foundations of Western culture. The entire project of transvaluation is Nietzsche's attempt to overcome nihilism. One of Nietzsche's characterizations of the philosopher is that he is a "physician of culture"; and he means this in two respects. First of all, the philosopher is the diagnostician of culture and he makes apparent the diseases which infect his culture. Functioning as a critic of contemporary culture, Nietzsche produced some of his finest insights as well as some of his bitterest condemnations. Many of the cultural illnesses which Nietzsche diagnosed are to be found as spiritual illnesses against which Nietzsche had to struggle as aspects of his own most intimate life-situation. Nietzsche's obsession with rooting out the diseases of culture tended at times toward a kind of fascination and pre-occupation rather like that of Hans Castorp's in Thomas Mann's *The Magic Mountain*.

The second aspect of the philosopher as a "physician of culture" is that of a healer of the spirit and it is here that Transvaluation comes in. Nietzsche could come to terms with physical and spiritual sickness only as something to be overcome. Such overcoming requires strength and a certain hardness toward oneself and others. In terms of the doctrine of the Superman, Nietzsche is merciless with regard to self-

[26] Sigmund Freud, "Thoughts on War and Death," in *On Creativity and the Unconscious*, ed. Benjamin Nelson (New York, 1965), pp. 222–23.

pity. The greatest danger, however, is that of pity for others, for such an attitude tends to indulge and excuse their follies. Thus, the Superman must harden himself and appear aloof and cruel, for otherwise there is no Transvaluation and everything collapses once again into nihilism. One is here reminded of Buber's remark that it is sometimes necessary to be cruel in order ultimately to be kind. It is in this manner that Nietzsche's humanism is grounded in contempt and a hardness toward oneself and others. Nietzsche firmly believed that any indulgence of weakness in human beings would lead ultimately to the destruction of humanity.

There are people who become hypochondriacal through their sympathy and concern for another person; the kind of sympathy which results therefrom is nothing but a disease. Thus there is also a Christian hypochondria, which afflicts those solitary, religiously-minded people who keep constantly before their eyes the sufferings and death of Christ.[27]

The allusion to Christianity here is no mere passing reference, for Nietzsche saw Christianity as one of the most virulent forms of nihilism. From this it should be clear that Nietzsche's characterization of himself as an anti-Christ *must also be understood as a characterization of himself as an anti-nihilist.*

In his very earliest works Nietzsche tackled this problem of nihilism in terms of the relationship between philosophy and culture. In his book *Philosophy in the Tragic Age of the Greeks*, he says:

A period which suffers from a so-called high level of liberal education but which is devoid of culture in the sense of a unity of style which characterizes all its life, will not quite know what to do with philosophy and wouldn't, if the Genius of Truth himself were to proclaim it in the streets and the market places. During such times philosophy remains the learned monologue of the lonely stroller, the accidental loot of the individual, the secret skeleton in the closet, or the harmless chatter between senile academics and children. No one may venture to fulfill philosophy's law with his own person, no one may live philosophically with that simple loyalty which compelled an ancient, no matter where he was or what he was doing, to deport himself as a Stoic if he once had pledged faith to the Stoa. All modern philosophizing is political, policed by governments, churches, academies, custom, fashion, and human cowardice, all of which limit it to a fake learnedness.[28]

For Nietzsche, a healthy culture is one in which philosophy flourishes as something intrinsic to the culture and even promotes that culture and helps guarantee its survival. Thus, by its very nature philosophy

[27] Friedrich Nietzsche, *Human, All Too Human*, Vol. I in *The Philosophy of Nietzsche*, ed. Geoffrey Clive (New York, 1965), p. 600.

[28] Nietzsche, *Philosophy in the Tragic Age of the Greeks*, pp. 37–38.

stands opposed to nihilism. Again, it is important to note that this model of culture, like the model of the Superman, is drawn from the Greeks. Nietzsche's orientation toward the Greeks was in large part, no doubt, a result of his philological investigations, but the roots of the matter go much deeper; for there was a profound spiritual affinity for Nietzsche between the Greek temperament and his own.

Nietzsche's fixation with regard to the notion of Transvaluation is now intelligible, since we can see that Transvaluation is the key to the Superman and to authentic culture as well. To reach its ultimate goals, this process of Transvaluation must take place on two levels, the individual existential level and the institutional cultural level. Nietzsche was never so much an idealist as to believe that every human being would seek the path to the Superman, and so it became supremely important to transform the institutions of culture to nurture and preserve those great individuals who could bring culture to its highest expression. This is the foundation of his "aristocratic radicalism." It parallels the position of Socrates, that only the best and the wisest should rule. Nietzsche, like his spiritual ancestors Heraclitus and Socrates, possessed a deeply rooted suspicion of the masses or the "herd," and strongly rejected democracy (not to mention, socialism and communism) as a form of nihilism which created precisely the same types of cultural disease and insanity which Christianity perpetuated. Ultimately, however, Transvaluation and aristocratic radicalism are not directed toward the production of this or that kind of political state, but rather are directed toward the creation of a great culture. This is politics in the manner of what Nietzsche calls "great politics." Great politics concerns itself with the whole range of man's expression and organization of himself and seeks to create a life-situation which raises the spirit to its highest manifestation as authentic culture. It is here in terms of the notion of great politics that we see Nietzsche as the physician of culture going beyond his role as diagnostician to begin to function as the healer of the spirit.

Aesthetics versus Positivism

Nietzsche's fixation on an aesthetic perspective as a foundation for his philosophizing is evident from his earliest works through his latest. In fact, for Nietzsche the questions of values and morality are inextricably bound up with aesthetics. This aestheticism is, in large part, the result of two extremely important influences; the ancient Greeks (especially relevant is the effect of Heraclitus) and Schopenhauer with his doctrine of creative Will. From the early Greeks he inherited a sense for philosophy as conceptual drama and was profoundly influenced by the power and vitality of their language. For Nietzsche, the pre-Socratics were involved in the unfolding and revelation of a cosmic drama which achieved its highest expression in the tragedies of Aeschylus and Sophocles. Already in *The Birth of Tragedy* Nietzsche regards the Greek way of life, perhaps somewhat romantically, as itself an art form. Greek tragedy was the highest expression of the synthesis of the Apollonian and the Dionysian which human culture has ever achieved. He argues that such an expression was possible only on the basis that the Greek culture was itself already pervaded by these Apollonian and Dionysian elements. Thus, for Nietzsche, the ultimate achievement of culture is a manner of living such that its everyday life is an artistic expression. During his early years of study he was deeply affected by the quest of the ancient Greeks for unity and harmony. He achieved what for him was a basic insight which was to pervade his philosophy ever after, namely, that the highest and ultimate form of philosophy is cosmology. Nietzsche's cosmology, like the pre-Socratic cosmologies, is monistic. "The decisive point of Nietzsche's cosmology . . . . can be expressed in two words: Nietzsche was a *dialectical monist.*" [29] For Nietzsche, as for the pre-Socratics, philosophy must "begin" with cosmology and, of course, cosmology is the "science of beginnings" (*archai*). It is only in terms of the ultimate principles (*archai*) of harmony and unity that there is any possibility of truly ordering man's individual existence and the institutions of his social existence. Thus, all the "true" manifestations of man's existence are grounded in aesthetics as *mimesis*, since the highest and therefore truest institutions are those which "imitate" and are modelled on the "ultimate principles," for, as Nietzsche puts it, "it is only as an *aesthetic phenomenon* that existence and the world are eternally justified." [30] How this view is compatible with Nietzsche's theory of truth as "perspectivism" is a question which we will have to consider later.

The other major influence which helped produce Nietzsche's aestheticism was Schopenhauer. The general orientation of Schopenhauer's philosophy, his metaphysics of the Will, his elevation of art and especially of music, all had a pronounced effect in guiding Nietz-

[29] Walter Kaufmann, *Nietzsche: Philosopher, Psychologist, Antichrist* (Cleveland and New York, 1965), p. 204.
[30] Friedrich Nietzsche, *The Birth of Tragedy*, trans. Walter Kaufmann (New York, 1967), p. 52.

sche's thought into new dimensions. In one respect it is possible to discuss Schopenhauer's effect on Nietzsche only in very general terms, since it is quite clear that from the earliest encounter with Schopenhauer's thought Nietzsche interpreted him for his own purposes and, in fact, projected many of his own ideas into Schopenhauer's position. Nietzsche evidently had some awareness of this, for in *Schopenhauer as Educator*, he remarks:

> And Schopenhauer's philosophy should always be first of all interpreted in this way: individually, by the individual for himself alone, in order to gain insight into his own misery, needs, and limitations and to know the antidotes and consolations; namely sacrifice of the ego, submission to the noblest intentions, and above all justice and mercy.[31]

It is significant to note that the "antidotes and consolations" which are mentioned at the end of this quotation are later radically reinterpreted or rejected by Nietzsche. The influence of Schopenhauer is not to be understood in terms of specific doctrines, but rather in terms of a metaphysical re-orientation of Nietzsche's thought. It is also interesting to observe that the elevated stance Nietzsche gives to art parallels Hegel's position and, furthermore, Nietzsche, like Hegel is first and finally involved in developing a metaphysic of the Spirit.[32] Needless to say, Wagner also exerted an important influence on the development of Nietzsche's aesthetic perspective and this influence has been well documented both by Nietzsche himself and by his critics.

In the middle period of Nietzsche's creative life a new influence comes into play and is to have lasting effects through the rest of his writings.

> For a time, in what is known as his second or "Positivistic" period, Nietzsche entertained the possibility that science might answer such questions as we can meaningfully ask, and that, if through anything, "through science does one really approach the real nature of the world and a knowledge of it."[33]

This scientific perspective has some peculiar consequences for Nietzsche's philosophy. An opposition arises between a view of the world grounded in aesthetics and a view grounded in the causalities of the physical sciences. The effects of these positivistic leanings are still present in the fragments which compose *The Will to Power*, where

---

[31] Friedrich Nietzsche, *Schopenhauer as Educator*, trans. James W. Hillesheim and Malcolm R. Simpson (Chicago, 1965), p. 26.

[32] For a discussion of the parallels between Nietzsche and Hegel, see Kaufmann's *Nietzsche*, pp. 204–13.

[33] Arthur C. Danto, *Nietzsche as Philosopher* (New York, 1965), p. 69.

Nietzsche claims of the Doctrine of Eternal Recurrence that, "It is the most *scientific* of all possible hypotheses."[34] The fragment from which this quotation is taken is a late one, having been written in June of 1887. Thus, it is clear that a concern with this scientific perspective is present from the middle years of Nietzsche's productivity right up until the end. During this time Nietzsche oscillated between this scientific perspective and the aesthetic perspective which had been established earlier. As any careful reader of Nietzsche would expect, Nietzsche remains critical of both perspectives and there is a growing awareness in his later works of an opposition between these perspectives. At first, there is no evidence that Nietzsche was concerned about reconciling this opposition, but as he progressed he seemed to feel a greater and greater demand to provide a unified systematic presentation of his philosophy. During the period from 1882 to 1888, Nietzsche drew up five different plans for such a comprehensive work and in each plan the doctrine of Eternal Recurrence plays a central role. All of the other facets of his philosophy were evidently to be brought into relation to his doctrine.[35] That Nietzsche felt the necessity to reconcile this opposition is a fact of the utmost significance as we shall later discover.

For Nietzsche all of the pre-occupations discussed above were deeply rooted in his most intimate life-situation. The unfolding of his own spiritual dimension was a project which simultaneously revealed a cultural and world view characterized by an incredible sensitivity to the spiritual dislocations of the modern age. In a significant sense Nietzsche's philosophy is a personalized version of Hegel. Both Nietzsche and Hegel were dominated by a cosmic vision which they sought to express in terms of Spirit. In spite of their many significant differences, both philosophers present a view that is characterized by a grandeur which has been lost to most contemporary philosophy, and both have a vision of man which extends far beyond the chaos and despiritualization which characterizes the contemporary life-situation of most men.

[34] Friedrich Nietzsche, *The Will to Power*, trans. Walter Kaufmann and R. J. Hollingdale (New York, 1967), pp. 36.
[35] Friedrich Nietzsche, *Vorspiel einer Philosophie der Zukunft*, ed. Karl Löwith (Frankfurt am Main, 1959), pp. 169–78.

Jaspers on the Relevance of Nietzsche's
Life to his Thought

As we have already observed, Jaspers devotes almost one-fifth of his Nietzsche book to a consideration of Nietzsche's life. In these sections Jaspers, on the whole, proceeds descriptively, offering very many quotations from Nietzsche as support for interpretive remarks. In fact, Jaspers' method of proceeding here might be characterized as "hermeneutic phenomenology," although certainly not in the sense in which Heidegger uses this phrase. The phenomenologically descriptive aspect of Jaspers' discussion consists in allowing Nietzsche to present himself as he is by means of constant direct quotation without presupposing or imposing any critical models of interpretation. From Jaspers' point of view the first task is to let Nietzsche speak for himself, while the interpreter keeps his mind free of all external theories and biases. The "hermeneutic" or interpretive aspect of the enterprise is for Jaspers primarily internal. Interpretation is the unfolding of what is already implicit; genuine interpretation can impose nothing external; it must work within the context of the self-revelation of the thinker himself. This, of course, does not exclude the use of biographical material which is not presented by the thinker himself, but Jaspers insists, and rightly so, that such material must always be understood in relation to the total context of the thinker with special emphasis on its relation to the self-revelation and self-understanding of the thinker.

The hermeneutic model which Jaspers employs (and there must be such a model, for hermeneutics by its very nature demands a model) is *Existenz*. The question now arises as to how Jaspers can escape violating his own criterion for interpretation, namely, that no external interpretive model be imposed. Jaspers is very careful to point out here that *Existenz* is not an *external* model but rather a *dialectically developed internal* model. But what is *Existenz?* Jaspers who philosophizes in terms of an elaborate dialectic, characteristically provides no simple description of *Existenz*. However, William Earle in his introduction to Jaspers' *Reason and Existenz* presents an accurate and relatively succinct description.

This fundamental center, each individual in his inwardness as he is to himself as just this unique, historical self, is *Existenz*. "Existenz," again, is an index; it names without characterizing. What it names is not the individual in his organic vitality, his abstract understanding, or his spirit; it is the individual himself, as he comprehends himself, in his freedom and authenticity standing before Transcendence. It is the ultimate ground, basis, or root of each historical self; it is not the content of any concept. And since Existenz is actual only in authentic self-awareness, a corruption of that awareness may corrupt Existenz itself. Existenz is but a possibility for men; it is not a property with which we are endowed by nature. It must be enacted inwardly if it is to be at all; and it need not ever be. It is the possibility in men of coming to themselves, of the self rejoining itself for a moment. Existenz is only a possibility for human nature; things in the world have no such possibility.[36]

For Jaspers, then, to interpret Nietzsche means to enter into dialogue with Nietzsche's *Existenz* as it finds expression in Nietzsche's writings. Here we must understand Jaspers' position very carefully. This dialogue is a dialogue between Jaspers' *Existenz* and Nietzsche's *Existenz*. However, Jaspers himself warns that *Existenz* as possibility is subject to corruption. This means that Jaspers is confronted with two problems. First of all, Jaspers must be certain that within this dialogue he is interacting as *authentic Existenz* and then he must establish criteria for determining when Nietzsche is speaking out of his authentic *Existenz* and when he is not. The second problem revolves around a criterion of validity for the dialogue itself. Jaspers emphatically denies that such dialogue is "merely subjective," and, since it is clearly not "objective" in any ordinary empirical sense, this suggests that there is some kind of self-validating objectivity which resides with the transcendental character of *Existenz* itself. Since Jaspers regards truth as a dialectical consequence and this dialectic is always open-ended, there is no final "objectivity," no final truth. Truth is a relation which can only exist as a relation between one *Existenz* and another and so truth is always a becoming. Even though this middle ground which Jaspers occupies between subjectivity and objectivity is well protected, it is nonetheless problematic and we shall have to keep the two above-mentioned problems clearly in mind as we examine Jaspers' specific interpretations of Nietzsche's doctrines. Finally, it is clear that in terms of Jaspers' conception of interpretation, biography (in its extended sense as contributory to a grasping of *Existenz*) is not only relevant to an interpretation of Nietzsche, but absolutely essential. A congruent view of interpretation is to be found in Nietzsche himself as expressed in his preface to *Philosophy in the Tragic Age of the Greeks*. For Jaspers and Nietzsche both, genuine interpretation can only be *"ad hominem."*

---

[36] William Earle, "Introduction" to Karl Jaspers' *Reason and Existenz*, (New York, 1960), p. 11.

Heidegger on the Relevance of Nietzsche's
Life to his Thought

In addition to his two volume *Nietzsche*, Heidegger has written a number of essays that deal with various facets of Nietzsche's works, but in none of these works does he concern himself with the biographical aspect of Nietzsche. There is less than ten pages devoted to biographical considerations in his 1155 page *Nietzsche:* and most of the material is in relation to *The Will to Power* plus a few references to works where biographical information may be obtained. He specially mentions Baeumler and Frau Förster-Nietzsche and refers to her *Das Leben Friedrich Nietzsche's* after which he adds the cautionary remark, "However, this publication like all that is biographical requires much reflection."[37] He then adds, "We shall forgo any further statement and discussion of the highly heterogenous literature about Nietzsche, since none of it could be useful for the task of this course of lectures."[38] The only concern that Heidegger has for biographical materials is a few letters which mention either Eternal Recurrence or the doctrine of the Will to Power and some sketches for the book, *The Will to Power*, which are to be found in the *Nachlass*. This already tells us that the basic approaches of Heidegger and Jaspers are radically different.

Michael Hamburger in his book *From Prophecy to Exorcism* comments harshly on Heidegger's position on Nietzsche.

In the case of a writer whose thought flowed so directly out of his life, who was consistent only in being unreservedly true to his own nature and his own moods, it is absurd to argue, as Heidegger did, that the biographical approach is outdated and irrelevant. Nietzsche himself claimed that only what is personal remains forever incontrovertible.[39]

If, then, Heidegger rejects any biographical or life-situational approach, what approach does he adopt? At this point only a brief indication can be given. Heidegger is most fundamentally concerned with Nietzsche's metaphysics, but not just Nietzsche's metaphysics as the culmination of the historical unfolding of metaphysics. For those acquainted with almost any of Heidegger's writings it is a familiar story. Heidegger argues that the pre-Socratics and especially Heraclitus and Parmenides were moving in the direction of genuine ontology, i.e., the asking of the question about the meaning of Being as such. However, a confusion arises in Plato and becomes firmly

---

[37] Heidegger, *Nietzsche*, p. 19.
[38] *Ibid.*, p. 19.
[39] Michael Hamburger, *From Prophecy to Exorcism* (London, 1965), p. 32.

rooted in Aristotle and the inquiry goes astray. Philosophers no longer ask the genuine question about Being *as such*, but now instead ask the question about the Being of beings, thus going off on the tangent of metaphysics. This tangent, according to Heidegger, reaches its final expression in Hegel and especially Nietzsche, who thereby opened up the way to a "return" to the possibility of a genuine fundamental ontology (which, of course, for Heidegger is his own philosophy). Briefly, then, Heidegger's interpretive approach is a metaphysical-historical one and in all fairness we should recognize that in spite of its one-sidedness this kind of interpretation has a long and rich history which has yielded many important insights. The existential life-situational approach is after all relatively recent and, one might even say, begins in earnest with Nietzsche himself. It should also be noted that Heidegger does place great emphasis on the texts and establishes as a criterion for genuine interpretation a "thinking along with" Nietzsche through the corpus of his writings and this approach also includes for Heidegger a "thinking through" of Nietzsche's ideas to their full conclusions even where Nietzsche himself did not do this.

NIETZSCHE'S EXTREMISM AND HONESTY: A THEORY OF COMMUNICATION

Nietzsche was a passionate thinker. He was also a critical one. It is well known that he worked and reworked his fragments before arriving at their final published form. Why, then, are so many of his statements cast in such extreme forms of expression? At times Nietzsche thunders like a penitential preacher or shrieks like a mad prophet. It is difficult to believe that this extremism is unintentional and yet, in his later work, he becomes critical of extremism. In August of 1881, in a letter to Peter Gast, he says, "Do I speak as one who has had a revelation? If so despise me and do not listen to me."[40] Nonetheless, Nietzsche was firmly convinced that authentic philosophy could not be communicated in abstract systems. For Nietzsche philosophy is an activity, a process – philosophizing. Jaspers makes much of this notion of philosophizing and to such an extreme that he virtually denies that Nietzsche has any philosophical doctrines. This dynamic conception of philosophy permitted Nietzsche to adopt an experimental attitude in his attempts to communicate his ideas and as a result we

[40] Jaspers, *Nietzsche*, p. 405.

find great variety in his modes of expression: aphorism, metaphor, simile, poetry, symbol, and indirectness as in Kierkegaard (although Nietzsche did not know of Kierkegaard's work until 1888). In all of these modes, Nietzsche sometimes used the technique of exaggeration, thus giving rise to extremism. Nietzsche, like many other writers, realized that the majority of readers are somewhat casual and so Nietzsche frequently uses the technique of exaggeration as a shock tactic to "awaken" the reader, to sting him to thought. This, of course, is a technique as old as Socrates, but Nietzsche uses it with a fine precision. Also involved here is Nietzsche's conviction that philosophy is a passionate and vital concern, and he frequently uses the simile of dancing as an illustration and contrast to the traditional view that philosophy is something solemn and ponderous.

That genuinely philosophical combination, for example, of a bold and exuberant spirituality that runs *presto* and a dialectic severity and necessity that takes no false step is unknown to most thinkers and scholars from their own experience, and therefore would seem incredible to them if somebody should speak of it in their presence. They picture every necessity as a kind of need, as a painstaking having-to-follow and being-compelled. And thinking itself they consider as something slow and hesitant, almost as toil, and often enough as "worthy of the *sweat* of the noble" – but not in the least as something light, divine, closely related to dancing and high spirits. "Thinking" and taking a matter "seriously," considering it "grave" – for them all this belongs together: that is the only way they have "experienced" it.[41]

Thus, for Nietzsche, there is in philosophical communication a certain amount of play and lightness and a considerable amount of irony. Nietzsche's extremism is no accident of temperament, but rather a quite intentional attempt to enhance communication and stimulate thought.

A second fundamental aspect of Nietzsche's concept of communication is honesty and self-criticism. No matter how extreme the formulation and expression of his ideas, it was never his intention to deceive or misguide, for his will to communicate was too strong. In spite of his celebration of deception as a "virtue" and his castigation of "serious-mindedness," the simple fact is that Nietzsche was too serious about his ideas to undertake any project of deception regarding their communication. Again and again he complains of being misunderstood in his most "honest" efforts. Nietzsche was merciless in applying his standard of honesty to other persons, as we have seen in the case of Wagner; yet he was equally strict with himself and

[41] Nietzsche, *Beyond Good and Evil*, p. 139.

even demanded strict honesty from others in their criticisms of him. An amusing example of this occurred when Nietzsche sent one of his musical compositions to Hans von Bülow. Von Bülow's reply is an astonishing critical devastation.

Your *Manfred Meditation* is the most fantastically extravagant, the most unedifying, the most anti-musical thing I have come across for a long time in the way of notes put on paper. Several times I had to ask myself whether it is all a joke, whether, perhaps, your object was to produce a parody of the so-called music of the future. Is it by intent that you persistently defy every rule of tonal connection, from the higher syntax down to the merest spelling? Apart from its psychological interest – for your musical fever suggests, for all its aberrations, an uncommon, a distinguished mind – your *Meditation*, looked at from a musical standpoint, is the precise equivalent of a crime in the moral sphere. Of the Apollonian element I have not been able to discover the smallest trace; and as for the Dionysian, I must say frankly that I have been reminded less of this than of the "day after" a bacchanal. If you really feel a passionate urge to express yourself in music, you should master the rudiments of the musical language: a frenzied imagination, revelling in reminiscences of Wagnerian harmonies, is not the sort of foundation to build upon. Wagner's most unprecedented audacities, apart from the fact that they derive from a dramatic web and are justified by the words – for in his purely instrumental works he wisely denies himself prodigious things of the kind – are without exception grammatically correct, down to the tiniest detail of notation . . . . But if you, highly esteemed Herr professor, really take this aberration of yours into the field of music quite seriously (as to which I am still doubtful), then at least confine yourself to vocal music and surrender to the words the helm of the boat in which you rove the raging seas of tone. You yourself, not without reason, describe your music as "terrible." It is indeed more terrible than you think — not detrimental to the common weal, of course, but something worse than that, detrimental to yourself, seeing that you can find no worse way of killing time than raping Euterpe in this fashion.[42]

And Nietzsche's response to this letter is equally astonishing, for he discusses von Bülow's criticisms objectively, accepts them, and thanks him for them. Years later, he even ventures to send another composition to von Bülow and in the accompanying letter he remarks, "Once upon a time I sent you a piece of my music and you passed sentence of death upon it in the most justifiable manner possible."[43] However, it must be admitted that Nietzsche did not receive criticism of his philosophy with such equanimity. His justification for the rejection of his philosophical critics was his claim that they misunderstood him and in most cases he was probably right. Yet, intrinsic in Nietzsche's mode of philosophizing is a repeated struggle with himself and his

[42] Ernest Newman, *The Life of Richard Wagner* (New York, 1946), IV, 324.
[43] Nietzsche, *The Philosophy of Nietzsche*, ed. Clive, p. 91.

ideas, a self-criticism which is epitomized in his evaluation of *The Birth of Tragedy* in *Ecce Homo*.

> Let me repeat that today the book appears impossible to me, – I consider it badly written, heavy, painful, full of a straining after images, maudlin, sugared at times to the point of effeminacy, uneven in tempo, devoid of the will to logical clarity, utterly convinced and therefore contemptuous of demonstration, distrustful even of the propriety of demonstration." [44]

Nietzsche was never quite satisfied with his attempts to communicate, and his compulsion to honesty, itself a form of extremism, drove him more and more to consider a final comprehensive "systematic" formulation of his entire philosophy. Lacking this "system," the interpreter must be as self-critical of himself as was Nietzsche, and must continually re-examine his interpretation with the framework of Nietzsche's texts in order to avoid reading into Nietzsche that which is external.

NIETZSCHE: POET, PHILOSOPHER, PSYCHOLOGIST, OR SOCIAL CRITIC

Numerous critics, including some philosophers, have contended that Nietzsche was not primarily a philosopher. For example, the literary critic James Huneker says, "Friedrich Nietzsche was more poet than original thinker." [45] Santayana makes a similar judgment: "It is hardly fair to a writer like Nietzsche, so poetical, fragmentary, and immature, to judge him as a philosopher." [46] Santayana's critical essays on Nietzsche are excellent examples of what criticism and interpretation should *not* be. Santayana's misunderstandings of Nietzsche are truly monumental. Fortunately, in dealing with Jaspers and Heidegger, we have no such gross and superficial distortions to deal with. Despite the problems inherent in their interpretive approaches, Jaspers and Heidegger have carefully studied Nietzsche's writings and make profoundly serious attempts to be faithful to the character of his philosophy.

Jaspers' View

Jaspers attempts to understand Nietzsche in terms of Nietzsche's own *Existenz*, but more specifically in terms of Nietzsche's *Existenz*

---

[44] Friedrich Nietzsche, *Ecce Homo* in *The Philosophy of Nietzsche*, ed. Willard Huntington Wright (New York, 1954), pp. 937–38.

[45] James Huneker, *Egoist: A Book of Superman* (New York, 1910), p. 238.

[46] George Santayana, *Egotism in German Philosophy* (New York, n.d.), p. 114.

as a philosopher. There can be no doubt that, for Jaspers, Nietzsche must, first and foremost, be understood as a philosopher. That Nietzsche was a brilliant psychologist, a penetrating social critic and, at times, superbly poetic, is undeniable; but for Jaspers all of these other facets must be understood in terms of Nietzsche's being as a philosopher, but as a "new" kind of philosopher; one who speaks from the destiny of his own *Existenz*.

> They [Kierkegaard and Nietzsche] cannot be classed under any earlier type (poet, philosopher, prophet, savior, genius). With them a new form of human reality appears in history. They are, so to speak, representative destinies, sacrifices whose way out of the world leads to experiences for others. They are by the total staking of their whole natures like modern martyrs, which however, they precisely denied being. Through their character as exceptions, they solved their problem.[47]

Thus, although Nietzsche is to be understood primarily as a philosopher, he must be understood as an initiator of a new kind of philosophizing, a philosophizing out of *Existenz*.

Heidegger's View

Heidegger, too, is critical of any interpretation of Nietzsche which does not retain Nietzsche's being as a philosopher at its core. In fact, in this respect, Heidegger is much more traditional than Jaspers. This is evident from the fact that Heidegger's concern with Nietzsche is primarily a concern with Nietzsche's metaphysics and with how this metaphysics fits into the historical unfolding of Being. Heidegger rejects the idea that Nietzsche is primarily a poet-philosopher and also attacks the notion that Nietzsche's philosophy is a "philosophy of life" (*Lebensphilosophie*). Here he seems to have Jaspers in mind, among others.

> However, for a long time it has been passed down from the German chairs of philosophy that Nietzsche is not a rigorous thinker, but rather a "poet-philosopher." Nietzsche does not belong to the philosophers, who think out only abstract and shadowy matters remote from life. If, however, one does call him a philosopher, then he must be understood as a "philosopher of life." This title, already popular for some time, should at once cause suspicion, as though philosophy is otherwise for the dead and therefore basically superfluous. Such a view corresponds fully with the opinion of those who welcome in Nietzsche "the philosopher of life" who has finally done away with abstract thinking. These customary judgments regarding Nietzsche are erroneous.[48]

---

[47] Karl Jaspers, *Reason and Existenz*, trans. William Earle (New York, 1960), p. 38.
[48] Heidegger, *Nietzsche*, I, 13–14.

For Heidegger, also, there is no question that Nietzsche must be fundamentally understood and interpreted as a philosopher, and Heidegger, like Jaspers, sees Nietzsche as the advent of a "new kind of philosophy." For Heidegger, this new kind of philosophy is not an *Existenz*-philosophy, but rather, Heidegger believes, metaphysics reaches its culmination in Nietzsche, and thereby the possibility for fundamental ontology has been opened up once more.

SUMMARY

It should now be quite clear that both, Heidegger and Jaspers, approach Nietzsche as a serious and profound philosopher. However, it should also be clear that their respective grounds for doing so are radically different. Jaspers wishes to concern himself with Nietzsche's philosophy in terms of the vital core of Nietzsche's *Existenz* and thereby to enter into existential dialogue with Nietzsche. Heidegger, too, emphasizes the notion of dialogue, but for him it is a dialogue with Nietzsche's metaphysics rather than an existential dialogue. Jaspers' approach to Nietzsche is many-faceted, whereas Heidegger's approach remains fundamentally one-sided. Each approach has its virtues and its inadequacies and in the following chapters we shall concern ourselves with the adequacy of these two interpretations in terms of explicit examinations of the major ideas in Nietzsche's philosophy.

CHAPTER II

NIETZSCHE'S METAPHYSICS AND EPISTEMOLOGY

It is necessary for us here to remind ourselves of the direction in which we wish to proceed. The thesis which we wish to demonstrate is that there is a fundamental dualism at the heart of Nietzsche's philosophy. We have already discussed how Jaspers and Heidegger arrive at radically different interpretations. Thus, we are here going to undertake a detailed examination of these two interpretations regarding the central ideas in Nietzsche's philosophy in order to show that this dualism of which we have spoken is the ground for the possibility of two such radically different interpretations. How is it to be characterized? Here we can give only a brief indication. We have already suggested that there is an opposition between an aesthetic perspective and a positivistic perspective. However, this dualism is more fundamentally stated in terms of an opposition between Nietzsche's metaphysics and epistemology, on the one hand, and his philosophical anthropology on the other. What makes this problem all the more fascinating is that Nietzsche himself was aware of this opposition. We must be very careful here as to how we understand this notion of a dualism. First of all, it in no way denies the fact that there are extremely important and even consistent relationships between Nietzsche's metaphysics and epistemology and his philosophical anthropology. Secondly, the basic opposition which defines this dualism is a radical one which goes to the very heart of the manner in which Nietzsche chose to philosophize. As radical as this opposition is, it is by no means simple, for, in its most fundamental aspect, it raises the question of the very nature of thought itself. Finally, although this dualism does have a single focus, its ramifications touch every aspect of Nietzsche's philosophy and it manifests itself in terms of many specific, less fundamental oppositions, such as the one we have already mentioned – the opposition between an aesthetic perspective and a positivistic one.

By far the majority of Nietzsche's discussions of the problems of Being and Becoming are to be found in *The Will to Power*. We have previously remarked that cosmology constitutes the center of Nietzsche's thought and as soon as we begin to examine the questions about the nature of Being and Becoming, this becomes evident. Ultimately, Nietzsche's theory of reality is the ground for his theory of truth which, in turn, is the ground for all values. In other words, Nietzsche approaches metaphysics as "First Philosophy." Nietzsche's metaphysics has two aspects which it is important to distinguish carefully. The first is a critical or "destructive" aspect which constitutes a critique of traditional metaphysical notions of Being and reality. The second aspect consists of Nietzsche's own positive contributions to metaphysics, which we shall call his theory of REALITY in order to distinguish it from the traditional notions which he is criticizing.[1] Nietzsche's conception of the problem of REALITY is inseparably bound up with the conceptions of logic and rationality, i.e., with the nature of thought, conceptualization, and categorization.

Nietzsche's critique of traditional metaphysics is of considerable interest in that we once again discover strong parallels with the pre-Socratics, especially with Heraclitus.

Today we are again getting close to all those fundamental forms of world interpretation devised by the Greek spirit through Anaximander, Heraclitus, Parmenides, Empedocles, Democritus, and Anaxagoras – we are growing more Greek by the day; at first, as is only fair, in concepts and evaluations, as Hellenizing ghosts, as it were: but one day, let us hope, also in our bodies![2]

Nietzsche believes that metaphysics was led astray by the categories of Being, reality, and truth. At first, it appears that Nietzsche totally

---

[1] In various places throughout the text full capitalization has been used for seven words: VIRTUE, TRANSCENDENCE, TRUTH, NIHILISM, REALITY, THOUGHT, and KNOWLEDGE. This has been done in order to indicate clearly the fundamental differences between the perspectives of philosophical anthropology and the cosmological perspective. Whenever any of the seven words is written in the above manner with full capitalization, this is to indicate that the statement containing such capitalized words is made from the perspective of cosmology. If these words are not capitalized they refer to the perspectives of philosophical anthropology. For example, Nietzsche's theory of TRUTH (cosmological perspective) states that there are no truths (philosophical anthropological perspectives).

[2] Nietzsche, *The Will to Power*, pp. 225–26.

rejects the classical metaphysical two-world view of Appearance and reality, or Becoming and Being. However, on closer examination, it becomes clear that Nietzsche wishes to transform what has been traditionally regarded as a dualism into a "dialectical monism," thus achieving a synthesis of Heraclitus and Parmenides. "To impose upon becoming the character of being – that is the supreme will to power."[3] But the question which remains for us here is that of how such a "unification" is possible. Again at this point we can only give a brief anticipatory indication. The key to this "unity" is time or, more specifically in Nietzsche's terminology, the doctrine of Eternal Recurrence. A fundamental grasp of the "unification" of Being and Becoming depends upon the elaboration of this doctrine with which we shall concern ourselves shortly. However, at the moment, let us take a closer look at the grounds for Nietzsche's critique of traditional metaphysics.

Nietzsche believes that traditional metaphysics is based on a fundamental deception grounded in the very nature of thought itself.

In order to think and infer it is necessary to assume beings: logic handles only formulas for what remains the same. That is why this assumption would not be proof of reality: "beings" are part of our perspective.[4]

For Nietzsche, all things are in continuous Becoming; all forms of permanence and endurance are apparent and illusory; are *necessary* fictions. That they are necessary does not, however, change their ontological status – they remain deceptions. Here we have the presentation of an ontological limitation of human being; namely, that human knowledge is by its very nature grounded in the fictions of permanence and endurance, that is, in the illusion of Being. Thus, in this respect, we can say of Nietzsche's metaphysical and epistemological position that it is anti-anthropocentric.

Knowledge and becoming exclude one another. Consequently, "knowledge" must be something else: there must first of all be a will to make knowable, a kind of becoming must itself create the deception of beings.[5]

Nonetheless, Nietzsche recognizes the fact that we *must* act *as if* there were Being both in our practical lives and in our pursuit of science.[6]

---

[3] *Ibid.*, p. 330.
[4] *Ibid.*, p. 280.
[5] *Ibid.*, p. 280.
[6] For a discussion of Nietzsche's notion of fictions in relation to the Kantian "as if" see Hans Vaihinger, *The Philosophy of 'As If,'* trans. C. K. Ogden (New York, 1924), pp. 341–62.

For Nietzsche, REALITY must be understood as Becoming, and Being is simply a conceptual illusion we have created in order to think and communicate. Thus, logic becomes a kind of necessary mistake which we need for conceptualization, but here again we need to make a distinction between thought in the traditional metaphysical sense and the special kind of THOUGHT by means of which Nietzsche, in one sense, transcends traditional metaphysics and thereby arrives at the diagnosis of necessary fictions and goes beyond this to establish his own conception of REALITY. What we must remember here is that Nietzsche grounds his metaphysics in Becoming, and that the other aspects of his metaphysics and epistemology are to be derived from this grounding.

Jaspers' View

Jaspers is highly suspicious of any and every attempt to interpret Nietzsche in terms of specific doctrines. Jaspers rejects the notion that Nietzsche had any coherent doctrine of Being and instead places emphasis on the dialectical aspects of Nietzsche's thinking about Being and Becoming. Jaspers repeatedly concerns himself with the dynamic aspect of Nietzsche's thought and thus prefers to discuss Nietzsche's "philosophizing" rather than his concepts. This approach seems, at first, consistent with Nietzsche's own approach to the character of philosophy as conceptualization. Jaspers seems to place more importance on the process of Nietzsche's thinking than in any "results" at which he arrived.

> The movement of Nietzsche's thinking seems to become stranded whenever, as frequently occurs, the will to truth requires its own surrender. But always a new progression begins; for the goal is authentic being rather than nothingness. It is authentic being toward which the passionate will to truth, in the form of an ineradicable skepticism, strives with ever renewed insistence .... As though driven by fate, he seems compelled to expose every intellectual triumph immediately to unlimited skepticism. He does not relapse into the nothingness of the theory of truth that annihilates itself by moving in a circle, but he fills the circle with ever new developments through which his will to truth reasserts itself. He does not get bogged down on any purportedly definitive correct insight into the nature of truth but draws all such insights back into the whirlpool of his thoughts.[7]

This passage is important for two reasons. First of all, Jaspers points out that dialectic is not a random process, but must be directed toward some goal. In this case the goal is "authentic being." However, we should note that there is a fundamental ambiguity in this phrase.

[7] Jaspers, *Nietzsche*, p. 211.

There is the metaphysical sense of Being with which we are concerned here, and there is the anthropological-philosophical sense of Being which we shall consider in the next chapter. This brings us to the second point regarding the above quotation. Jaspers suggests that Nietzsche never really attains the goal of his dialectic, that what insights he does attain are always thrown "back into the whirlpool of his thoughts." Thus, Jaspers tends to minimize the importance of Nietzsche's metaphysical insights in favor of the dialectical anthropological-philosophical sense of Being which he explicates out of Nietzsche's *Existenz*.

Jaspers' approach to the problems of Being and Becoming is peculiar in that he tends to shift emphases in order to create an interpretive method consistent with his notions of dialectic and contradiction. Jaspers sees three aspects to Nietzsche's "philosophizing" about Being.

But though Nietzsche's philosophizing is immersed in "becoming," he does not stop with it, but again lays hold of being (1) as the *intelligible necessity of life* within existence, (2) in his transcending philosophy that aims at *being* per se and (3) by virtue of his *existential attitude*.[8]

The first aspect is that of the necessary or "life-preserving" fictions about which we have already spoken. They provide, in part, the bridge between Nietzsche's metaphysics and epistemology and his philosophical anthropology. They are, therefore, also the bridge between the anti-anthropocentric perspective of the metaphysics and epistemology and the anthropocentric perspective of his philosophical anthropology.

The second aspect is the metaphysical, which Jaspers regards as fragmentary, inconsistent, and confused. The third aspect is, of course, the one to which Jaspers gives most emphasis as it involves interpretation out of Nietzsche's *Existenz* understood as "real dialectic." At the moment we are concerned with the second aspect – the metaphysical one. Jaspers wishes to interpret Nietzsche's conception of Being as essentially contradictory and regards this contradictoriness as one which arises out of Nietzsche's existential-psychological situation, rather than as an essential metaphysical contradictoriness which lies at the heart of the meaning of Nietzsche's metaphysics.

As a young man Nietzsche tried out the metaphysical thought: "If contradiction, if . . . . true being, and if becoming belongs to appearance, then profound understanding of the world consists in understanding contradiction." . . . . The question arises: Do oppositions and contradictions inhere in being itself, or are they merely modes of appearance devoid of real existence? Is becoming an ultimate reality that resolves all opposition and overcomes all contradictoriness,

8 *Ibid.*, p. 350.

or are contradictions the reality which the appearance of becoming merely obscures? Nietzsche did not think with any consistency beyond these beginnings, but again and again he touched upon this perennial problem of philosophy in which logic and metaphysics meet.[9]

This passage is strange for two reasons. Jaspers does not seem to take Nietzsche's youthful remark very seriously and he repeatedly remarks on the strangeness (and inconsistency!) of Nietzsche's remarks on "logic." Yet as late as 1888, in a fragment, Nietzsche wrote, "The conceptual ban on contradiction proceeds from the belief that we are *able* to form concepts, that the concept not only designates the essence of a thing but comprehends it."[10] Also in a fragmentary note of 1887 he wrote, "The character of the world in a state of becoming as incapable of formulation, as 'false,' as 'self-contradictory.'"[11] Thus, this problem of Being and Becoming and the nature of the "logic" for formulating these notions was of perennial concern to Nietzsche, as Jaspers himself admits, which makes his remark that Nietzsche "did not think with any consistency beyond these beginnings" seem all the stranger. Secondly, Jaspers' questions in the passage quoted above seem merely rhetorical and there is the implication that Nietzsche never really thought these problems through. However, once we realize what Jaspers has done some of the strangeness disappears. Unfortunately, Jaspers' interpretive methodology does not in practice remain true to the theory of interpretation which he originally presents and which we have already sketched.

Jaspers violates his own theoretical model of interpretation in two important ways. This in no way, however, undermines Jaspers' enterprise which contains much that is enlightening and stimulating, but it does underline the fact that we must be very cautious about accepting any interpretation of Nietzsche until we have carefully examined its foundations. First of all, as we have already observed, Jaspers uses the notion of *Existenz* as a hermeneutic model and attempts to justify it as a model on the grounds that it is developed internally rather than being imposed externally. We also noted that this interpretation is to be understood as a dialectic between Jaspers' *Existenz* and Nietzsche's *Existenz* or, more accurately, Nietzsche's *Existenz as Jaspers interprets it*. Jaspers denies that the notion of *Existenz* is purely subjective and, of course, it is not purely objective either, and so it is

9 *Ibid.*, pp. 395–96.
10 Nietzsche, *The Will to Power*, p. 280.
11 *Ibid.*, p. 280.

a matter of interpretation. Thus, already hidden in Jaspers' hermeneutic model is a presumptive interpretation. However, someone might
argue that Jaspers' *Nietzsche* is itself the elucidation of Nietzsche's
Existenz. If, however, that were the case, then Jaspers could not
legitimately appeal to the notion of *Existenz* as the supporting foundation of various facets of his interpretation. Furthermore, it is clear
that with regard to Nietzsche's metaphysical notions, Jaspers is
disinclined to take them very seriously and almost hints that they are
aberrations of Nietzsche's *Existenz*. Thus, we can see that a clarification
and elucidation of the notion of *Existenz* in general and the criteria of
interpretation of Nietzsche's *Existenz* in particular are crucial to
Jaspers' Nietzsche interpretation. Unfortunately, Jaspers does not
directly face this problem and, as a result, some of his attitudes and
criticisms, especially in the areas of Nietzsche's metaphysics and
epistemology, seem somewhat arbitrary.

Jaspers' second violation is considerably more subtle and centers
around the notion of contradiction. Here again there are two aspects
to the problem. First, when Jaspers uses the phrase "real dialectic,"
he means a *dialectic of contradiction*.

In any case, it is the task of the interpreter to be forever dissatisfied until he
has *also* found the contradiction, to search out contradictions in all their forms,
and then, if possible, to gain direct experience of their necessity. Instead of being
occasionally provoked by contradiction, one should pursue contradictoriness to
its source.[12]

If this were put forth simply as a general suggestion, it would have to be
accepted as good advice, but presented, as it is, as a *methodological
principle*, it is quite misleading. It is true that an interpretation which
omitted taking into account Nietzsche's dialectic of contradiction
would be deficient, but Jaspers' overemphasis on this aspect of Nietzsche's thinking is reductive.

The second aspect of the problem about this notion of contradiction
involves Jaspers' use of the conception of transcendence. Transcendence
plays an extremely important role in Jaspers' own philosophy and
carries with it certain dynamic overtones which provide connective
links to the notion of *Existenz*. Here, in relation to the problem of
interpreting Nietzsche's conceptions of Being and Becoming, Jaspers
has imported his own notion of transcendence. What is Nietzsche's
notion of Being, according to Jaspers?

---

[12] Jaspers, *Nietzsche*, p. 10.

His metaphysical doctrine tells us what that being per se, conceived as nothing but pure this-worldliness, actually is: Being is *the eternal recurrence of all things*. The insight into this recurrence, with its consequences for our awareness of being, our conduct, and our experience, has taken the place of belief in God. Being is *will to power;* all that occurs is nothing but a mode of the will to power which in its endless appearances furnishes the sole propulsion of becoming. Being is *life;* it is designated by the mythical symbol, Dionysus. The meaning of being is the *superman*.[13]

But how is it possible that Being is all of these things? According to Jaspers, it is the result of a contradiction in Nietzsche's notion of Being which leads him to posit a kind of transcendence which is total immanence, since Nietzsche was a severe critic of all the traditional forms of transcendence.

In each case, being is no longer the transcendence of God; instead it is the immanence that I can discover, investigate, and produce .... The being that Nietzsche has in mind can only be observed and conceived in actual specific objects within the world. Hence the constant transformation of transcending total immanence into the known immanence of particularity pertaining only to specific mundane things. This comes about because, having previously identified the essence of being metaphysically with an absolutized specific world-being, he can always return to the latter. Thus his meaning is constantly changing from transcending thinking to discursive thinking within the world as he shifts from one method of thinking to another.[14]

One's first impulse is to dismiss this as sophistry. However, upon taking a closer look, one can see what leads Jaspers to adopt this peculiar position. First, let us remind ourselves of three things: (1) Jaspers' interpretation based on *Existenz* emphasizes that aspect of Nietzsche's thought which we have called philosophical anthropology; (2) there are significant disparities between Jaspers' own metaphysics and Nietzsche's; and (3) Jaspers believes that there is a contradiction in Nietzsche's notion of Being. However, not even Jaspers can deny that there is a metaphysical dimension to Nietzsche's philosophy and, since Nietzsche *appears* to reject all forms of transcendence, Jaspers is led to his notion of transcendence in immanence in order to distinguish a metaphysical and a mundane level, which at the same time reinforces his notion that there is a contradiction in Nietzsche's thought about Being. It is possible that Nietzsche, who was very subtle as a psychologist, was exceptionally clumsy as a metaphysician; but it is also possible that Nietzsche's youthful thought about contradiction, which persisted throughout his active life, was the attempt to open up a new

---

[13] *Ibid.*, pp. 430–31.
[14] *Ibid.*, p. 431.

dimension of metaphysical thought or, as Heidegger would put it, an attempt to prepare the ground for the "overcoming" of metaphysics, which is precisely Heidegger's view, as we shall now see.

Heidegger's View

For Heidegger, the problems of Being and Becoming are central to the interpretation of Nietzsche. In fact, Heidegger believes that the really great philosophers, in spite of the great variety of concerns and methodologies, are all ultimately concerned with a single question – the question about the nature of Being. However, Heidegger also feels that this question is just that question which the history of philosophy has not unfolded. The reason for this is, of course, from Heidegger's point of view, the historical "mistake" which the Greeks made in turning from fundamental ontology to metaphysics. Nietzsche is the culmination of the historical development of metaphysics and at the same time he opens up the possibility for an authentic re-orientation to Being itself. Nonetheless, Nietzsche failed to "stand beyond" the tradition of metaphysics and thus is its culmination, since he forced metaphysics to its most extreme conclusion – nihilism.

Nietzsche's failure to "stand beyond" traditional metaphysics is a result of the way in which he directed his thought about Being. In several places Nietzsche describes his own philosophy as a "reversal of Platonism." Platonism is guilty of having made Being into something static and permanent – namely "idea" – in conformity with the limitations of the human epistemological situation. Thus, "metaphysics is anthropomorphism – the forming and viewing of the world according to the image of man."[15] However, anthropomorphism is precisely what Nietzsche hopes to escape through his reversal of Platonism, but, according to Heidegger, he cannot, "for this metaphysics, to which the doctrine of the superman belongs, places man, as no previous metaphysics has, in the role of the unconditioned and only measure of all things."[16] Thus Nietzsche's metaphysics is not only Heraclitean, but leads to a kind of hyper-Protagoreanism as well.

However, at the moment, we must take a closer look at this problem of Being. Our discussion here must necessarily remain incomplete and can only be fully developed in the following sections, since for both, Jaspers and Heidegger, Nietzsche's notion of Being is fully intelligible only in relation to the notions of the Will to Power, Transvaluation,

[15] Heidegger, *Nietzsche*, II, 127.
[16] *Ibid.*, II, 127.

Eternal Recurrence, and truth. An examination, not to mention an evaluation, of Heidegger's interpretation of Nietzsche's doctrine of Being is difficult for several reasons. First of all, Heidegger's manner of proceeding is ponderous and he is highly repetitious. At times it seems as though the preliminaries and preparations for discussing the "basic questions" are interminable and Heidegger has the annoying habit of making frequent important, but poorly integrated, digressions. Secondly, it is a major undertaking in itself to untangle Heidegger's ideas from Nietzsche's. Heidegger rather blithely assumes that Nietzsche fits comfortably into his conception of the historicity of metaphysics as the unfolding of the question about Being. Finally, Heidegger uses Nietzsche's philosophy as an occasion for philosophizing "beyond" Nietzsche, and toward the end of the second volume of his *Nietzsche*, Nietzsche virtually disappears from the discussion.

With these difficulties in mind, let us attempt to present the nucleus of Heidegger's interpretation of Nietzsche's notion of Being. Like Jaspers, Heidegger emphasizes that for Nietzsche, Being must be grasped as Becoming, and also that Nietzsche's "theory" of REALITY has two aspects – a critique of traditional metaphysics and an attempt to provide the groundwork for a "new" metaphysics. It is this latter aspect that is of primary importance here. Nietzsche's critique of the traditional conceptions of Being or, more accurately, of all the traditional forms of transcendence immediately directs our attention to this second "creative" aspect which is an attempt on Nietzsche's part to "transcend" traditional metaphysical thinking.

In the first third of the first volume of his *Nietzsche*, Heidegger approaches Nietzsche's notion of Being through an analysis of his aesthetic perspective and the "reversal of Platonism." These two facets of Nietzsche's thought are inextricably bound up with one another. For Platonism truth is more valuable than art, but in Nietzsche's reversal "Art is more valuable than truth."[17] For the Platonist, reality and truth are to be found only in the realm of the supersensible and with respect to reality and truth the realm of the sensible is deficient. For Nietzsche, however, art is the fundamental ground for the revelation of Being, since in his early period when Nietzsche's aesthetic perspective pre-dominates, art is the highest expression of the Will to Power. In part, Heidegger is very sympathetic with this view since it strongly parallels his own position that poetry and painting can be

---

[17] *Ibid.*, I, 250.

revelations of Being.[18] Nietzsche rejects the translation of Being by the Platonists to a supersensible plane, since this imposes static anthropomorphic categories on that which is continually in process. REALITY must be grasped as Becoming and can, therefore, only be grasped in terms of the sensible. Genuine Art is that which reveals to us the sensible as Becoming and, understood as the Will to Power, leads us to a genuine apprehension of REALITY.

Ultimately, however, Heidegger rejects Nietzsche's attempt at a reversal of Platonism and calls him "the most unbridled Platonist in the history of Western metaphysics."[19] Heidegger goes even further for he argues that Nietzsche never really asks the fundamental question, "What is Being?," but instead asks only the introductory question (*Leitfrage*), "What is the being (*das Seiende*)?"[20] The fundamental question remains as foreign to Nietzsche as to the history of thinking before him."[21] We must keep in mind, however, that Heidegger's criticisms of Nietzsche are based on what Heidegger apprehends as an incongruence between his own thinking and Nietzsche's. We shall also have to consider the degree to which Heidegger's interpretation has been conditioned by his own philosophical project; and this raises the question of the adequacy and unbiasedness of Heidegger's interpretation.

Comparison and Contrast

Heidegger and Jaspers agree that Nietzsche's notion of Being must be grasped as a dialectic of Becoming. They further agree that Nietzsche's metaphysical project must be understood as a critique of traditional metaphysics, which then leads into the attempt to provide a "new" kind of metaphysics. Both agree that this attempt fails, but their reasons for this opinion are radically different. For Jaspers, these reasons stem from what he regards as Nietzsche's inability as *Existenz* to escape the fundamental impulse toward transcendence. For Heidegger, Nietzsche's project fails because Nietzsche does not "overcome" metaphysics by asking the fundamental question about Being as such. Basically Jaspers believes that Nietzsche fails because there is a contradiction inherent in his notion of Being. Heidegger, on the other hand, emphasizes Nietzsche's failure in terms of what he regards as

[18] See Heidegger's essay, *The Origin of the Work of Art.*
[19] William B. Macomber, *The Anatomy of Disillusion: Martin Heidegger's Notion of Truth* (Evanston, 1967), p. 197.
[20] Heidegger, *Nietzsche*, I, 80.
[21] *Ibid.*, I, 80.

Nietzsche's anthropomorphism of metaphysics. This is a curious situation. Jaspers ignores the consequences of Nietzsche's attack on conceptualization, especially as it applies to the notion of contradiction. As Jaspers himself points out, Nietzsche very early in his philosophical career became convinced of the necessity for thinking through the nature of metaphysics as a contradiction. Thus, Jaspers fails to make the distinction between Nietzsche's notion of Being containing a contradiction – which view is a misunderstanding on Jaspers' part – and the view Nietzsche actually presents, namely, that Being itself as apprehended by the thought of traditional metaphysics is inherently a contradiction. This is a direct consequence of Nietzsche's critique of metaphysics. In other words, Nietzsche is saying that a new kind of THOUGHT is necessary in order to grasp REALITY. The traditional modes of thought, due to their notion of "logic," have imposed static categories to create a permanent notion of Being as the essence of reality. True REALITY, however, requires a different kind of THOUGHT, one which can grasp the essentially contradictory nature of the ordinary conceptualization of Being.

Heidegger, too, curiously ignores Nietzsche's own suggestions and guidelines. Nietzsche, in his criticisms of Platonism, makes it quite clear that he rejects the anthropomorphism of metaphysics and epistemology. Heidegger, however, believes that Nietzsche is guilty to the extreme of just such an anthropomorphism. It is, of course, possible that Nietzsche does violate his own prohibition, but before deciding that this is the case we should first examine Nietzsche's position in this regard with great care. Heidegger, however, makes no such examination and takes it as self-evident that Nietzsche is guilty. In anticipation we might suggest that Heidegger arrives at this verdict because he fails to recognize the fundamental dualism between Nietzsche's metaphysics and epistemology and his philosophical anthropology. Heidegger attempts to subsume all aspects of Nietzsche's thought under his metaphysics. Jaspers, on the other hand, basically attempts to subsume all of Nietzsche's thought under philosophical anthropology and thus produces similar distortions from the other side. Ultimately we hope to show that two such radically different interpretations are possible precisely because of this fundamental dualism at the heart of Nietzsche's philosophy and, further, that any interpretation which fails to take into account this dualism will of necessity be one-sided. To grasp fully Nietzsche's THOUGHT about REALITY, we must examine the other basic aspects of his metaphysics and, finally, attempt to understand these in relation to his notion of Being.

THE WILL TO POWER

The doctrine of the Will to Power is central to any attempt to gain an understanding of Nietzsche's metaphysics. Nonetheless, this doctrine has been repeatedly and perversely misunderstood. It is with regard to this doctrine that we once again encounter Nietzsche as a cosmologist in much the same way in which the pre-Socratics were cosmologists. There is, of course, also the influence here of Schopenhauer in terms of the general doctrine of the metaphysical primordiality of the Will. Nietzsche, however, very soon rejected Schopenhauer's conception as associated with negativity and pessimism, and transformed his own doctrine of Will into a doctrine of cosmic affirmation. In most of the pre-Socratics the primordial *arché* was conceived of as dynamic, that is, it was imbued with the power of self-differentiation and, in fact, the life-force was thought of as itself a specific manifestation of this power which characterized the primordial *arché*. This is the doctrine of "animism" and in this sense Nietzsche's conception is "animistic."

The mechanistic representation of a "lifeless" Nature is only an hypothesis for the purposes of calculation; it overlooks the fact that here too power relations and therewith relationships of perspective held sway. Every point of power is in itself perspectival. From this it becomes clear, "that there is no inorganic World." Everything "real" is alive, it is in itself "perspectival" and asserts itself in its perspective against others.[22]

For Nietzsche, the doctrine of the Will to Power is the foundation of metaphysics; it is the ultimate expression of the primordial *arché*, that is, the Will to Power *is* in the most radical metaphysical sense, *what there is*. As Danto puts it:

It is hardly avoidable that we think of Will-to-Power in almost exactly the terms in which men once thought of substance, as that which underlies everything else and was the most fundamental of all. For Will-to-Power is not something we *have*, but something we *are*. Not only are *we* Will-to-Power, but so is everything, human and animal, animate and material. The entire world is Will-to-Power; there is nothing more basic, for there is nothing other than it and its modifications.

Plainly, then, Will-to-Power is an elemental concept in Nietzsche's thinking, a concept in whose terms everything is to be understood and to which everything is finally to be reduced. It is metaphysical or, better, an ontological concept, for "Will-to-Power" is Nietzsche's answer to the question "What is there?"[23]

---

[22] *Ibid.*, I, 245.
[23] Danto, *Nietzsche as Philosopher*, p. 215.

Clearly, then, this metaphysical doctrine of power has nothing to do with a "politics of power" as it is ordinarily understood.

Here we must make a distinction between the Will to Power as such, understood as *arché*, and the specific manifestations of the Will to Power as individualized "beings" or, as Nietzsche might put it, as individualized "becomings." Metaphysically considered the Will to Power is, with regard to the question of value, *neutral*. That is to say, the Will to Power in itself is neither good nor bad; it simply *is*. However, a man, as an individuation of the Will to Power, "exists" as a valuational creature, that is, the very becoming of man *essentially is* as a creator of values, as is exemplified in Nietzsche's doctrine of the Superman as the "goal" of man's Becoming. In the next chapter, we shall consider the human being as a specific manifestation of the Will to Power. We ought, however, to note here that there are two corresponding senses of *kosmos*. In the metaphysical sense the Will to Power is the structural and regulative principle as well as the dynamic one. The philosophical anthropological sense of *kosmos*, man, by means of conceptualization and abstraction, *imposes order* on "Chaos." There are many sub-types of this second notion of *kosmos*, such as, political order, social order, and religious order.

On the metaphysical level, however, Nietzsche sharply contrasts his sense of *kosmos* as Will to Power with the mechanistic physicalistic interpretation of *kosmos*. He thus says:

Physicists believe in a "true world" in their own fashion: a firm systematization of atoms in necessary motion, the same for all beings – so for them the "apparent world" is reduced to the side of universal and universally necessary being which is accessible to every being in its own way (accessible and also already adapted – made "subjective"). But they are in error. The atom they posit is inferred according to the logic of perspectivism of consciousness – and is therefore itself a subjective fiction. This world picture that they sketch differs in no essential way from the subjective world picture: it is only construed with more extended senses, but with *our* senses nonetheless – And in any case they left something out of the constellation without knowing it: precisely this necessary perspectivism by virtue of which every center of force – and not only man – construes all the rest of the world from its own viewpoint, i.e., measures, feels, forms, according to its own force – They forgot to include this perspective-setting force in "true being" – in school language: the subject.[24]

Here we have again an underscoring of perspectivism and another statement of Nietzsche's rejection of anthropomorphism in metaphysics and epistemology. As we shall see later, the becoming of human being certainly relates to the Will to Power, "for life is merely a special

[24] Nietzsche, *The Will to Power*, p. 339.

case of the will to power,"[25] but this is not grounds, for Nietzsche, for anthropomorphic projections into metaphysics.

Jaspers' View

Jaspers begins his discussion of the Will to Power with a brief statement of Nietzsche's earlier "world-exegesis" and then contrasts this with the notion of the Will to Power. Nietzsche's earlier position belongs to his critique of traditional metaphysics.

> Nietzsche warns us against *all* notions of the whole: "Let us guard against thinking that the world is a living being .... or that the universe is a machine .... Let us guard against saying that there are laws of nature .... Let us guard against thinking that the world eternally creates novelties." All these "shadows of God" darken actuality. We are within the world, and the whole of the world is, *as a whole*, not accessible to us.[26]

In view of this position, Jaspers is "astonished" that Nietzsche arrives at the notion of the Will to Power.

> He rejects every determinate species of entity that as such is supposed to express the nature of Being. Nevertheless, his world exegesis appears in fact to revive just the sort of specification that he rejects.[27]

This position of Jaspers is an amplification of his belief that Nietzsche's notion of Being is contradictory.

Jaspers continues his discussion with a brief consideration of the development of the Will to Power out of the concept of "life." He argues that Nietzsche observed that wherever there is life, there is a manifestation of the Will to Power. He further argues that, initially, Will to Power is simply a specification of the notion of life. Later, however, Nietzsche states that life is merely one way in which the Will to Power manifests itself. Jaspers chooses to view this as a contradiction rather than as a progression and development. This dual tendency of Jaspers to see everything in Nietzsche through the lenses of contradiction and to ignore the possibility of conceptual sophistication and development is, perhaps, the greatest weakness of Jaspers' interpretation, for it forces Jaspers to deny again and again that Nietzsche expressed anything like "doctrines." Furthermore, it creates a situation in which Jaspers has to accept the principle that the whole of Nietzsche's philosophy is *essentially* ambiguous. To be sure, there are

---

[25] *Ibid.*, p. 369.
[26] Jaspers, *Nietzsche*, p. 293.
[27] *Ibid.*, p. 294.

ambiguities in Nietzsche and the general suggestion that we be aware of these and attempt to account for them is excellent. However, the characterization of Nietzsche's philosophy as essentially ambiguous and the adoption of the search for ambiguities as a methodological principle is extremely dubious.

The major part of Jaspers' discussion of the Will to Power relates to specific manifestations, which we shall consider in the next chapter. However, toward the end of his discussion he does present a "critical characterization" of the Will to Power as a metaphysical notion. First of all, he charges that Nietzsche is guilty of reifying the Will to Power.

Thus Nietzsche, who does everything he can to arouse and preserve our awareness of what is possible, to reveal every last perspective, and to discover countless interpretations, appears to conclude by absolutizing something specific. Instead of reacting to the liberating questions that can no longer be answered in general terms by referring back to the historicity of contemporary autonomous *Existenz*, he seems rather to reply in universal terms when he accounts for authentic being by reifying the will to power.[28]

This charge of reification is itself ambiguous, because the notion "thing-like" is ambiguous. Nietzsche nowhere suggests that the Will to Power is anything at all like a perceptual "object." He repeatedly emphasizes the process character of the Will to Power. Will to Power is dynamic – it is Becoming – and, therefore, certainly not "thing-like" in any usual sense. However, the Will to Power *qua* concept and *qua* abstraction is something static which suggests unity and permanence; but this is a problem which is rooted in the very nature of language, as Nietzsche himself was well aware. "In order to think and infer it is necessary to assume beings: logic handles only formulas for what remains the same."[29] This, then, points at a radical experiment on Nietzsche's part to communicate "beyond" the radical structures of the "logic of language." "There is no such thing as 'will'; it is only a simplifying conception of understanding, as is 'matter.'"[30] Here we can see a kinship with Berkeley, who was also attempting to communicate beyond the boundaries of traditional conceptualization. It is curious that Jaspers, who strongly emphasizes Nietzsche's radical "experiments in communication," persists in evaluating these in traditional terms.

---

[28] *Ibid.*, p. 309.
[29] Nietzsche, *The Will to Power*, p. 280.
[30] *Ibid.*, p. 254.

A second criticism which Jaspers has of the Will to Power is that Nietzsche's monism is the result of an illegitimate "absolutizing."

The many sense-verifications in empirical observation are fused with an interpretative construct as absolutizing thinking applies them to being itself in a manner that is no longer empirically verifiable or controllable.[31]

The real root of the problem, for Jaspers, however, is once again transcendence. Here also Jaspers understands Nietzsche's critique of the traditional notions of transcendence to mean a total rejection of the very notion of transcendence. We noted previously, that Jaspers spoke of Nietzsche's position as "transcendence in immanence," but here Jaspers' formulation is even stronger and he suggests an absolute separation of immanence and transcendence. It is strange that Jaspers *does not* advance this same criticism against Spinoza's monism.[32] Jaspers believes that Nietzsche's exegesis in terms of the Will to Power is fundamentally deficient in that it omits a facet of human *Existenz* which cannot be grasped in terms of a doctrine of immanence.

However, the exegesis misses something within the original being of human *Existenz* that has nothing to do with will to power and is, in fact, only discoverable apart from it. The will to power is unrelated to the self-being that acknowledges responsibility for itself, to the independent point that is unconditioned and exists only in relation to transcendence, to communication as loving struggle that neither wills nor exerts power, and to the truly free and open horizon. To be sure Nietzsche's metaphysics unveils the perversions of these types of essential being, but their true substance remains untouched.

The essential point here is that this metaphysics of radical immanence undertakes to read the ciphers of being as will to power *apart from transcendence.* He who knows himself to exist in relation to transcendence cannot see himself as having any kinship within its confines. Existence reveals a being that struggles against the possibility of this metaphysics (although the struggle for power is alien to its nature) and that refuses to be encompassed by this exegesis. It accepts Nietzsche's endeavor to illumine specific aspects of the world in a realistic manner, but it turns away when he thereby attempts to apprehend being itself.[33]

It is interesting to contemplate how Nietzsche himself might have reacted to this criticism. It seems likely that he would have accused Jaspers of introducing a surreptitious theology with his notion of transcendence. Jaspers' judgments here are not the result of an "*internal* hermeneutic"; rather, they are rooted in Jaspers' own metaphysics. Jaspers is using his own special notions of transcendence and

[21] Jaspers, *Nietzsche*, p. 316.
[32] Karl Jaspers, *The Great Philosophers*, ed., Hannah Arendt, trans. Ralph Manheim (New York, 1966), II, 273–387.
[33] Jaspers, *Nietzsche*, pp. 317–18.

"ciphers of being" as the foundation for a critique of Nietzsche's position. This would seem to be a more subtle and sophisticated version of the charge that Nietzsche's philosophy is deficient because it rejects the traditional notions of God as espoused by the "Christian" interpreters of Nietzsche. The fact that Jaspers' bias here is a metaphysical one, makes it no less a bias. When we regard Jaspers' conclusion about the doctrine of the Will to Power, it becomes further evident that Jaspers imposes his own conception of metaphysics in evaluating Nietzsche. *"The doctrine of the will to power is not his definitive metaphysics, but a thought-experiment performed within the more extensive whole of his investigation of being."* [34] Jaspers' insistence upon an interpretive methodology with regard to Nietzsche which centers around a "dialectic of contradiction" leads him to view Nietzsche's metaphysics as essentially fragmented in such a manner that other aspects of Nietzsche's metaphysics are not harmoniously related to the doctrine of the Will to Power.

His discontent with this metaphysics is shown by the fact that it contrasts with and supplements his account of *life* and by the further fact that it is overshadowed by his doctrine of *eternal recurrence*, which, in its turn, proves to be merely relative.[35]

Heidegger, however, emphatically rejects any such notion of fragmentation and insists upon the essential unity of the basic aspects of Nietzsche's metaphysics, as we shall now see.

Heidegger's View

For Heidegger, the key to Nietzsche's metaphysics is to be found in the doctrine of the Will to Power understood in relation to Eternal Recurrence and Transvaluation.

All Being is, for Nietzsche, a Becoming. This Becoming has the character of the action and activity of Willing. Will, however, is, in its essence, Will to Power.[36]

Later Heidegger adds:

The doctrine of Eternal Recurrence of the same belongs together with the doctrine of Will to Power in the most intimate fashion. The unifiedness of this doctrine manifests itself historically as Transvaluation of all previous values.[37]

---

[34] *Ibid.*, p. 318.
[35] *Ibid.*, p. 318.
[36] Heidegger, *Nietzsche*, I, 15.
[37] *Ibid.*, I, 26.

Thus a full grasp of Heidegger's interpretation of Nietzsche's metaphysics will have to wait upon a discussion of Eternal Recurrence and Transvaluation. However, in the last third of the first volume of his *Nietzsche*, Heidegger approaches the Will to Power from a somewhat different direction, which we shall pursue here and in the section on truth, which is to follow. The second approach involves not only the notion of truth, but Nietzsche's conceptions of knowledge and life as well.

Let us begin, then, with a general outline of this approach. First, we should note that Heidegger is here less concerned with the book, *The Will to Power*, than with following out the course of Nietzsche's thought concerning the doctrine of the Will to Power. [38] Heidegger titles this part of his book, "The Will to Power as Knowledge" and begins it with a discussion of Nietzsche's thought as the culmination of metaphysics. Let us here introduce the word "entity" as a translation for Heidegger's "das Seiende," since its literal translation as "that which is" tends to be awkward. We may now reformulate Heidegger's diagnosis of Nietzsche's metaphysics as a culmination. According to Heidegger's view, Nietzsche presents a critique of traditional metaphysics as the basis for the "overcoming" of traditional metaphysics. However, Heidegger believes that Nietzsche's attempt is a failure and that he remains firmly rooted in the tradition of metaphysics, for Nietzsche asks only the question of metaphysics – What is the Being of entities? – and does not ask the fundamental question for the "overcoming" of metaphysics – What is Being as such? The basis for Nietzsche's attempt at the "overcoming" of metaphysics is his doctrine of the Will to Power, and Heidegger believes that his elaboration of this doctrine is a demonstration of Nietzsche's "failure." This elaboration begins with a presentation of the Will to Power as "the principle of a new establishment of value." [39] Also, Nietzsche uses the word "world" as "the totality of entities" to mean "life" and Heidegger quotes him as saying, "*'This world is the Will to Power – and nothing besides!* And you also are this Will to Power – and nothing besides!'"; [40] and then concludes that "the totality of entities is 'life'" and that "the essence of life is 'Will to Power'." [41] Further, "Knowledge, according to Nietzsche is a form of the Will to Power." [42] Thus, it would appear that we are now

[38] *Ibid.*, I, 481–87.
[39] *Ibid.*, I, 487.
[40] Nietzsche as quoted in Heidegger, *Nietzsche*, I, 492.
[41] *Ibid.*, I, 492.
[42] *Ibid.*, I, 494.

in a position to begin the main discussion; unfortunately, however, Heidegger's discussion is full of linguistic gymnastics that seem endlessly involved. We are being told that knowledge can be understood only in terms of the essence of truth and also in terms of knowing as *techné*, but the essence of truth must be grasped in the sense of "correctness" as an "establishing of value," which notion, Heidegger insists, must be approached through Nietzsche's "biologism."[43] And this is not the end of it, for Heidegger now proceeds by connecting Nietzsche's "biologism" with "logic," since it is the "trust in Reason" that creates "truths" – life-preserving fictions – and man projects these "truths" out of his confrontation with Chaos, which is understood in relation to the "collapse" of the Aristotelian law of contradiction.[44] Finally, this "collapse" of the law of contradiction results in a "destruction" of the distinction between the real and the apparent world and, thus, the metaphysics of truth is subjectivism understood as anthropomorphism and the "ground" of the "justification" for truth is "justice" or "correctness" (*Gerechtigkeit*).[45] Stated in this bald and incomplete manner, Heidegger's "analysis" sounds like a self-parody.

This "analysis," however, is important for three reasons: (1) it does contain some genuine and profound insights into Nietzsche's metaphysics, (2) it presents some new insights into Heidegger's own philosophy, and (3) it presents hints of an implicit critique of Husserlian phenomenology. The first and the third points are the ones of interest to us here, and it may be that the third point will help us to understand why there is so much of Heidegger's own thought super-imposed upon Nietzsche's. For example, in another discussion on the Will to Power, Heidegger again presents his criticism that Nietzsche remained rooted in the realm of metaphysics and never attained ontology. Ontology, in Heidegger's sense, is concerned with the distinction between Being and beings or entities. Heidegger then comments that it is ontology in this sense that is the concern of his book, *Being and Time*.[46] In another discussion of Heidegger's, this time on Eternal Recurrence, he argues, as we shall see later, that in his doctrine of Eternal Recurrence, Nietzsche attempted to think Being through the notion of time. But, of course, Nietzsche fails, for otherwise he would have produced Heidegger's fundamental ontology. From this it is clear that Heidegger's interpretation is, indeed, of a very special kind. Heidegger

[43] *Ibid.*, I, 495–527.
[44] *Ibid.*, I, 527–625.
[45] *Ibid.*, 625–658.
[46] *Ibid.*, II, 209.

uses Nietzsche's philosophy as an occasion for doing his own philosophizing. However, let us see what insight we can gain about the Will to Power from Heidegger's "analysis."

Heidegger and Jaspers agree that Nietzsche's doctrine of the Will to Power is a radical experiment in communication. Furthermore, Heidegger reminds us, as does Jaspers, that we should be most careful not to be misled by the language, for as Nietzsche himself says, Will "is merely a word."[47] Nietzsche uses various linguistic means to approach the essential nucleus of the idea which he most fundamentally calls the Will to Power. Like Jaspers, Heidegger notes that Nietzsche sometimes speaks of the Will to Power as life and that, at other times, he speaks of life as one form of the Will to Power; but also like Jaspers, Heidegger fails to distinguish between the metaphysical doctrine of the Will to Power and the doctrine of the Will to Power as philosophical anthropology. For Heidegger, Nietzsche's philosophy is metaphysics with occasional excursions into the mundane world, whereas for Jaspers, Nietzsche's philosophy is philosophical anthropology with occasional excursions into metaphysics.

For Heidegger, Nietzsche's epistemology is a direct consequence of his metaphysics and is, in fact, inseparable from it, since "Knowledge is, according to Nietzsche, a form of the Will to Power."[48] But what is knowledge? Nietzsche's conception of knowledge, Heidegger argues, is graspable only in terms of an understanding of the essence of truth. So, let us now proceed to a discussion of Nietzsche's notion of truth.

NIETZSCHE'S DOCTRINE OF TRUTH

Here we have one of the most original and most interesting facets of Nietzsche's philosophy. His doctrine of truth is also an illustration of his philosophical "extremism." It is here that we discover the "crisis point" of Nietzsche's philosophy. It is in Nietzsche's epistemology that we find the attempt to lay the groundwork for a "new" metaphysics. Nietzsche himself characterizes his epistemology as "perspectivism." Human knowledge is always to be understood as the adoption of a particular perspective and this is the case for scientific, cultural, or individual forms of knowledge. Thus, at first glance, it would appear that Nietzsche's epistemology provides a consistent link between his metaphysics and his philosophical anthropology, since the episte-

---

[47] *Ibid.*, I, 650.
[48] *Ibid.*, I, 494.

mological notion of perspectivism is quite compatible with the meta-physical notion of the Will to Power as Becoming. However, if we look closer, we find a radical critique of the traditional notions of truth – a critique which lies at the heart of Nietzsche's own notion of TRUTH. Nietzsche denies repeatedly that truth is an absolute and views truth and knowledge as forms of the Will to Power which human beings have "created" for their own self-perpetuation. In a posthumously published fragment from 1873 titled "On Truth and Lie in an Extra-Moral Sense," Nietzsche makes it clear that he regards the Will to truth as the "creation" of "necessary" life-preserving fictions; necessary, in that they preserve and promote the *human* Will to Power.

In some remote corner of the universe, poured out and glittering in innumerable solar systems, there once was a star on which clever animals invented knowledge. That was the haughtiest and most mendacious minute of "world history" – yet only a minute. After nature had drawn a few breaths the star grew cold, and the clever animals had to die.

One might invent such a fable and still not have illustrated sufficiently how wretched, how shadowy and flighty, how aimless and arbitrary, the human intellect appears in nature. There have been eternities when it did not exist; and when it is done for again, nothing will have happened. For this intellect has no further mission that would lead beyond human life. It is human, rather, and only its owner and producer gives it such importance, as if the world pivoted around it.[49]

But what about the passage just quoted? Is it true? Here we come to understand the necessity for making a distinction between the traditional theories of truth and Nietzsche's theory of TRUTH. For Nietzsche, there is a fundamental perspective, namely, the cosmological perspective, which so to speak, puts all other perspectives "in perspective."

Nietzsche's critique of the traditional theories of truth goes even further, for ultimately it turns out to be an attack on the very foundations of logic and rational thinking. Sometime in the year 1887 or 1888 Nietzsche decisively formulated his attack on the "law of contradiction."

We are unable to affirm and to deny one and the same thing: this is a subjective empirical law, not the expression of any "necessity" but only of an inability.

If, according to Aristotle, the law of contradiction is the most certain of all principles, if it is the ultimate and most basic, upon which every demonstrative proof rests, if the principle of every axiom lies in it; then one should consider all the more rigorously what *presuppositions* already lie at the bottom of it. Either it asserts something about actuality, about being, as if one already knew this from another source; that is, as if opposite attributes *could* not be ascribed

<hr />

[49] Nietzsche, *The Portable Nietzsche*, p. 42.

to it. Or the proposition means: opposite attributes *should* not be ascribed to it. In that case, logic would be an imperative, not to know the true, but to posit and arrange a world that shall be called true by us.

In short, the question remains open: are the axioms of logic adequate to reality or are they a means and measure for us to *create* reality, the concept "reality," for ourselves? – To affirm the former one would, as already said, have to have a previous knowledge of being – which is certainly not the case. The proposition therefore contains no *criterion of truth*, but an *imperative* concerning that which *should* count as true.[50]

Here Nietzsche emphasized that logic and, with it, knowledge, are *human* creations designed for the purposes of "rational" thought and communication. Again we have the implied distinction between traditional thought and Nietzsche's THOUGHT. For Nietzsche, THOUGHT about REALITY is the thinking through of the contradiction which defines and delimits the epistemological-ontological situation of being human. Thus, even though Nietzsche rejects all the traditional forms of transcendence, there is for him, nonetheless, a TRANSCENDENT perspective, namely, the cosmological perspective, which is THOUGHT about REALITY. This TRANSCENDENCE is rooted in the possibility of our Being, as human, to move "beyond" the context of knowledge and to grasp it as *life-preserving fictions*. That is to say, the cosmological perspective can grasp the TRUTH of the anthropological perspective and thereby achieve an understanding of REALITY. However, this conception of REALITY drives a wedge between thought and THOUGHT thus creating a fundamental dualism between Nietzsche's metaphysics and epistemology and his philosophical anthropology. TRUTH, then, for Nietzsche is the understanding that all truths are perspectival and, as such, are manifestations of the *human* Will to Power. KNOWLEDGE, then, is THOUGHT about knowledge, that is, the apprehension of truths as life-preserving fictions. Thus, THOUGHT creates a dualism which is irrevocably rooted in the epistemological-ontological situation of being human, since it depends upon the "rejection" of the "law of contradiction" in order to achieve TRUTH, i.e., the cosmological perspective, but at the same time human life, as the Will to Power, depends upon the "acceptance" of the "law of contradiction" as ontologically necessary from the perspective of philosophical anthropology. The same principle is at work here in the doctrine of Being as Becoming, for in TRUTH, Becoming is Being and it is only our anthropological perspective that "necessitates" our hypostatization of Becoming into "graspable" Being. As we shall see later, it is the ontological possibility

---

[50] Nietzsche, *The Will to Power*, p. 270.

of man's being able to take up a TRANSCENDENT perspective which creates this dualism at the heart of Nietzsche's philosophy, of which he himself was well aware.

Jaspers' View

Jaspers divides his discussion of Nietzsche's notion of truth into three major parts.

Nietzsche's various reflections as he seeks to discover *what it means to be true* can scarcely be brought into a single systematic order. Although they are actually fused with each other, we shall trace them from three independent sources indicated by Nietzsche himself: (1) *methodical science*, (2) *the theory that truth has its being in a construction* devised by living existents, and (3) *a boundless passion for truth*. In all cases we arrive at intelligible positions located on a route that seems to end in failure: Nietzsche is intent on the *dissolution of reason*. Finally, all of these reflections on truth lead to a *transcending breakthrough*.[51]

The notion of scientific truth belongs primarily to Nietzsche's so-called Positivistic phase. Nietzsche's emphasis here is on the methodological aspect and he seems more concerned with the discipline which such a method can provide than with any particular scientific results which accrue from the application of such a method. The most interesting and most important aspect of this part of Nietzsche's concern with truth is his exposition of the limitations of science, which Jaspers summarizes in five propositions. (1) *"Factual scientific knowledge is not knowledge of being."*[52] Here, of course, Nietzsche is already suggesting that there are "truths" that lie outside of the grasp of science. Science is concerned with particular realms of related "facts" and by its very nature cannot attempt to exposit the Whole which is the task of cosmological philosophy. (2) *"It is not the possession of the truth but the quest for it that is satisfying."*[53] Here we have an underscoring of Nietzsche's conviction that the quest for TRUTH is more important than any particular truths that are obtained. The Will to TRUTH is an open-ended dialectic which essentially characterizes Nietzsche's "new" kind of philosophizing. Even TRUTH, as grasped from the TRANSCENDENT perspective of cosmology, is fully intelligible only when understood dialectically. *"Scientific certainty provides no security in connection with the things that really matter most."*[54] For Nietzsche, there can never be any full certainty or absolute security and this is the KNOWLEDGE of knowledge, namely, that philosophy, in its inmost and most intimate

---

[51] Jaspers, *Nietzsche*, p. 171.
[52] *Ibid.*, p. 176.
[53] *Ibid.*, p. 176.
[54] *Ibid.*, p. 177.

Being, is forever dynamic. Every absolute is a degeneration from the TRUTH of philosophy to the dogma of the generalized perspective. (4) *"Scientific knowledge simply cannot give purpose to life."*[55] For Nietzsche, the Knowledge which science achieves, may or may not benefit man; there is no necessary relation between scientific progress and human progress. (5) *"Science cannot answer the question concerning its own meaning."*[56] The meaning of science must be understood in relation to Life and, in particular to the *human* Will to Power. If, then, there is meaning to life, this is not discoverable by science, but remains rather in the province of philosophy. "The philosopher discovers his task where *being in its entirety* emerges, whereas science offers methodical certainty about particulars."[57] Thus, though science is relevant to philosophy, philosophy must go "beyond" it, for science offers only a certain range of possible perspectives or truths.

The second part of Jaspers' discussion of Nietzsche's views of truth centers around the conception of truth "as illusion." This is, of course, Nietzsche's conception of perspectivism with its implicit critique of the previous philosophical and theological theories of absolute truth.

All knowledge is an interpretation of being provided by a living and cognizing subject; there is no truth that is not entertained in thought and believed, that is, that is not found within that encompassing being that we are . . . ., and that is possibly all the being there is. Thus conceived, truth is not something independent, unconditioned, and absolutely universal. Rather it is inextricably involved with the being of a living subject and the world that he has constructed. But this world as it appears to us is, like ourselves, in a constant process of temporal change.[58]

This insight that human knowledge is by its very nature defined and delimited by the facticity of the possible *human* perspectives is one that has been stated by many philosophers, but none has pushed it to the radical extremes that Nietzsche has. However, Jaspers also insists that this view forces Nietzsche to distinguish between two "levels of truth."

Such utterances can surely be meaningful only from the standpoint of a kind of truth – unattainable as it may be from the level of life – that can detect the erroneousness of the knowledge that serves life. This involves two distinct concepts of truth: To begin with, truth appears as the kind of error that supports life. But again it appears as remote from life, as though one must abandon life in order to arrive at the criterion through which life's errors can be recognized.[59]

---

[55] *Ibid.*, p. 177.
[56] *Ibid.*, p. 177.
[57] *Ibid.*, p. 182.
[58] *Ibid.*, pp. 184–85.
[59] *Ibid.*, p. 186.

This second concept is what we have called "TRUTH." Jaspers also recognizes that along with this TRUTH there is a kind of KNOWLEDGE which is not the knowledge gained from the perspective of life. As Jaspers points out, this notion of TRUTH raises some difficult questions. It would now seem that in spite of himself Nietzsche has posited an absolute truth, since, as Jaspers also points out, Nietzsche's position here does imply a TRANSCENDENT perspective. However, we must be very careful here not to jump to conclusions, especially since Nietzsche himself repeatedly criticizes all the traditional absolutistic theories of truth. This should lead us to suspect that Nietzsche is trying to communicate something else about the nature of TRUTH.

It is here that we encounter the third phase of Jaspers' discussion concerning Nietzsche's theory of TRUTH. Jaspers correctly observes that Nietzsche cannot accept any theory which posits some final truth, since this would be a betrayal of the dialectical character which essentially determines the course of Nietzsche's philosophizing. Thus, "his thoughts about truth, since they deny what is required for their formulation, must run into incessant contradictions."[60] The contradictions, according to Jaspers, arise because Nietzsche's notion of TRUTH repeatedly points to a TRANSCENDENCE. We have already taken note of this fact and must now carefully examine how Jaspers interprets it. For Jaspers, these contradictions are the result of Nietzsche's radically dialectical approach to the problem of TRUTH.

His theory is not a theory about a given state of affairs; it is a philosophical means of expressing first the existential appeal to the essential truth born by essential life and, second, the possibility of a life-transcending intimate awareness of being.[61]

The first point is, of course, a reference to the notion of *Existenz*. The second point is an interpretation of the first in terms of *Existenz* as transcendence (in Jaspers' sense). According to Jaspers' interpretation, then, TRUTH turns out to be something very much like the existentialist notion of authenticity. Ultimately, TRUTH resides in *Existenz* and *Existenz* as an essential and positive notion, when used by Jaspers, already implicitly contains the idea of a positive form of transcendence. Jaspers believes that Nietzsche attempts this "transcending breakthrough to truth," because he could not fully accept the consequences of his "dissolution of reason."[62] Jaspers is convinced that while

[60] *Ibid.*, 190.
[61] *Ibid.*, p. 190.
[62] *Ibid.*, pp. 218–19.

Nietzsche never truly resolved this "opposition," he did at least point to TRUTH through the use of poetic devices, thus implying, according to Jaspers, that TRUTH is by its very nature "indeterminate."

When Nietzsche views truth in its determinacy as error required by life, always and inevitably the idea of a *truth per se* stands in the background, not only as the negation of all determinate truth, but as the possibility of making contact with being itself. This truth that is at once negative and positive, insofar as it lies beyond all determinacy, and is simply itself, and insofar as it also can appear as knowledge of being, must in every form prove dangerous to life, i.e., to existence that is bound up with error. Consequently from the standpoint of life itself, the will to truth is questionable.[63]

If the TRUTH is that there are no truths, then TRUTH is a great danger to life and results finally in the most extreme of all nihilisms. Thus, the heart of the conflict resides in the fact that TRUTH is death. However, Jaspers asserts that there is also a positive aspect to TRUTH.

The passion for truth, in the guise of radical and incessant doubt, causes all determinate appearances to perish. While truth as transcendence – as the completely indeterminate and indeterminable truth itself – cannot lie, yet every specific truth within the world can. Only the concrete historicity of *Existenz*, indubitably present though uncognizable, is then true. What sets a limit to doubt is not some truth or other, not the thought of an absolute truth, but this *Existenz*.[64]

Here Jaspers' use of his hermeneutic model of Existenz has provided an impressive and plausible interpretation, but if we look more closely we shall see that Jaspers has made some subtle, but nonetheless extremely important, shifts of emphasis. However, from this part of Jaspers' interpretation, we can now understand how he grounds his "justification" for emphasizing Nietzsche's philosophical anthropology and minimizing the importance of the metaphysics and epistemology.

Jaspers exposits very well the dialectical tension which characterizes Nietzsche's discussion of TRUTH, yet it seems rather odd to conclude that Nietzsche, who was so intimately concerned with the notion of contradiction, ultimately ends up with a theory of TRUTH that is contradictory (in the sense of "unresolved" and "confused"). Jaspers softens this judgment somewhat by reference to the implicit positive notion of transcendence as a form of quasi-resolution. Here we need to remind ourselves of the nature of philosophical inquiry for Nietzsche. Jaspers arrives at his interpretation of Nietzsche's theory of TRUTH partly as a result of his insistence on viewing Nietzsche's conception

63 *Ibid.*, pp. 221–22.
64 *Ibid.*, p. 227.

of philosophical THOUGHT strictly through the lenses of philosophical anthropology, thus grounding THOUGHT primarily in life. Heidegger, however, grasps the essential nature of philosophical THOUGHT in almost precisely the same way in which Nietzsche did.

Nietzsche once said (Werke, 7, 269): "A philosopher is a man who never ceases to experience, see, hear, suspect, hope, and dream extraordinary things . . . ."
   To philosophize is to inquire into the *extra*-ordinary. But because, as we have just suggested, this questioning recoils upon itself, not only what is asked after is extraordinary but also the asking itself. In other words: this questioning does not lie along the way so that we bump into it one day unexpectedly. Nor is it part of everyday life: there is no requirement or regulation that forces us into it; it gratifies no urgent or prevailing need. The questioning itself is "out of order." It is entirely voluntary, based wholly and uniquely on the mystery of freedom, on what we have called the leap. The same Nietzsche said: "Philosophy . . . . is a voluntary living amid ice and mountain heights" (Werke, 15, 2). To philosophize, we may now say, is an extra-ordinary inquiry into the extra-ordinary.[65]

Thus, philosophical THOUGHT is not grounded in life and is possible only on the ground of a TRANSCENDENCE which inheres in the very nature of being human. Man *qua* THINKER is an anomaly of Being. THOUGHT is a philosophical enterprise and discovers that thought in its service to Life is always perspectival, but THOUGHT is also a perspective – a cosmological one. However, the THINKER is also a thinker, i.e., he is enmeshed in concerns of everyday Life. As a result there is an opposition, a "contradiction," but it is not a contradiction contained in THOUGHT, rather it is contradiction *between* THOUGHT and thought. This means two things: (1) that contradiction is rooted in the nature of dialectic itself, and (2) that Nietzsche's theory of TRUTH implies an ontology. If man were simply limited to the perspectives of life, this conflict would not occur. However, through the dialectic of philosophy, man has the possibility of taking up a perspective which TRANSCENDS life and which, thereby, places him in the position of being able to *TRANS*value. The entire metaphysics of Nietzsche requires this form of TRANSCENDENCE which we have characterized as the possibility of taking up a cosmological perspective, for without this TRANSCENDENCE no "evaluation" of life would be possible and, therefore, no Trans-valuation as an attempt to overcome nihilism would be possible. Nietzsche's doctrine of contradiction goes much further than Jaspers suggests. It is not simply that there is a contradiction in Nietzsche's notion of TRUTH, but rather that we here truly have Nietzsche's "dialectic of contradiction." In fact, we might even say that Nietzsche's

[65] Heidegger, *Introduction to Metaphysics*, pp. 12–13.

position here is a phenomenological description of the nature of the dialectic between the perspectives of life and the perspective of philosophy as cosmology. That there is such a dialectical opposition between these perspectives has to do with the nature of Being in general and man's Being in particular.

It is at this point that we arrive at Nietzsche's implicit ontology. This position is a "negative" ontology in two ways. First of all, man's grasp of Being as static and permanent is error and this error may be understood through THOUGHT which grasps Being as Becoming. Here, as Jaspers points out, THOUGHT *threatens* life and in an attempt to resolve this opposition Jaspers introduces his notion of *Existenz* as a positive form of transcendence. However, this move would seem to subvert the basic goal of Nietzsche's philosophy, *for it is only on the ground of this dialectical negativity that human Being as the Will to Power can ever achieve the Transvaluation of all values.* In fact, it is just this dialectical negativity which is the *motive force* of Nietzsche's philosophy. The second form of negativity is also dialectical and centers around man's discovery of the limitations of his Being as Will to Power. Nietzsche again and again emphasizes, in Heraclitean fashion, the constant struggle between the individual Will to Power and the World Obstacle. His emphasis on struggle is another reason for accepting the notion of the *essential* negativity of the dialectic between life and philosophy. It is through this discovery of his own defining limitations, that man comes to have a vague glimmer of the vast number of possible perspectives that lie forever outside of his realm of experience and thereby he can attain some small notion of Being by understanding what is denied him. Thus man's self-understanding becomes immensely important philosophically, for it results in a sharpening and clarification of the dialectical poles and enhances the quality of genuine THINKING.

Jaspers sees certain ontological implications in Nietzsche's theory of TRUTH and ultimately grounds Nietzsche's conception in man's "inner Being" or *Existenz*. "Only this attitude of unlimited openness to the possible under the strict leadership of something unknown, *Existenz* itself, can truly say: 'Nothing is true.'"[66] Somewhat later Jaspers adds:

As we deliberately go through the dialectical movements in which the truth never attains its goal (since it can never be possessed but in the end even denies itself), we are forced back to find fulfillment in our own historically present *Existenz*. Through our knowledge of this movement we become aware of not

[66] Jaspers, *Nietzsche*, p. 227.

possessing the truth. Only perseverance in this movement can overcome the danger of deception which will result if we thoughtlessly use Nietzsche's isolated and isolating formulae as deadsure dicta and, with the aid of these dialectical thoughts, arbitrarily justify or condemn everything.[67]

This notion of *Existenz*, as "something unknown" which resides at the core of the individual human Being, is something that we shall have to examine in the next chapter, in terms of Nietzsche's theory of man. However, it is clear that the TRANSCENDENCE which is relevant here to Nietzsche's metaphysics and epistemology is *not* unknown and *is* describable in terms of man's possibility of taking up a cosmological perspective. Jaspers' notion of *Existenz* may be a part of the dialectical relationship between TRUTH and truth, but it is certainly not a complete picture. The strength of Jaspers' interpretation lies in what we have called the aspect of philosophical anthropology, but the corresponding weaknesses on the side of metaphysics and epistemology produce distortions of the essential core of Nietzsche's philosophy.

Heidegger's View

We are now in a position to return to our examination of Heidegger's interpretation of the relationship between the Will to Power and TRUTH. Heidegger's "analysis" is composed of very many "sub-analyses" which are provocative in the dual sense of stimulating and irritating. The "logic" of the relationships between these various sub-parts is not always clear; therefore, we shall not follow Heidegger's "analysis" step by step, but rather we shall here be concerned with extracting the essential core of his interpretation. We shall postpone an examination of certain aspects of Heidegger's discussion until the next chapter.

Heidegger regards Nietzsche's theory of TRUTH as the "crisis point" in his philosophy and, like Jaspers, he distinguishes between two forms – what we have called TRUTH and truth. The initial exposition of truth as illusion and error follows the basic pattern that we have already discovered in Jaspers. However, Heidegger then introduces a new facet into the discussion, namely ,the notion of truth, when grasped in its essence as TRUTH, is to be understood as *homoiosis* – a likeness or correspondence between the "glance" and what it grasps.

And in the age in which the fulfillment of modern times commences Nietzsche sharpens the above statement even more: *"Truth is the kind of error* without which a definite kind of living species would not be able to live. The value of *life* decides in the end."* (Notation made in 1885, *Der Wille zur Macht*, n. 493).

---

[67] *Ibid.*, p. 228.

If truth according to Nietzsche is a kind of error, then its essence lies in a manner of thinking which always and necessarily falsifies the real in so far as every act of representation causes the unexposed "becoming" to be still and set up something that does not correspond (i.e. something incorrect) with what has thus been established in contradistinction to the fluent "becoming," thereby establishing something erroneous as the alledgedly real.

In Nietzsche's defining of truth as incorrectness of thinking there lies the concession to thinking of the traditional essence of truth as the correctness of making an assertion .... Nietzsche's concept of truth is an example of the last reflection of the extreme consequence of that changing of truth from the unhiddenness of beings to the correctness of the glance. The change itself takes place in the definition of the Being of beings.[68]

In Heidegger's judgment, Nietzsche's theory of TRUTH is not at all an "overcoming" of metaphysics, but, on the contrary, remains deeply rooted in the historical unfolding of traditional metaphysics. We should also note that Heidegger here criticizes Nietzsche's notion of TRUTH by contrasting it with his own theory of truth as "unhiddenness" or *aletheia*. Heidegger also introduces another approach to interpreting Nietzsche's conception of TRUTH. TRUTH is to be understood as "holding-something-to-be-true."[69] This, Heidegger argues, is a consequence of Nietzsche's "destruction" of the distinction between an apparent world and a real world. Thus, as Heidegger interprets Nietzsche, TRUTH no longer transcends man, since this "holding-something-to-be-true has in terms of its origin the character of a command."[70] Here we have one of the more ingenious facets of Heidegger's interpretation. Where does this command originate? The command arises out of the individual Will as an expression of his Will to Power. The command is not, however, simply the arbitrary expression of Power, but rather this Will is conditioned by "justice" (*Gerechtigkeit*). Heidegger plays with the word *Gerechtigkeit* in such a way that it also comes to mean "correctness," "rightness," "correspondence," and "justification."[71] Thus, TRUTH understood as *homoiosis* is *Gerechtigkeit* and both "possess" the same essence, namely, assimilation into and identification (*Eingleichung*) with Chaos.[72] And what is Chaos? Chaos here has a twofold meaning: (1) In its broadest sense it means the "world" or, in other words, the to- tality of entities (*das Seiende im Ganzen*) and (2) in a more specific sense it means "our realm of sensation, which we recognize as the realm of the

---

[68] Martin Heidegger, *Plato's Doctrine of Truth* in *Philosophy in the Twentieth Century* trans. John Barlow (New York, 1962), III, 267.
[69] Heidegger, *Nietzsche*, I, 634.
[70] *Ibid.*, I, 634.
[71] *Ibid.*, I, 636.
[72] *Ibid.*, I, 636–37.

body" and which is "only a *section* of the great Chaos that is the world itself." [73] Now let us see what sense we can make out of these vertiginous tergiversations.

Heidegger is here playing with certain words in order to create metaphorical (and, therefore, for him, *metaphysical*) connections between various facets of Nietzsche's philosophy. TRUTH as *homoiosis* consists of a holding-something-to-be-true as the result of a command. Traditionally this command has been the Aristotelian "law of contradiction." However, we have already seen how Nietzsche attacks this "law" and concludes that this life-preserving fiction tells us what we *should* regard as true. Heidegger adds that, due to the intimate connection between TRUTH and Being, this imperative also legislates what shall count as Being. [74] Nietzsche claims that his attack on this imperative and, thereby, on traditional metaphysics, opens up the ground for the possibility of a new command – a command which arises out of the individual Will to Power itself. However, the primordial confrontation of the individual Will to Power with its world, i.e., with Chaos, provides no directive. Man must *create* order, that is, he must transform Chaos into *kosmos*. TRUTH tells us that there is no *telos*, so man must create a *telos*, but this cannot be done arbitrarily. The *telos* arises out of the individual Will to Power in its TRUTH as "justice" (*Gerechtigkeit*). The new command, then, arises out of "justice" as a kind of terrible freedom, for this freedom is in its essence a "self-overcoming." [75] As Zarathustra asks:

Can you give ourself your own evil and your own good and hang your own will over yourself as a law? Can you be our own judge and avenger of your law? Terrible it is to be alone with the judge and avenger of one's own law. Thus is a star thrown out into the void and into the icy breath of solitude.[76]

Such creative freedom is the "Way of the Creator" and it is in this self-overcoming that man himself becomes an artistic creation and, as such, the highest expression of the Will to Power. Power in its highest form, then, is power over one's Self and this is the greatest of all struggles as well as the most difficult. For Zarathustra adds, "But the worst enemy you can encounter will always be you, yourself; you lie in wait for yourself in caves and woods." [77]

The new command, with which Nietzsche replaces the old "law of

[73] *Ibid.*, I, 566–67.
[74] *Ibid.*, I, 609.
[75] *Ibid.*, I, 639.
[76] Nietzsche, *Zarathustra*, p. 175.
[77] *Ibid.*, p. 176.

contradiction," originates from the innermost Being of man as Will to Power. It is only in terms of this "justice" which characterizes man's *telos* – the Superman – that Transvaluation becomes possible. It is this "justice" which lays the foundation for the highest of all forms of art – the creation of new values. For Heidegger, Nietzsche's conception of Will is to be understood ultimately as command and the Will to Power is a self-domination out of which one "overcomes" oneself.

Heidegger's final judgment is that Nietzsche does not succeed in "overcoming" metaphysics, but, to the contrary, is so deeply rooted in the historical tradition that his philosophy is the "consummation" of metaphysics. In addition, Heidegger makes two further charges which are of interest. The first is that Nietzsche is "guilty" of "humanizing" all entities. "Is not the world thought of after the image of man? Is not such thought pure anthropomorphism?" [78] Heidegger's answer to both of these questions is affirmative and he then adds that Nietzsche was not only aware of this "humanization," but *intended* it. [79] The second charge is that, ultimately, Nietzsche's position is a kind of necessary "subjectivism" which brings the history of traditional metaphysics to an end. Thus, Nietzsche does not attain the "true" heights of fundamental ontology, since he does not think the question of Being as such, but, nonetheless, Heidegger admits that Nietzsche's "subjectivism" and anthropomorphism are in "the grand style." This charge of "subjectivism" is also the charge of nihilism and, for Heidegger, nihilism is equatable with metaphysics.

What we must now concern ourselves with is an evaluation of Heidegger's interpretation and critique. There are a number of criticisms which could be advanced against some of Heidegger's more extreme linguistic machinations, but, on the whole, they are peripheral and we shall try to focus on the central issues. The first point to be considered is Heidegger's somewhat dubious rendering of Nietzsche's notion of TRUTH as *homoiosis*. Heidegger seems obsessed with finding unifying connections between everything. Whenever Heidegger explicates a theory of TRUTH, be it his own or someone else's, he invariably attempts to link the problem of TRUTH to some form of perceptual immediacy. In his own philosophy he subsumes epistemology under the rubric of fundamental ontology, thereby creating the impression that he has avoided the charges of "subjectivism" and anthropomorphism. However, this avoidance is, it would seem, purely formal and

---

[78] Heidegger, *Nietzsche*, I, 653.
[79] *Ibid.*, I, 653–54.

structural. Richardson, in explicating Heidegger's interpretation of how Zarathustra creates a path to the Superman by teaching the doctrine of Eternal Recurrence, says:

Zarathustra preaches the super-man *because*, and only inasmuch as, he preaches the eternal return. He proclaims both at once, *for they are correlative: The Being of beings and the nature of man*. [italics mine] . . . .
But farther than this Nietzsche cannot go. To go farther would be to think the correlation between Being and the nature of man *as such* . . . . To think it means to go beyond metaphysics with its interpretation of man as rational animal. It means to pass from present-ative thinking into foundational thought. Nietzsche, slave to present-ative thinking, could not take this step. That is why Heidegger feels he has the right to ask if this "bridge to the highest hope" does not in fact lead to a desolation still more profound, the desolate nihilism of remaining oblivious to the Being-process itself.[80]

Unfortunately, this notion of "Being-process" does not really provide a basis for an evaluation of Nietzsche, for Heidegger has not yet provided us with his fundamental ontology. What Richardson does say about "Being-process" makes Heidegger's charges of "subjectivism" and anthropomorphism seem all the more suspicious.

The shelter for the Being-process comes-to-presence along with this positive-negative process itself in the very moment of its arrival among being. In fact, ". . . . this arrival of Being is in itself the arrival of a shelter for Being . . . ." And where precisely *is* the shelter for Being among beings? In the nature of man! This explains the intimacy between Being and man.[81]

Here it is difficult to see what precisely distinguishes Heidegger's own position from Heidegger's interpretation of Nietzsche's position. That Heidegger claims a kind of "objectivity" for his position and further claims that he has escaped "subjectivism," is quite empty. Simply to label a position "fundamental ontology" does not exempt it from the demand for an explication. Without having the statement of Heidegger's fundamental ontology, all criticisms which are based on a comparison and contrast with it are vacuous. Furthermore, Heidegger's discussion of the relationship between the ontological and perceptual facets of TRUTH as *homoiosis* and as *aletheia* are at best ambiguous. However, his discussion of *homoiosis* in relation to "justice" and the Will to Power is thought-provoking.

Heidegger's charge that Nietzsche's metaphysics is anthropomorphic is somewhat strange. First of all, in the most extensive sense, every-

---

[80] William J. Richardson, *Heidegger: Through Phenomenology to Thought* (The Hague, 1963), pp. 380–81.
[81] *Ibid.*, pp. 510–11.

thing that man conceives of, does, perceives, and creates is a direct consequence of the nature of his Being as *anthropos*. But this is merely tautological. Even if, as Heidegger claims, Being thinks us, we still have in some way to appropriate that thinking and make it our own; otherwise it would remain forever beyond us and, therefore, would be irrelevant to us. However, Nietzsche repeatedly emphasizes – and as we have already seen his whole philosophy depends upon it – that inherent in man is the possibility for a kind of TRANSCENDENCE which through the THINKING of philosophy can place man in a perspective "beyond" and "outside" of himself, namely, the cosmological perspective. It is precisely when man takes up this cosmological perspective that he encounters the limitations of all of his other perspectives as an *anthropos* which lives and thinks in the context of a world. This is the paradox that is grounded in the very core of the Being of man and as such constitutes the fundamental dualism between the cosmological perspective of metaphysics and the utilitarian perspectives of life. Again, without Heidegger's fundamental ontology, Heidegger's charge of anthropomorphism is vacuous.

Excursus: An Implicit Critique
of Phenomenology?

We have already observed that Heidegger's Nietzsche interpretation is not simply interpretation, but serves as an occasion for Heidegger to do some philosophizing of his own. We also suggested that parts of his Nietzsche interpretation might contain hints of a critique of Husserlian phenomenology and its derivatives. If this is the case, this suggestion would go a long way toward explaining why it is that certain facets of Heidegger's interpretation seem rather foreign and out of place in connection with Nietzsche. We certainly cannot fully explore here the possibility of such an implicit critique, but there are certain rather provocative hints worth noting. This possibility may also enable us to gain a better perspective on Heidegger's interpretation and lead us to a partial understanding of the motivating forces behind some of the more radical aspects of Heidegger's "analysis." Let us, therefore, briefly take note of a few of the more important "parallels."

It is well known that after Heidegger's so-called "turning point" in the thirties, phenomenology virtually disappears from this work. However, Heidegger has said almost nothing explicit about the reasons for this "abandonment." Nonetheless, in the preface to Richardson's book, which is a letter from Heidegger, there are several very interesting remarks by Heidegger.

As my familiarity with phenomenology grew, no longer merely through literature but by actual practice, the question about Being, aroused by Brentano's work, nevertheless remained always in view. So it was the doubt arose whether the "thing itself" was to be characterized as intentional consciousness, or even as the transcendental ego. If, indeed, phenomenology, as the process of letting things manifest themselves, should characterize the standard method of philosophy, and if from ancient times the guide-question of philosophy has perdured in the most diverse forms as the question about the Being of beings, then Being had to remain the first and last thing-itself of thought.
Meanwhile "phenomenology" in Husserl's sense was elaborated into a distinctive philosophical position according to a pattern set by Descartes, Kant and Fichte. The historicity of thought remained completely foreign to such a position . . . . The Being-question, unfolded in *Being and Time*, parted company with this philosophical position, and that on the basis of what to this day I still consider a more faithful adherence to the principle of phenomenology . . . . Now if in the title of your book, *From Phenomenology to Thought*, you understand "Phenomenology" in the sense just described as a philosophical position of Husserl, the title is to the point, insofar as the Being-question as posed by me is something completely different from that position.[82]

There are several things here worth noting. First of all, part of Heidegger's Nietzsche interpretation is an attempt to show that Nietzsche's philosophy is grounded in a "subjectivism," which in its modern form begins with Descartes and continues through Leibniz and Kant. In the passage quoted above, Heidegger's rejection of the "thing itself" as "intentional consciousness, or even as the transcendental ego," and his connecting the elaboration of Husserlian phenomenology with the tradition established by Descartes, Kant, and Fichte, all of this suggests that, ultimately, Husserl, like Nietzsche, was caught in "subjectivism" and never succeeded in "overcoming" metaphysics. If this is so, then Husserl, too, must be understood as a part of the "consummation" of metaphysics. This, then, would mean that Heidegger's critique of the tradition of "subjectivism," using Nietzsche as its culminative example, would also be an implicit critique of Husserl's phenomenology.

It is also well known that Heidegger, in order to create and nurture the impression of "objectivity," scrupulously avoids the use of words such as "subjectivity," "ego," "consciousness," and "subject" when expounding his own position. In Richardson, we find the following in a passage in which he is explicating Heidegger's interpretation of Nietzsche's conception of Will: "Nietzsche so conceives pure Will(ing) that the immutable 'was' or time is dissolved in a 'now' that abides,

[82] Richardson, *Heidegger*, trans. William J. Richardson, pp. XII–XIV.

a *nunc stans."* [83] But it is precisely this phrase, *"nunc stans,"* that Husserl uses to describe his most fully developed conception of the ego! [84]

A significant portion of the third part of volume I of Heidegger's *Nietzsche* is quite consistent with Heidegger's general criticisms of Husserlian phenomenology, including especially the analyses of human "bodily" life as "Chaos" (pure sensation), the notion of a creative Will, and the charges of subjectivism and anthropomorphism. It is a nice irony that Husserl, in a marginal note in his copy of Heidegger's *Being and Time,* attacks Heidegger *for anthropomorphism!* "H. [Heidegger] transposes or transverses the constitutive phenomenological clarification of all of the regions of entities and universals – the total region, world – into the realm of the anthropological." [85]

It may be, then, that through his Nietzsche interpretation, Heidegger is implicitly giving an account of the reasons for his movement away from phenomenology as Husserl conceived it. Furthermore, there are suggestions here and there of further elaborations of the "new" "hermeneutic" phenomenology which Heidegger creates "beyond" the Husserlian version. As provocative as these possibilities are, we cannot pursue them further here. Such an investigation requires a separate study.

Comparison and Contrast

There are three major points which we should consider here. First of all, Heidegger and Jaspers agree that Nietzsche's attempt to "go beyond" or "overcome" traditional metaphysics does not succeed. Both arrive at this judgement on the basis of their own specific, and radically different, philosophical positions. That this procedure results in distortions of certain perspectives of Nietzsche, is, of course, unavoidable, even by Nietzsche's own criteria. Nonetheless, there are two objections we can advance against this manner of proceeding. Both Heidegger and Jaspers read certain facets of their own philosophy into that of Nietzsche's. This is an explicit violation of Jaspers' own canons of interpretation and an implicit one of Heidegger's. However, the other point is even more important: both use their own philosophical position as a critical foil for evaluating Nietzsche's philosophy, yet nowhere does either of them explicitly present a statement of the foil.

[83] *Ibid.,* p. 379.
[84] Alwin Diemer, *Edmund Husserl: Versuch einer systematischen Darstellung seiner Phäno-menologie* (Meisenheim am Glan, 1956), p. 45.
[85] *Ibid.,* p. 29. My translation.

Heidegger remains the silent ontologist, who throws out only vague hints and clues, but certainly nothing substantial enough to constitute a critical foil and Jaspers is the philosopher of ambiguity, who insists that we must *somehow* "sense" through our own *Existenz* – "an unknown" – what this critical foil is. Clearly, these are both rather tenuous grounds for critical evaluation.

The second major point concerns Jaspers' and Heidegger's criticisms of Nietzsche's notion of TRANSCENDENCE. Nietzsche's meaning is, on the whole, quite clear. Man is the being who contains within himself, at the very core of his Being, a dualism, a paradox. Man is that being who exists with the possibility of taking up a perspective "outside" of and "beyond" himself – a cosmological perspective which stands opposed to and threatens the perspectives of his life as *anthropos*. However, neither Jaspers nor Heidegger finds this position acceptable. Jaspers suggests that Nietzsche hints at another, more positive, kind of transcendence, and Jaspers' tentative explication of this other kind of transcendence is presented in terms of his own conceptions of *Existenz* and the Encompassing. Heidegger simply says that Nietzsche's notion of TRANSCENDENCE is not really transcendence at all, for Nietzsche remains rooted in traditional metaphysics and does not raise the question of Being as such at all. From Heidegger's standpoint, the raising of the Being-question is decisive, for *"Being is the transcendens pure and simple."* [86] One would suspect that with regard to these two notions, Nietzsche would accuse both, Heidegger and Jaspers, of surreptitious theology. At this point we need to take careful note of one aspect of the problem of transcendence in relation to Heidegger. The view as presented here is the "early" Heidegger of *Being and Time* which, as Heidegger himself emphasizes, remains the core for all of his later investigations including those which go to the very limits of language in the attempt to sketch out the topography of fundamental ontology. In these later works Heidegger attempts an overcoming of the traditional dichotomy between transcendence and immanence. However, the outcome of this effort is problematic and its full significance rests on an understanding of the foundation provided in *Being and Time*. As a consequence we have used the earlier view as a basis for exposition recognizing that we may later find it necessary to expand our interpretation in light of the later works. In Chapter IV we shall explicitly concern ourselves with this problem.

[86] Martin Heidegger, *Being and Time*, trans. John Macquarrie and Edward Robinson (London, 1962), p. 62.

The final point is of special interest. Both Heidegger and Jaspers seek to find connecting links between what we have called the cosmological and the anthropological perspectives. Both are concerned with grounding values in ontology, and both believe that there are hints of such an attempt on Nietzsche's part, although he did not succeed because of the nature of his conception of TRANSCENDENCE as discussed above. However, according to Jaspers, Nietzsche pinpoints the source of the creation of values in some unknown aspect within the Being of the individual man, and this notion Jaspers interprets as a parallel to his notion of *Existenz*. Also, in Heidegger's explication of Nietzsche's notion of *Gerechtigkeit*, there are strong parallels to Heidegger's own notion of authenticity as the ontological manifestation of Care as the call of conscience. [87] Whether or not these parallels are truly significant, we shall have to consider when we discuss Nietzsche's conception of the ultimate source of the creation of values.

ETERNAL RECURRENCE

The problem of Eternal Recurrence is without question the most vexatious aspect of Nietzsche's whole philosophy. On the whole, even Nietzsche's most sympathetic critics have found this doctrine to be a maze of confusion and inconsistencies. Many have simply dismissed this part of Nietzsche's philosophy as "a phantastic hypothesis" or as a "half-mystic doctrine." [88] Others, such as Danto, have made careful examinations of the manifold inconsistencies of this doctrine and have attempted to discover the historical and scientific influences that led Nietzsche to this peculiar view. [89] Some, of course, have even suggested that this doctrine is a revelation of Nietzsche's incipient insanity. However, if we remain true to the spirit of Nietzsche's philosophy, we shall discover that Nietzsche's own struggle with this doctrine, is far from being insane or even "phantastic." What is necessary for us to do here is to attempt to understand those elements *within* Nietzsche's philosophy which led to this position. Here the search for external influence, which may be of interest historically, will not lead us to an understanding of the *philosophical* grounds for Nietzsche's promulgation of this troublesome doctrine. Furthermore, anyone with a course in freshman logic can sit down and point out several egregious in-

---

[87] Heidegger, *Nietzsche*, I, 632–48. See also *Being and Time*, pp. 312–48.
[88] William Salter, *Nietzsche the Thinker: A Study* (New York, 1917), p. 163.
[89] Danto, *Nietzsche as Philosopher*, pp. 200–13.

consistencies. A piano student, after hearing a recital by Arthur Rubenstein, went to his piano lesson the next day and asked his teacher in a triumphant manner, "Did you notice that Rubenstein made three mistakes last night?" His teacher replied, "Any idiot can hear mistakes, but did you hear the music?" The inconsistencies in the doctrine of Eternal Recurrence have already been sufficiently exposed; what we are after is Nietzsche's "music."

Here we need to take note of two things. First of all, Nietzsche himself was profoundly ambivalent toward the idea of Eternal Recurrence. In *The Joyful Wisdom*, Nietzsche speaks of this idea as "the heaviest burden." [90] He also speaks of the conditions which are necessary in order to *"endure"* this idea. [91] He even goes so far as to say, "perhaps it is not true; let others wrestle with it." [92] were it not for the fact that Nietzsche took this idea of Eternal Recurrence so seriously, one would be tempted to take this last statement as an expression of mischievious delight, for "wrestle" with it others certainly have. On the other hand, he speaks of Eternal Recurrence as "the triumphant idea." [93] He also goes on to speak of the ecstatic joy which this idea can bring to those who are strong enough for it. Secondly, it is also important to note that there are less than half a dozen references to Eternal Recurrence in Nietzsche's published works and even in the *Nachlass*, there are only about twenty-five fragments which deal with it, and then only in a very sketchy fashion. Yet, in spite of all this, Nietzsche placed such extraordinary importance on this idea that he wanted to be known as "the teacher of the eternal recurrence." [94]

With all this in mind, let us now consider the "structure" of Nietzsche's philosophy in relation to Eternal Recurrence. As a "metaphysician" Nietzsche is a philosopher of Becoming, but he is also an "aesthetician" in the profoundest sense, since for him art is higher than truth. For Nietzsche, only aesthetics can ultimately provide a "justification" for existence. In spite of his physical and mental anguish, Nietzsche found so much in life to affirm, so much that was ecstatically beautiful, that he could not bear the idea that all things simply perish and disappear forever in the folds of time. This feeling is, as Nietzsche himself describes it, "the longing for Eternity."

[90] Friedrich Nietzsche, *The Joyful Wisdom*, trans. Thomas Common (New York, 1960), pp. 270–71.

[91] Nietzsche, *The Will to Power*, pp. 545–46.

[92] Nietzsche quoted in Salter, *Nietzsche the Thinker*, p. 176.

[93] Nietzsche, *The Will to Power*, p. 544.

[94] Friedrich Nietzsche, *The Twilight of the Gods* in *The Portable Nietzsche*, trans. Walter Kaufmann, p. 563.

A certain emperor always bore in mind the transitoriness of all things so as not to take them too seriously and to live at peace among them. To me, on the contrary, everything seems far too valuable to be so fleeting: I seek an eternity for everything: ought one to pour the most precious salves and wines into the sea? – My consolation is that everything that has been is eternal: the sea will cast it up again.[95]

Thus the doctrine of Eternal Recurrence becomes a surrogate for a doctrine of Being! "To impose upon becoming the character of being – that is the supreme will to power .... That *everything recurs* is the closest *approximation of a world of becoming to a world of being.*" [96] Here Nietzsche as a man enmeshed in the perspectives of Life becomes a "victim" of the THOUGHT of Nietzsche as a philosopher. Nietzsche's THOUGHT about the TRANSCENDENCE of man as philosopher, who can take up the cosmological perspective, grasps the Being of man as an inescapable paradox; that is, there is an irreconcilable and irrevocable dualism in the Being of man, namely, the unbridgeable opposition between the perspectives of life and the cosmological perspective. It is precisely here that Nietzsche violates the ultimate foundations of his own metaphysics by attempting to bridge the unbridgeable dualism through the doctrine of Eternal Recurrence. As a man, Nietzsche finds the idea that all things perish, never to return, "unbearable." As a philosopher, he rejects the anthropomorphism of metaphysics and with it the idea of Being. As a result, man is the Being in which there is a metaphysical opposition and struggle between the eternally opposed perspectives of Heraclitus and Parmenides. This dialectic of opposition rests at the heart of Nietzsche's philosophy, yet, at the same time, Nietzsche's "religious" impulse demanded at least a partial resolution and this he attempted to achieve through the doctrine of Eternal Recurrence. Partly as a result of his suffering, Nietzsche had a great passion for that which was beautiful in life and, therefore, his attempt to resolve the very dualism, which he himself so persistently elucidated as irresolvable, is the most human of failings. Thus, a vast problem comes to haunt the late philosophy of Nietzsche: which is primary, the perspective of life or the cosmological perspective? Either position taken by itself seems to collapse into nihilism, and thus Nietzsche began to sketch the foundations for the doctrine of Eternal Recurrence as a way of overcoming "meaninglessness." However, philosophically the cost was too great, for, ultimately, this doctrine was a rejection of the most basic groundwork of Nietzsche's metaphysics and, as a consequence,

[95] Nietzsche, *The Will to Power*, pp. 547–48.
[96] *Ibid.*, p. 330.

we find the ramifications of the fundamental dualism in the Being of man thrusting deeper and deeper into the whole fabric of Nietzsche's philosophy. As we shall soon see this opposition penetrates into the innermost recesses of Nietzsche's philosophical anthropology and accounts for much of what has been labeled "Nietzsche's extremism."

Jaspers' View

Jaspers places his discussion of the problem of Eternal Recurrence under a general section titled, "The Affirmation of the Concept of Being." His discussion is divided into three main parts which take up three perspectives on the problem of Eternal Recurrence: metaphysical, individual existential, and historical. The last two, to which Jaspers gives the greatest emphasis, we shall consider in the next chapter under Nietzsche's philosophical anthropology. However, we should once again notice the consistent emphasis which Jaspers gives to this side of Nietzsche's philosophy. Jaspers' treatment of the metaphysical aspect reveals a certain impatience which verges on irritation.

He begins his discussion with a series of questions which reveals the general direction of his interpretive approach.

But what if the philosopher nevertheless insists upon comprehending becoming as the true essence of being? If life cannot be satisfied by a view of becoming and cannot renounce cognition of being without dying as a result of it, is this true also of *philosophizing* which, after all, is a form of *life?*[97]

Philosophizing – a form of life? Yes and no. There is the philosophizing about life which is grounded in the Transvaluation, but the Transvaluation itself is grounded in a philosophical THOUGHT which TRANSCENDS the perspectives of life. This cosmological perspective is *not* grounded in life and is, in fact, antithetical to life in the sense that it provides the necessary opposition to life in the most radical philosophical dialectic that makes Transvaluation possible. However, Jaspers does recognize that the doctrine of Eternal Recurrence and the idea of the Superman are inextricably related. Thus, from the very beginning, Jaspers sets up a pattern of interpretation in which the idea of Eternal Recurrence "is philosophically as essential as it is questionable." [98] Jaspers then adds, "To him it was most overpowering, while probably no one since then has taken it seriously." [99]

Jaspers does say that Nietzsche was pointing by means of this

[97] Jaspers, *Nietzsche*, p. 351.
[98] *Ibid.*, p. 352.
[99] *Ibid.*, p. 352.

doctrine to a transcending to a different kind of Being, but in what follows he virtually ignores this possibility in favor of the existential form of transcendence in relation to *Existenz*. In general, Jaspers has very little that is positive to say about Eternal Recurrence.

When we deal analytically and critically with this idea, we encounter on its *physical* side a form of scientific argument that in this case cannot but fail. Its *metaphysical* meaning proves to be a version of dogmatic metaphysics of the pre-Kantian variety, while its existential significance simply expresses godlessness.[100]

Jaspers proceeds by examining the presuppositions of Nietzsche's "arguments" for Eternal Recurrence. Nietzsche presupposes unceasing change, infinite time, and a limitation of space and energy.[101] From these "unproved assumptions" Nietzsche argues that there must be a very large, but nonetheless, finite number of possible energy states and that, given infinite time, the cosmos would have to achieve a state of equilibrium or else would have to repeat previous combinations. He further argues that the fact that a state of equilibrium has not been achieved, again given infinite time, is proof that it is not possible. But surely, Jaspers' assumptions are no more "scientific" nor less unproved than are Nietzsche's when he says:

Because of the irreversibility of time and the unrepeatability of temporal existence, *Existenz* in its relation to transcendence, precisely because it never returns, can mean either eternal fulfillment or final and irreparable loss. When we say with reference to Nietzsche that his thought is without transcendence, we are right only with respect to the way in which *we* can conceive of it but not about the way in which *he* experienced it. Through it, Nietzsche, as it were, enters an atmosphere that is inaccessible to us; it is as though he left us and sank into a void.[102]

Strictly speaking, this last criticism of Jaspers is a fallacy of relevance known as *tu quoque*, but it does, nonetheless, point up the essentially speculative character of "scientific" cosmology and we should after all remember that Nietzsche does call Eternal Recurrence an "hypothesis." It is, of course, true that Nietzsche did try to find some "evidence" for his hypothesis, but it is also clear that the primary significance of this doctrine is rooted in his metaphysics and not in some quasi-scientific demonstration. It is on this point that we must take issue with Jaspers.

---

[100] *Ibid.*, p. 353.
[101] *Ibid.*, pp. 353–54.
[102] *Ibid.*, p. 365.

Eternal Recurrence is, in the first place, a *physico-cosmological hypothesis*. Nietzsche, as its author, succumbs to the charm of its presumptive harmony with the convincingly demonstrable knowledge of science. As a result he loses the philosophical substance of the thought without succeeding scientifically.[103]

Eternal Recurrence *is not itself* a "physico-cosmological hypothesis," but rather it is to be the bridge between the perspectives of philosophical anthropology and the cosmological perspective, which means that its foundations must be discovered in *both* realms.

Jaspers also raises the question about possible historical roots for Eternal Recurrence and considers Christianity and pre-Socratic philosophy as possible sources, but he finally decides that Nietzsche regarded this doctrine as something essentially new.

Since the thought of recurrence, as Nietzsche viewed it, is rooted neither in the Christian nor in the Greek world and is thus devoid of history, it may be said to have been forcibly fashioned out of a state of historical forlornness – out of nothingness, so to speak – and to be all-inclusive only in its historical nullity. It might be considered as Nietzsche's means of catching man, as it were, after his total rejection of all traditional matters of belief, with a view to keeping humanity going and – what is even more important – forcing it upwards.[104]

Basically this is the accusation that Eternal Recurrence is a "noble lie." But surely such an interpretation would be radically at odds with Nietzsche's conception of "breeding," for it is only through the TRUTH of the doctrine of Eternal Recurrence that the weak are selected out.

Thus Nietzsche does occasionally speak of "natural selection" – but in his conception of it "the spirit" is *not* "forgotten," as it is in biologistic constructions and "breeding" is at least as spiritual as it is physical. One would go wrong, however, if one assumed that Nietzsche had specifically devised his doctrine as a factor in a "breeding" scheme. The eternal recurrence was not meant to be a "noble lie," and it has been seen that Nietzsche had the greatest scorn for such unholy means.[105]

It seems rather odd that Jaspers would impute such a motive to Nietzsche in light of his analyses of Nietzsche's sense of "justice" and almost obsessive honesty.

Jaspers' interpretation of Eternal Recurrence seems to go astray as a result of his insistence on interpreting the notions of TRUTH and TRANSCENDENCE in relation to his own philosophy. Jaspers persists in attempting to re-orient the metaphysical aspects of Nietzsche's

---

[103] *Ibid.*, p. 363.
[104] *Ibid.*, pp. 366–67.
[105] Kaufmann, *Nietzsche*, p. 281.

philosophy in order to bring them into harmony with his own emphasis on philosophical anthropology. This shows up especially in his repeated attempts to subsume Nietzsche's cosmological perspective under his own conception of *Existenz*.[106]

Heidegger's View

Once again, in dealing with Heidegger's interpretation, we are forced to proceed selectively, since Heidegger's path is a tangled and torturous one, full of digressions and linguistic gymnastics. However, the essential form and structure of his interpretation are relatively straightforward and these are our concern here. In volume two of his *Nietzsche*, Heidegger gives a brief summary of his interpretation of the nature of the "argument" for Eternal Recurrence.

If the totality of entities as such is Will to Power and there with eternal Becoming and if Will to Power demands the absence of a goal and endless progression toward a goal is in itself excluded; if, at the same time, the eternal Becoming of Will to Power is limited in its possible forms and domain of creations, because it cannot be endlessly new, then the totality of entities as Will to Power must permit the return of the same and Recurrence of the same must be eternal. This "cycle" contains the "primordial law" of the totality of entities, if the totality of entities is the Will to Power.[107]

However, there is a hidden assumption here, for, a bit later, Heidegger interprets the Will to Power as life. "Life itself, that is the Will to Power."[108] This permits Heidegger to charge, once again, that Nietzsche has "humanized" knowledge and metaphysics and, therefore, in his view, Nietzsche has not "overcome" metaphysics. Also Heidegger here reduces the notion of TRUTH to truth as error and ignores TRUTH as TRANSCENDENCE.[109] We should also take note of the fact that Heidegger interprets Recurrence as that which transforms the transitoriness of the entity as Becoming into the permanence, duration, and fixedness classically attributed to Being.[110] However, Nietzsche, as we have already observed says that Recurrence is the most extreme *"approximation of a World of Becoming to that of Being."* It is curious that Heidegger with his fondness for linguistic nuances completely ignores the word "approximation."

Now let us take a closer look at some of these problems by examining a more extended discussion of Eternal Recurrence, which occurs in

---

106 Kaufmann, *Nietzsche*, p. 281.
107 Heidegger, *Nietzsche*, II, 286.
108 *Ibid.*, 290.
109 *Ibid.*, II, 288–89.
110 *Ibid.*, II, 287–88.

volume one. Heidegger regards Eternal Recurrence as the *fundamental* doctrine in Nietzsche's philosophy. Historically, Eternal Recurrence is to be understood as standing in opposition to the Christian and the Platonic traditions. The source of the doctrine itself with regard to Nietzsche is, Heidegger asserts, to be found in Nietzsche's own life. [111] Eternal Recurrence is an idea of great personal significance, which was not the result of a "logical" consideration of series of propositions, but rather it came to Nietzsche as an extremely forceful experience. In fact, Heidegger waxes mystical concerning this experience.

> The realm of vision, into which the thinker sees, is no longer the horizon of his "personal experiences," it is a something Other than he himself, something which passes over and under him and is henceforth there, something which no longer belongs to him, the thinker, rather something remains to which he only belongs. [112]

Here Heidegger seems to admit the possibility for a kind of TRAN-SCENDING TRUTH which man can attain. However, Heidegger's position on this point is not clear, as we shall soon see. At this point, Heidegger digresses in order to prepare a defense against the critics of his interpretation and, indirectly, of the whole of his philosophy. He asserts that "it belongs to the essence of every genuine philosophy, that it will necessarily be misunderstood by its contemporaries." [113]

Following a fairly detailed discussion of the various passages in Nietzsche's works, which deal with Eternal Recurrence, Heidegger begins his interpretation. Heidegger dismisses the idea that Eternal Recurrence is to be understood as a "scientific" doctrine at all. Heidegger attempts to impose a unity of interpretation upon the diverse character of the fragments concerning Eternal Recurrence and he adds a cautionary remark which is, indeed, an understatement: "The connection between the individual parts is in no way immediately clear." [114] Heidegger once again returns to the theme that Nietzsche is guilty of "humanizing" metaphysics and, according to Heidegger, the doctrine of Eternal Recurrence epitomized this "humanizing." For Heidegger, Hegel is clearly guilty of this "humanizing" when he asserts his famous principle, "That which is rational, is real; and that which is real, is rational"; but Nietzsche is no less guilty with his doctrine of "unreason." "However, if we posit unreason as a world-

---

[111] *Ibid.*, I, 261.
[112] *Ibid.*, I, 264.
[113] *Ibid.*, I, 268-69.
[114] *Ibid.*, I, 340.

principle, this also is a humanizing."[115] The consequence of this "humanizing" is that eternity and therewith the whole conception of time which is grounded in the doctrine of Eternal Recurrence, is not "objective" and, therefore, not truly ontological in Heidegger's sense. Yet Heidegger admits that his "humanizing" is something "which Nietzsche by all means and in all ways wants to avoid."[116] At this point we encounter a Heideggerian thesis which goes far beyond the interpretation of Nietzsche, yet, as a philosophical bias, absolutely conditions his interpretation of Nietzsche.

Every representation of the totality of entities, every world-interpretation is therefore unavoidable humanization.

Such considerations are so obvious, that even one who has followed this out only roughly must see that the human being with all of his representing, intuiting, and determining of entities is always pushed into the blind alley of his own humanness.[117]

Heidegger proceeds by raising the problem of meaning in such a way as to indulge his taste for philosophical puns. Once again, this passage below may be seen not only as a prelude to his critique of Nietzsche's "anthropomorphism," but also as an implicit critique of Husserl.

All of our representing and intuiting is such that in it we *mean* something, an entity. In every [act of] meaning [*Meinung*] I make the meant [*das Gemeinte*], simultaneously and inevitably, into my own [*zum Meinigen*]. All meaning [*Meinen*], which is apparently related only to the object itself, becomes a possessing and appropriation of the meant [*des Gemeinten*] by the human ego. [An act of] meaning [*Meinen*], is in itself simultaneously: to represent something and to make the represented into my own [*zu dem Meinigen machen*].[118]

This move is, of course, part of Heidegger's program to show that Nietzsche ends up in a subjectivistic nihilism. But how is it that Nietzsche is guilty of "humanizing" his position, when his explicit project is the "de-humanization" [*Entmenschung*] of metaphysics? Here Heidegger plays a game which we might call "the essential unity of antinomies." Heidegger argues that world-interpretation is inextricably bound up with "humanizing." The project of "de-humanizing" is also a *human* project and thus, ultimately it too is latently a "humanizing."[119] Heidegger is playing on the ambiguity of the notion of "humanization," for he adds that any thinking which regards "humanizing" as something which cannot be overcome, is superficial,

[115] *Ibid.*, I, 350.
[116] *Ibid.*, I, 357.
[117] *Ibid.*, I, 358.
[118] *Ibid.*, I, 358.
[119] *Ibid.*, I, 359.

regardless of how "critical" it pretends to be.[120] The solution to this problem is an inquiry into the Being of man or, more accurately, into the Being of *Dasein*. This, of course, is an implicit reference to Heidegger's own project in *Being and Time*. But is not this project of man attempting to understand his own essence also a "humanizing?" Heidegger admits that, *in one sense*, it is; however, in another sense, there is the possibility "that, the determination itself, its truth, raises man above himself and thereby this truth is *de*-humanized."[121] This is because the question about who man is, contains within itself a more fundamental question – the Being-question – *"which neither Nietzsche nor the philosophy before him unfolded or could unfold."*[122] This discussion permits us to understand more concretely, though not necessarily more clearly, Heidegger's basis for his charge of anthropomorphism. Here we run up against the question of the "justification" of "ontological propositions" as being somehow "objective." Heidegger wishes to argue that there are unique structures which uniquely define and delimit what it means to be human and that these are grounded in Being as such. Nietzsche, however, with his perspectivism persists in regarding philosophy, and ontology, too, in a special way, as "autobiographical." In this regard, William Earle presents a very interesting thesis, which he calls "ontological autobiography."

In the cases of both Heidegger and Sartre we have, properly speaking, "ontological autobiographies," that is, an analysis of a fundamental sense of life pushed to ontology. Heidegger's is 'fundamental-Ontologie," and Sartre's is "phenomenological ontology." In both, however, the analysis pushes toward a pretended universality, and the explicit autobiographical content is muted or absent. I should like to suggest that if ontology aims at what is ontologically richest, and therefore at what Being has become, it should reverse this traditional aspiration toward the universal, that which everything exemplifies or which all men exemplify, and aim at what Nietzsche aimed at when he said: Against the value of the forever unchanging, the value of the briefest, most perishable, the most seductive glints of gold on the belly of the serpent, *vita*. And even Hegel has shown, in his reiterated demonstrations, that Being as such is the emptiest of concepts, virtually nothing, whereas the richest is what these universals have become by differentiating themselves into the concrete universal, the historical and unrepeatable fulfillment of ontology.

It is then by no means certain that to be authentic is to pose a question about Being, or to confront the impossibility of being God, *or anything else formulable in advance.*[123]

---

[120] *Ibid.*, I, 359–60.
[121] *Ibid.*, I, 361.
[122] *Ibid.*, I, 365.
[123] William Earle, "Ontological Autobiography" in *Phenomenology in America*, ed. James Edie (Chicago, 1967), p. 78.

Thus, unless Heidegger can provide some "justification" for the move from the particular (Heidegger's analysis of *his own Dasein* and its structures) to the universal (fundamental ontology), he cannot exempt his own philosophy from the charge of anthropomorphism and his charge against Nietzsche is essentially vacuous.

Heidegger devotes several sections to a consideration of the character of Nietzsche's "proof" for Eternal Recurrence. He rejects the idea that there is any point in trying to affirm or deny Nietzsche's "proof" as "scientific." Heidegger insists that Eternal Recurrence must be understood metaphysically – the "scientific" aspect is to be interpreted as simply a sort of foreground to the essential metaphysical aspect. "What here counts and can count as proof, must be determined purely out of the unique essence of the thought of thoughts [Eternal Recurrence]."[124] The "essence" of this thought of thoughts is once more an occasion for Heidegger to return to the theme of "humanizing," this time in terms of the notion of perspectivism. Heidegger raises the question about the possibility of taking up a "standpoint" which is "standpointless."[125] He quotes Nietzsche as saying that each of us has a corner to stand in and we cannot see beyond that corner, yet Nietzsche also says that there is a TRANSCENDING standpoint, that is, a standpoint which is free from standpoint. How does Nietzsche decide between these two? Here we come to the crux of the problem which it has taken us so long to elucidate.

Either the exclusion of every humanization is regarded as possible, in which case it must be possible for there to be such a thing as the standpoint of freedom from standpoint; or else the human being is recognized in his essence as a corner-stander, in which case a non-humanizing conception of the World-whole must be rejected. How does Nietzsche decide this Either-Or? .... He decides for both; for the Will to the de-humanization of the totality of entities, as well as for the Will to take seriously the essence of man as corner-stander.[126]

This, of course, is the very dualism of which we have spoken and Heidegger does go on to admit the possibility of there being a TRANSCENDENT perspective – the perspective which we have called cosmological. The question which faces us now then is: How does Heidegger interpret this dualism and how does he understand its significance? Unfortunately, Heidegger postpones the consideration of this question and introduces another involution into his discussion – the problem

[124] Heidegger, *Nietzsche*, I, 381.
[125] *Ibid.*, I, 378–81.
[126] *Ibid.*, I, 380.

of freedom versus determinism, which, fortunately, we can summarize briefly.

This problem rises directly out of the heart of the doctrine of Eternal Recurrence. If each event in every existence is but a repetition of a previous cycle, then everything is already determined including all the individual acts of Willing. If, then, we interpret the doctrine of Eternal Recurrence literally, there can never be a Superman, for Zarathustra himself says:

> Never yet has there been an overman. Naked I saw both the greatest and the smallest man: they are still all-too-similar to each other. Verily, even the greatest I found all-too-human.[127]

Clearly Nietzsche could not have meant the doctrine of Eternal Recurrence to be interpreted literally as absolute determinism. Ultimately, Heidegger leaves this question suspended and says that Nietzsche never pursued the problem of these connections. He adds that it would be a mistake to attempt to push Nietzsche's doctrine into the antinomy of freedom and necessity. In a highly significant way this problem frustrates Heidegger's passion for discovering unities.

The same frustration "recurs" when Heidegger comes to make his concluding remarks about the doctrine of Eternal Recurrence as a whole. Here again he asserts that there is an intrinsic unity between the three poles which constitute the essential form of Nietzsche's philosophy: Eternal Recurrence, the Will to Power, and the Transvaluation of all values. Heidegger's conclusion is particularly exasperating after one has worked through literally hundreds of pages of highly involved discussion, for Heidegger's conclusion is not a conclusion at all, but rather a resignation from the discussion. He refers to the various plans and outlines which are to be found in Nietzsche's *Nachlass* and then "concludes":

> However, these plans and the dry arrangements of titles and numbers *speak* for us only if they are illuminated and fulfilled by a knowledge of that which they wish to master. *We do not have such knowledge. It will require decades for it to arise.*[128] (My italics.)

The reasons for this resignation are apparent if we reflect for a moment on Heidegger's insistence on discovering a "unified" interpretation of Nietzsche's philosophy. The dualism of which Heidegger himself does take partial note, is not resolvable through the rather artificial device

---

127 Nietzsche, *Zarathustra*, p. 205.
128 Heidegger, *Nietzsche*, I, 430–31.

ot imposing unities. The "coherence" of Nietzsche's philosophy is intelligible only insofar as we understand the notion of Eternal Recurrence dialectically as the attempt to provide a bridge between the two essentially irreconcilable perspectives of life and cosmology. Heidegger's very method of proceeding is, of necessity, frustrated by the most fundamental character of Nietzsche's approach to philosophy.

TRANSVALUATION AND NIHILISM

The doctrine of Eternal Recurrence was Nietzsche's rather desperate and desultory attempt to reconcile the dualism that he knew was ultimately irreconcilable. It is highly significant that right up until his breakdown, Nietzsche continued to work on the problems of Transvaluation and nihilism and wrote hundreds of pages on these topics, while writing only a relatively few pages on Eternal Recurrence. Unlike Eternal Recurrence, Transvaluation and nihilism are consonant with the rest of Nietzsche's philosophy and remain grounded in the metaphysics of Becoming. In fact, it is the problem of nihilism which is the motive force for the dialectic between the perspectives of life and cosmology and which finally leads to the doctrine of Transvaluation. Thus, it is through nihilism and Transvaluation that a dialectical relation is established between Nietzsche's metaphysics and epistemology as the cosmological perspective and his philosophical anthropology as the anthropological or life perspective, but we do not find here the attempt to stabilize Becoming as a kind of quasi-Being. The dialectic with which we are concerned here is, like Hegel's, open ended.

Here we must be very careful, for Nietzsche approaches the problem of nihilism from a variety of directions, which can be divided into three basic senses. The *first* sense of nihilism, which we shall continue to write as "nihilism," is pejorative. It refers to all traditional forms of transcendence which result in the positing of some principle or entity which is absolutized as an essential unity. It also includes any value system, such as "Socratism" and Christianity, which grounds its values in a non-human or trans-human principle or entity. And finally, it includes any "truths" derivative from such value systems. Sometime between November 1887 and March 1888, Nietzsche wrote: "Nihilism .... is reached .... when one has posited a totality, a systematization, indeed any organization in all events, and underneath all events."[129]

---

[129] Nietzsche, *The Will to Power*, p. 12.

It is for this very reason, that ultimately the doctrine of Eterna Recurrence must be rejected within the context of Nietzsche's metaphysics. The *second* sense of "nihilism," which we shall hereafter call "radical nihilism," is a more or less positive sense. Radical nihilism is a position of strength insofar as it recognizes the "meaninglessness" of all values grounded in a transcendent principle and further recognizes the "relativity" of all humanly grounded values.

Radical nihilism is the conviction of an absolute untenability of existence when it comes to the highest values one recognizes; plus the realization that we lack the least right to posit a beyond or an in-itself of things that might be "divine" or morality incarnate.[130]

However, "meaninglessness" cannot be the final stage. The *third* sense of nihilism and the one which primarily concerns us here, for which we shall hereafter write NIHILISM, is that TRUTH which we arrive at through the TRANSCENDING or cosmological perspective. TRUTH as an endless Becoming without a goal, TRUTH as a threat to all of the truths of life, TRUTH as the recognition of ultimate annihilation of the individual – this is, to say the least, not a comforting view. However, this is not yet the final state, for in this form of NIHILISM, Nietzsche sees the motive force for a dialectic with life which focuses on man and the creation of values with an intensity which no philosopher prior to Nietzsche achieved. The prospect of such a dialectic was extremely exciting to Nietzsche and because of its possibility, Nietzsche came to believe that, even though the human struggle was finally tragic, it nonetheless could achieve an extraordinary kind of dignity and nobility. For Nietzsche, this dialectic, like Becoming itself, must be understood as endless. There are no final answers, no final truths – there is only the endless challenge of the dialectic for man to create himself as a higher and ever higher type of Becoming.

But how does this dialectic manifest itself? The answer: as Transvaluation! There are two aspects to Transvaluation. The first is a critique of all the traditionally highest values, and we have already seen how, in terms of metaphysics, Nietzsche would proceed against all doctrines which rest on the foundation of transcendence. We shall have to raise the question of a critique again, however, in the next chapter, where we shall be concerned with the anthropological perspective. The second aspect centers around providing principles for a new evaluation. Nietzsche gives a clue to the method of proceeding

[130] *Ibid.*, p. 9.

in a fragment from 1885–1886. "Profound aversion to reposing once and for all in any one total view of the world. Fascination of the opposing point of view: refusal to be deprived of the stimulus of the enigmatic."[131] The dialectic of Transvaluation must, then, be a dialectic of opposition or even a "dialectic of contradiction." This insight goes a long way toward explaining the fragmentary and "contradictory" style in Nietzsche's method of communication, which some writers have attributed to Nietzsche's failing eyesight. Clearly, even with bad eyes, Nietzsche could have written "systematically" and "logically." Nietzsche placed great emphasis on the idea of method, but rejected almost totally the idea of "system," although he was tempted from time to time to attempt a "system", as we have seen in connection with the doctrine of Eternal Recurrence.

The metaphysical content of NIHILISM we have already elucidated in our discussions of TRUTH and the Will to Power. Transvaluation manifests itself within the anthropological perspective. However, it is NIHILISM which provides the impetus for *anthropocentrism* in its profoundest sense and emphasizes man as the creator of value, who can achieve his highest spiritual expression *only in terms of his dialectical relationship to the cosmological perspective.* Transvaluation is the creation of the "Self" in the face of the Nothingness revealed by the cosmological perspective.

Jaspers' View

Jaspers' exposition of the metaphysical aspects of NIHILISM and Transvaluation is brief and once again betrays Jaspers' fundamentally ambivalent attitude toward Nietzsche's philosophy. In the opening of his discussion, Jaspers' implicitly recognized the cosmological perspective, but he again shifts the emphasis of his interpretation to *Existenz* along with its implication of a Being that stands related to a kind of transcendence which Nietzsche does not recognize.

From the question about meaning and value his philosophizing gains its overwhelming impetus, and from the way in which he affirms being, or rather from his *thinking of the affirmation* – synonymous for him with being itself – it attains fulfillment.

The question of the value and meaning of existence is unlike any other question: man does not seem to become really serious until he faces it. Nietzsche is astonished by the fact that it is rarely asked and even more astonished by the observation that man's desire for knowledge can proceed without it . . . . Once the question has been raised, existence is deprived of its veil and appears

---

[131] *Ibid.*, p. 262.

desolate to the scrutinizing eye: it is "nothing but an uninterpreted has-been, a thing that lives by denying, consuming, and contradicting itself." One who views the whole in this way seeks solace and support in his despair. But reflective thinking only increases the despair by making it more and more clear that mankind has no goals, so that all human life seems inundated by a sense of aimlessness. When the question of ultimate meaning and value arises, life no doubt gains seriousness through the possibility of an *Existenz* that can now be truly grasped, but at the same time it loses its unquestioned security.[132]

Even if the model of *Existenz* and its accompanying affirmation of Being prove adequate in the context of Nietzsche's philosophical anthropology, the cosmological perspective cannot be subsumed under it without radically altering the structure and meaning of Nietzsche's metaphysics and at the same time robbing his whole philosophy of the motive force for its essential dialectic.

Jaspers remarks that Nietzsche even goes on to attack the question of the value of existence, because it cannot be answered. We can never have a perspective of the whole of life and, therefore, we are never in a position to formulate any final view or ultimate answer.

Nietzsche thus arrives at the basis of his philosophizing by calling in question the question concerning the value of life, the fact that the question is asked, and the very way in which it is answered. Instead of still raising the question concerning the value of existence, he questions the value of the question and the value of affirming and negating life; and he does so in order to arrive at the sources where the inviolable, unquestionably unbiased affirmation of existence will be revealed.[133]

Here again we discover a subtle twisting of Nietzsche's idea in order that Jaspers might insert the existential categories of his own philosophy into the interpretation. Jaspers cites a passage in which Zarathustra asks himself this question about the value of existence and then, Jaspers observes, Zarathustra asks pardon for his "weakness of mood." Jaspers understands this as a rejection of the question of the value of existence, but surely this is not so. Zarathustra is *not* the Superman, but he is on the path to the Superman – a dialectical path, in part conditioned by this very question of the value of existence. There can be no final judgment on existence; Nietzsche does not "affirm being," as Jaspers says. What Nietzsche does affirm is the potentiality of life as a *Willed* Becoming – it is the richness and superabundance of possibility that Nietzsche exuberantly affirms. It

---

[132] Jaspers, *Nietzsche*, pp. 333–34.
[133] *Ibid.*, p. 335.

is as though Nietzsche were speaking, when Kierkegaard says:

If I were to wish for anything, I should not wish for wealth and power, but for the passionate sense of the potential, for the eye which, ever young and ardent, sees the possible. Pleasure disappoints, possibility never. And what wine is so sparkling, what so fragrant, what so intoxicating as possibility![134]

In this respect Nietzsche is a thorough-going Heraclitean, for it is not a philosophy of life prescribed by rules which he presents, but rather a philosophy of *living*, the nature of whose dialectic precludes any circumscription by rules.

In terms of the problem of overcoming radical nihilism, Jaspers once more introduces the idea of *Existenz*, but this time in a fashion so direct, that there can be little question that he is reading his own philosophy into Nietzsche's.

Nietzsche discovers what is of genuine consequence precisely when reason seems to terminate in a void .... He finds it beyond all reason in the being revealed to him through his own actual self .... It is the existence (*Dasein*) of *Existenz* which as such never really becomes an object; it is the disclosure of being which experiences its own self and never *is* except through this self-experience. It does not experience anything foreign; on the contrary, it experiences that which truly *is* only through itself. It is basis, source, and boundary of all our self-awareness and therewith of our affirmation and negation of existence.[135]

It is this notion of *Existenz* that Jaspers proposes as the ground of Transvaluation, but even Jaspers is not altogether satisfied with this model. His dissatisfaction, however, is not with his interpretation, but rather with Nietzsche, since Nietzsche does not ground his notion in transcendence!

In grandiose illumination, Nietzsche brings into focus the absolute awareness of *Existenz* that is self-sufficient and heroically independent; and so he utters the immortal truth concerning the human condition. But this turns into a paradoxical autonomous being without God, a depth of godlessness whose independence, contrary to its very meaning, seems to surrender itself to particular causalities in the world by way of literalness of deviating formulas.[136]

And so it is that Nietzsche, in spite of himself, becomes the discoverer of an "immortal truth." The remainder of Jaspers' interpretation is devoted to the problem of nihilism and values in relation to the perspectives of life and we shall consider that discussion in the next chapter.

---

[134] Søren Kierkegaard, *Either/Or*, trans. David F. Swenson and Lillian Marvin Swenson (New York, 1959), I, 40.
[135] Jaspers, *Nietzsche*, pp. 336–37.
[136] *Ibid.*, pp. 348–49.

Heidegger's View

Heidegger's discussion of the three forms of nihilism and Transvaluation is in part repetitive, for he once again advances his thesis of the essential unity of the "five main parts" of Nietzsche's metaphysics: nihilism, Transvaluation, Will to Power, Eternal Recurrence, and the Superman. [137] The main discussion is in volume two of his *Nietzsche* and is of special interest in that here he presents his strongest critical "destruction" of Nietzsche's metaphysics. The conception of Transvaluation stands in direct relation to radical nihilism as something to be "overcome." Heidegger's exposition of Transvaluation as a critique of previous values and a positing of new values, and his exposition of the three forms of nihilism, follow the outline which we presented above. However, from this point on his interpretation re-instates itself in full Heideggerian peculiarity.

In seeking unity of the basic themes, Heidegger grounds Transvaluation and the forms of nihilism in the Will to Power. [138] This means that the Will to Power is the ground of the principle for the positing of new values, and since Nietzsche rejects all the traditional forms of transcendence, this principle "can have no other goal external to the totality of entities." [139] Transvaluation according to Heidegger, is grounded in the Will to Power *as* an attempt to "overcome" radical nihilism. At this point, Heidegger digresses for a discussion of one of his favorite themes – the Nothing. He accomplishes this by raising the question of the relation between the Nothing and radical nihilism and he arrives at the conclusion that, "perhaps the essence of nihilism lies in the fact that one has not taken seriously the question of the Nothing." [140]

When Heidegger returns to the main stream of the discussion, he makes a "distinction" between Nietzsche's cosmology and his psychology. The reason for the quotation marks is that a few pages later Heidegger "dissolves" the "distinction." Cosmology, as we have understood it, is that TRANSCENDENT perspective which arrives at the TRUTH of Becoming. Heidegger points out that Nietzsche's cosmology is not to be understood in the traditional sense i.e., in its relation to man and God, but rather, it is to be understood as another name for

[137] Heidegger, *Nietzsche*, II, 40.
[138] *Ibid.*, II, 36.
[139] *Ibid.*, II, 37.
[140] *Ibid.*, p. 37.

"world" and "world is the name for the totality of entities."[141] And what is the totality of entities? Heidegger answers: the Will to Power. Thus, cosmology, as grounded in the Will to Power, is *metaphysics*. However, Heidegger admits that the NIHILISM of cosmology "in no way leads into the Nothing."[142] The other pole of the "distinction" is psychology, which, Heidegger warns, is not to be understood as the experimental science nor as character analysis. When Nietzsche speaks of psychology, he means it in the sense of "anthropology," "if 'anthropology' is understood as: *philosophical* inquiry about the essence of man with regard to the essential relations of man to the totality of entities. 'Anthropology' is then the 'metaphysics' of man."[143] Heidegger then presents a series of connections, which are as imaginative as they are dubious. He states that psychology is the inquiry into the "psychic," which is to be understood in the sense of "life," which is to be understood in the sense of "Becoming," which is to be understood in the sense of "the Will to Power."[144] From this Heidegger concludes that "psychology" is metaphysics and, since cosmology is metaphysics, it follows that "psychology" and "cosmology" mean the same as "metaphysics"! From this Heidegger further "concludes" that, since "psychology" is in its primary aspect the "psychology of *man*" and, since man as the measure of entities is the "subject," Nietzsche has ended up in a radical doctrine of "subjectivity" and has thus "anthropomorphized" metaphysics, because "psychology" is metaphysics!![145] This is surely nothing more than a bad pun. Such a distortion of Nietzsche's thought is much too high a price to pay in order to achieve a unity of interpretation. It is, however, significant that Heidegger does arrive at the notion of two essential perspectives in Nietzsche's thought – the anthropological and the cosmological. If we interpret the doctrine of Eternal Recurrence as Nietzsche's own ambivalent attempt to bridge these two perspectives, then this alone would be enough to show that Nietzsche could not accept Heidegger's attempt at "unification."

Heidegger presents a second approach when he comes to consider the question of values themselves. He observes that Nietzsche speaks of the superiority of "instinct" over "categorical" reason. According to Heidegger, the ultimate source of value is grounded in "instinct" which

141 *Ibid.*, II, 37.
142 *Ibid.*, II, 60.
143 *Ibid.*, II, 61.
144 *Ibid.*, II, 61.
145 *Ibid.*, II, 61.

is "subjective" and a manifestation of the Will to Power. The direction in which Heidegger's criticism is moving is quite clear. He wishes to reduce Nietzsche's principle for the positing of new values to "psychology" understood as "anthropology" which is "metaphysics" and so, once again, Nietzsche is charged with not having "overcome" metaphysics. Heidegger refuses to recognize the possibility of a genuine "value theory," which is ontologically grounded in a philosophical anthropology. In fact, Heidegger dismisses the philosophy and phenomenology of value as pseudo-objective, i.e., as "subjective," "systems."[146] Heidegger observes that Nietzsche does claim that there is a hierarchy of values and that the particular manifestations of value are the result of the individual Will to Power.[147] From this, he draws the conclusion that the whole problem of values collapses inward upon itself as absolute "subjectivity." For Heidegger, Nietzsche's theory of value is the most radical expression, and therefore the culmination of a tradition initiated by Protagoras and brought into its modern form by Descartes. The direct consequence of the "subjectivity" is the relativizing of value such that value is posited in terms of its "utility" in increasing the Power of the individual Will to Power.[148] But if all of this is so, how can we understand Nietzsche's claim that there is a hierarchy of values? This is a complex question which we shall have to consider in connection with Nietzsche's theory of man, but this much is clear: Heidegger has arrived at his position partially as a result of his failure to distinguish the different senses of the Will to Power. In terms of his project of "unifying" Nietzsche's Metaphysics, Heidegger interprets the Will to Power exclusively and reductively as metaphysical.

However, even a cursory examination of Nietzsche's philosophy reveals that the metaphysical notion of the Will to Power is valuewise "neutral," whereas the particular manifestations of the Will to Power in the realm of the institutions of *anthropos* can be understood either "negatively" or "positively." Certainly the "egalitarianism" of Christianity and democracy is an expression of the Will to Power, but one which Nietzsche *rejects*. Nietzsche's whole project of providing a critique of previous values demands a hierarchy which differentiates between positive and negative manifestations of the individual and institutional forms of the Will to Power.

---

[146] *Ibid.*, 98–99.
[147] *Ibid.*, II, 101–05.
[148] *Ibid.*, II, 106.

Heidegger's interpretation finally arrives at two basic conclusions with regard to Nietzsche's philosophy. The first is that, *"We must grasp Nietzsche's philosophy as the metaphysics of subjectivity."* [149] The second is that, *"Metaphysics is, as metaphysics, the genuine nihilism."* [150] These conclusions still leave us with a question: What kind of an analysis would, for Heidegger, count as "overcoming" this "subjectivity"? The answer is, of course, no surprise. According to Heidegger, this analysis must be an ontological analytic of man or *Dasein* grounded in "fundamental ontology." [151] However, we have already seen how the absence of such a "fundamental ontology" renders vacuous any attempt to use it as a critical foil.

SOME CONCLUDING REMARKS

With respect to the interpretations of both Heidegger and Jaspers, we have seen how the attempt to "unify" Nietzsche's philosophy is disastrous. In Jaspers' confrontation with Nietzsche there is a certain anxiety. Jaspers insists that some form of transcendence must be found as a means of "overcoming" nihilism, "or else Nietzsche in the end will leave us nothing but a collection of absurdities." [152] Heidegger in his metaphysical flights, on the other hand, often seems remote and abstracted from the vitality of Nietzsche's philosophy. There is a sense in which it is fair to say that Jaspers is too involved with Nietzsche and Heidegger not involved enough.

It is extremely significant that both Jaspers and Heidegger take cognizance of what we have called a dualism in Nietzsche's philosophy, yet both, each in his own individual way, attempt to impose a unity of interpretation. Nietzsche himself regards the category of unity as a fiction of interpretation which arises out of the category of Being. Not only is Becoming the *arché* of Nietzsche's metaphysics, it is the ultimate principle of philosophy as dialectic.

For both Jaspers and Heidegger, the doctrine of Eternal Recurrence is an embarrassment. Heidegger attempts to escape the interpretive problem which it presents by saying that this idea has not yet been sufficiently thought and Jaspers attempts to dismiss it as a mystical aberration. The fact that this doctrine is an embarrassment arises

---

[149] *Ibid.*, II, 199.
[150] *Ibid.*, II, 343.
[151] *Ibid.*, II, 209.
[152] Jaspers, *Nietzsche and Christianity*, p. 87.

directly out of their respective attempts to "bridge" the fundamental dualism which characterizes the essential nature of Nietzsche's philosophy. Heidegger attempts to "reduce" Nietzsche's philosophy to metaphysics and Jaspers attempts a similar "reduction" to *Existenz*-philosophy or what we have called philosophical anthropology. To ignore either of these poles of Nietzsche's philosophy necessitates a warping and distortion of that philosophy, in such a way, that certain aspects become virtually impossible to account for.

The strength of Heidegger's interpretation is to be found in the "manner" in which he thinks about Nietzsche and also in the often penetrating questions which he raises. Heidegger's interpretation *forces* one to re-think all the basic doctrines of Nietzsche's metaphysics. It also forces a continual re-examination of the relationship of Nietzsche's metaphysics to the rest of his philosophy. There is no question but that some of the aspects of Heidegger's interpretation are artificial in the extreme, but, nonetheless, there is much to be learned from Heidegger's undertaking. The inordinate emphasis which Heidegger gives to Nietzsche's metaphysics is, at least, a corrective to the view that Nietzsche is merely a "philosopher-poet." Heidegger's interpretation also has the great virtue of placing Nietzsche's philosophy in an historical perspective, even though Heidegger's historical theses are sometimes dubious. Heidegger underscores the necessity for taking Nietzsche seriously as a metaphysician, who, rather than being a philosophical anomaly, belongs essentially to a rich philosophical tradition.

The real strength of Jaspers' interpretation remains to be seen, since he focuses primarily on Nietzsche's philosophical anthropology. Although Jaspers' actual interpretation sometimes falls short of the theoretical criteria which he himself establishes for interpretation, he nonetheless raises a number of provocative questions in relation to Nietzsche's metaphysics. Jaspers' attempts at dialogue with Nietzsche re-instate a human element which is lacking in Heidegger's interpretation. Jaspers reminds us that Nietzsche's ideas were the product of a very real, and very human struggle. In fact, it is precisely here that the real depths of Jaspers' interpretation are to be found. Genuine THINKING is the product of individual philosophers and an understanding of the full penetration of Nietzsche's insights must finally be understood in terms of Nietzsche himself.

CHAPTER III

NIETZSCHE'S PHILOSOPHICAL ANTHROPOLOGY

We must begin our discussion here by inquiring briefly into the meaning of the term "philosophical anthropology." Historically, philosophical anthropology has frequently been characterized as "metaphysical." However, in our discussion we wish to use the term in such a way as to create a contrast between metaphysics and philosophical anthropology. In the preceding chapter we used "metaphysics" to designate the cosmological perspective – a perspective which TRANSCENDS the "practical" concerns of man's life. Thus, by "philosophical anthropology," we shall mean those perspectives which center around the Life-concerns of the human being. It can be argued, as we shall see, that there is a "metaphysical" dimension to philosophical anthropology. We shall accept this argument with qualification, for ultimately even the TRANSCENDENT cosmological perspective is a human perspective, although *not* an anthropological one in the sense in which we wish to use the term "anthropological" here. At this point, we once again encounter the problem which Heidegger raised previously. There is a sense in which it is tautological to say that all of the perspectives which man can adopt are perspectives of *anthropos* and are, therefore, "anthropological." Heidegger attacks the notion of philosophical anthropology because, for him, anthropology is the highest, most radical, and therefore also the most nihilistic, form of "subjectivism." However, even Heidegger admits the possibility of an analysis of *anthropos*, which is itself not anthropological. Heidegger calls this analysis "an existential analytic of human *Dasein*," and argues that it is grounded in his "fundamental ontology." Heidegger's analysis of Nietzsche's philosophy as the "consummation" of Western metaphysics precludes, as far as Heidegger is concerned, any possibility that Nietzsche has escaped "subjectivism" and thereby "overcomes" metaphysics. This is a pre-judgment which, for the purposes of our discussion here, we must be careful to avoid. We shall be concerned with inquiring into Nietzsche's theory of man and investigating the nature of the dialectic which is operative between the perspectives of life and the cosmological perspective. This investigation will include a consideration of the question as to whether Nietzsche can escape the charge of "subjectivism." In this way, it is hoped that we shall arrive at an understanding of the innermost workings of Nietzsche's philosophy. There are already in existence several good expositions of various facets of Nietzsche's philosophical anthropology. We shall try to avoid duplication by thinking through Nietzsche's position in terms of the fundamental dualism which we are in the process of elucidating. However, a certain amount of repetition is unavoidable. Our primary purpose here is not simply to exposit Nietzsche, but rather to attempt a re-thinking of his philosophical anthropology from a new direction.

NIETZSCHE'S THEORY OF MAN AND
THE WILL TO POWER

There are two aspects to Nietzsche's theory of man. The first is his vision of man in terms of possibility and this he expounds in his doctrine of the Superman, which we shall consider in a later section. The second aspect, and the one with which we are concerned here, might be termed Nietzsche's "critique of man." Both Nietzsche's "critique" and his doctrine of the Superman are examples of Nietzsche's extremism, for he wished to create the greatest possible contrast between man as he is at his pettiest and his vision of a possible man at his noblest. Nietzsche thunders and rages and denounces man as he is in order to stir man out of his complacency and self-satisfaction, so that he might create "beyond" himself. This "beyond" is not other-worldly, but is, rather, man as a future and radical possibility. But before man can create beyond himself, he must first involve himself in a total reappraisal of what he is and what motivates him – thus, the necessity for the critique.

What is man's basic motivation? The Will to Power is Nietzsche's answer. But if everything is, metaphysically speaking, a manifestation of the Will to Power, then how is it possible for there to be a critique at all? From this the necessity for distinguishing between metaphysics and philosophical anthropology becomes immediately clear. Within the realm of *anthropos* there are positive and negative manifestations of the Will to Power. We shall use the terms "positive" and "negative" rather than the terms "good" and "evil" or "bad," since Nietzsche plays upon this latter set of terms in a dizzying fashion. Similarly, he plays ironically with the terms "virtue" and "vice." When we wish to designate unequivocally something which Nietzsche regards as positive we shall write it as "VIRTUE."

Let us begin with a consideration of those things which Nietzsche regards as negative manifestations of the Will to Power. These may be divided into two kinds. First, there are those which Nietzsche regards as simply base and despicable. Secondly, there are those manifestations which on the surface appear positive, but which in the long run turn out to be negative and destructive. Those of the first class all have, at bottom, the same basic motive – revenge or vengeance. It is revenge that motivates the "priest-type" and the "democrat," who are the preachers of equality; Nietzsche calls them the tarantulas.

"We shall wreak vengeance and abuse on all whose equals we are not" – thus do the tarantulas-hearts vow. "And 'will to equality' shall henceforth be the name for virtue; and against all that has power we want to raise our clamor!"[1]

Here we already have an indication that Nietzsche firmly believes that the Will to Power can be misdirected. Those who wish to dominate others hide their motives behind "virtues," which they wish to impose.

But thus I counsel you, my friends: Mistrust all in whom the impulse to punish is powerful. They are people of a low sort and stock; the hangman and the bloodhound look out of their faces. Mistrust all who talk much of their justice! Verily, their souls lack more than honey. And when they call themselves the good and the just, do not forget that they would be pharisees, if only they had – power.[2]

From this passage it is quite clear, that Nietzsche wishes to make value judgments with regard to the manner in which power is made manifest and the use to which it is put. Nietzsche also calls the tarantulas the "preachers of death." They deny life and wish to restrict and legislate against anything that threatens to surpass their "virtues." Scattered throughout the total corpus of Nietzsche's works, there are literally hundreds of passages in which he presents particular cases of this perverted Will to Power. Let us consider an example – chastity.

Do I counsel you to slay your senses? I counsel the innocence of the senses.
  Do I counsel you to chastity? Chastity is a virtue in some, but almost a vice in many. They abstain, but the bitch, sensuality, leers enviously out of everything they do. Even to the heights of their virtues and to the cold regions of the spirit this beast follows them with her lack of peace. And how nicely the bitch,

---

[1] Nietzsche, *Zarathustra*, p. 212.
[2] *Ibid.*, p. 212.

sensuality, knows how to beg for a piece of spirit when denied a piece of meat .... Those for whom chastity is difficult should be counseled against it, lest it become their road to hell – the mud and heat of their souls.[3]

This, of course, must not be taken as an apologia for indulgence in lust. The key sentence here is: "I counsel the innocence of the senses." What Nietzsche has presented here is the nucleus for a psychological (in the best and most human sense) theory of repression. Nietzsche realized that one can also become a slave to one's passions by denying them.

Chastity in and of itself cannot be said to be a virtue. However, the preachers of death wish to absolutize "virtues," for they would have us believe that all men are the same and are equal. For Nietzsche, there are no absolutes; there are no unconditionals. "Everything unconditional belongs in pathology."[4] It is the preachers of equality, who have strived so successfully to keep men from creating beyond themselves. To Nietzsche, it is imperative that men recognize their differences and preserve them. "I do not wish to be mixed up and confused with these preachers of equality. For, to *me* justice speaks thus: 'Men are not equal.' Nor shall they become equal!"[5] Equality breeds mediocrity, could almost be a motto for Nietzsche. In the realm of man, as in the realm of metaphysics, Nietzsche is a Heraclitean. It is only through struggle and opposition that one creates beyond himself. Metaphysically speaking, there is no telos; anthropologically speaking, man must create, out of his innermost nature, a *telos* – the Superman. An absolutely essential step in this direction is the overcoming of revenge. "For *that man be delivered from revenge*, that is for me the bridge to the highest hope, and a rainbow after long storms."[6] Nietzsche celebrates the struggle, extols the true enemy, and praises "war"; but this "war of opposites" is a spiritual war. "Your enemy you shall seek, your war you shall wage – *for your thoughts*. And if your thought be vanquished, then your honesty should still find cause for triumph in that."[7] (My italics).

From the above we can see that there are two kinds of "enemies." There are the negative enemies and the positive enemies. The negative enemies are the despisers of the body, the preachers of death, the preachers of equality, and the flies in the market place.

---

[3] *Ibid.*, p. 166.
[4] Nietzsche, *Beyond Good and Evil*, p. 90.
[5] Nietzsche, *Zarathustra*, p. 213.
[6] *Ibid.*, p. 211.
[7] *Ibid.*, p. 159.

Numberless are these small and miserable creatures; and many a proud building has perished of raindrops and weeds. You are no stone, but you have already become hollow from many drops. You will yet burst from many drops. I see you wearied by poisonous flies, bloody in a hundred places; and your pride refuses even to be angry. Blood is what they want from you in all innocence .... You are too proud to kill these greedy creatures. But beware lest it become your downfall that you suffer all their poisonous injustice.[8]

The positive enemies are those who, though still far from overcoming themselves, are on the path to the Superman. Nowhere does Nietzsche say that these "seekers of TRUTH" shall agree; the path he describes is not a path to Platonic absolutes, rather, it is a path of endless "war" or, philosophically speaking, of endless dialectic.

If the first type of negative manifestation is characterized by revenge, then the second type, that which on the surface appears positive, but is ultimately negative, is characterized by compassion (in the sense which we discussed in the first chapter). In the passage quoted above on the flies in the market place, Nietzsche warns against compassion, for even though they want blood "in all innocence," they will destroy those who act with compassion toward them. Compassion, it will be remembered, is "the last and greatest temptation" for Zarathustra. Here Nietzsche wrestles with the profoundest depths of the problem of humanism, and here we have a collision between the perspectives of life and the cosmological perspective. Man is the animal of insecurity, because he has self-consciousness and seeks a meaning for his existence which is grounded in some ultimate and absolute *telos*. Man's search for security has led him into a desperate chase after a principle, beyond himself, which would "justify" his existence.

"There is an ancient story that King Midas hunted in the forest a long time for the wise Silenus, the companion of Dionysus, without capturing him. When Silenus at last fell into his hands, the king asked what was the best and most desirable of all things for man. Fixed and immovable, the demigod said not a word, till at last, urged by the king, he gave a shrill laugh and broke out into these words: 'Oh, wretched ephemeral race, children of chance and misery, why do you compel me to tell you what it would be most expedient for you not to hear? What is best of all is utterly beyond your reach: not to be born, not to *be*, to be nothing. But the second best for you is – to die soon.'"[9]

Few can live with such a consciousness of life and even the Greeks found it necessary to project the fiction of the Olympians in order to make their existence tolerable. The many, the "superfluous ones" are too weak to accept the tragic character of existence and to create their

[8] *Ibid.*, p. 165.
[9] Nietzsche, *The Birth of Tragedy*, p. 42.

own existences as works of art out of the flux of Becoming. As a result they seek reassurances and comfort and fall victim to the preachers of death. They defend the absoluticity of their beliefs with enormous ferocity, because they recognize the threat to their security and fear their own weakness.

"No shepherd and one herd! Everybody wants the same, everybody is the same: whoever feels different goes voluntarily into a madhouse.
"'Formerly, all the world was mad,' say the most refined and they blink.
"One is clever and knows everything that has ever happened: so there is no end of derision. One still quarrels, but one is soon reconciled – else it might spoil the digestion.
"One has one's little pleasure for the day and one's little pleasure for the night: but one has a regard for health.
"'We have invented happiness,' say the last men, and they blink."[10]

Here we encounter a profound ambivalence in Nietzsche. He despises the last men, yet there is the omnipresent temptation of compassion, for Nietzsche realizes that there are many who need their absolutes, their life-preserving fictions, in order to survive. Ultimately, however, Nietzsche has to reject compassion, for it is futile. Compassion results in an implicit consent to indulge oneself in one's weakness. Compassion is destructive, in that it increases the suffering of the one who feels it and destroys the potential dignity of the one who is its object.

Nietzsche despises the last men for what they are, but he also loves them for what they could become.

Misunderstanding of love. There is a slavish love that submits and gives itself; that idealizes, and deceives itself – there is a divine love that despises and loves, and reshapes and elevates the beloved.[11]

Nietzsche, in his most extreme fashion, speaks of the necessity for war, suffering, and the annihilation of great numbers of men who are too weak to participate in the "Great Politics" of the future. He also speaks of the necessity for discipline, "breeding," and the "masters of the earth."[12] Here we must be very careful to balance the extremes, if we wish to arrive at a genuine understanding of Nietzsche's position. It is all too easy to distort this aspect of Nietzsche's philosophy and see him as a proto-Nazi. When Nietzsche speaks of annihilation, *he does not mean mass murder.* He wishes to "eliminate" the weak by creating conditions in which only the strong can survive. The war of which Nietzsche speaks has two aspects. The first is the "war" of self-

---

[10] Nietzsche, *Zarathustra*, p. 130.
[11] Nietzsche, *The Will to Power*, p. 506.
[12] *Ibid.*, pp. 500–04.

overcoming, which is the greatest and most difficult battle of all. The second is the "war" against the preachers of death and the last men, which is carried out by creating conditions in which they cannot survive, *except by overcoming* themselves.

Not to make men "better," *not* to preach morality to them in any form, as if "morality in itself," or any ideal kind of man, were given; but to *create conditions* that *require stronger men* who for their part need and consequently will *have*, a morality (more clearly: a physical-spiritual discipline) *that makes them strong!* 13

The "breeding" of which Nietzsche speaks is not so much a program of eugenics as it is the creation of conditions which require strength and also education in the sense of *paideia*.

Education in those rulers' virtues that master even one's benevolence and pity: the great cultivator's virtues ("forgiving one's enemies" is child's play by comparison), the affect of the creator must be elevated – no longer to work on marble! – The exceptional situation and powerful position of those beings (compared with any prince hitherto): the Roman Caesar with Christ's soul.14

This is hardly the design for a Hitlerian tyrant! It should now be clear that, for Nietzsche, the self-overcoming of the individual also requires an overcoming of the conditions that have led man to become what he is. This is the essential meaning of Nietzsche's "Great Politics." We shall see the ramifications of these transformations when we come to a consideration of the doctrine of the Superman.

The "critique" of man, as one aspect of Nietzsche's theory of man, reveals three central ideas. The first is the extension of the metaphysical principle of Becoming into the realm of *anthropos*. The second is that there are positive and negative manifestations of the Will to Power within the context of *anthropos* and, thus, there is an implicit hierarchy of values. Finally, there is the view that man's existence is potentially a work of art and that the highest expression of the Will to Power is man's self-overcoming.

Jaspers' View

Jaspers begins his discussion of Nietzsche's "critique" of man with an observation about Nietzsche's ambivalence in his attitude toward man.

Hence a fundamental feature of Nietzsche's thought is the movement of his love, that, when disillusioned, expressed itself as a most frightful denial of

12 *Ibid.*, p. 513.
13 *Ibid.*, p. 513.

human existence, only to reappear in the guise of a passionate affirmation of the essential nature of man.[15]

Nietzsche believed that genuine humanism was a dialectic between contempt for man and the vision of what man could become. The dialectic of self-overcoming operates between the pole of self-respect and self-contempt. For Nietzsche, only one who has despised mankind can truly love mankind and be, thereby, a genuine humanist. Jaspers argues rightly when he says that the priest-type has too little love for man and because of his dissatisfaction, the priest or saint projects his love "beyond" man into a Godhead, rather than helping to create the conditions that would lead man to an overcoming of himself.[16]

However, Nietzsche believes that even this disgust and contempt is something which must finally be overcome. It is Nietzsche's "longing for the genuine man," that leads him to his contempt and in his own life created strains in his relationships with Wagner, Rhode, and Lou Salomé. However, as Jaspers points out, Nietzsche's vision of authentic man was not some impossible ideal which he posited. In fact, ultimately, Nietzsche affirms man as he actually is *with his possibilities*. Nietzsche does not legislate particular possibilities for individuals which must be realized in order for them to strive toward authenticity. Rather, Nietzsche provides only a general framework which points a direction to the path of self-overcoming, but the particularities of the struggle must remain radically individual.

Nietzsche's *demands* cannot be of the sort that set up definite prescriptions and proscriptions which could guide the purposeful will. He starts much deeper because he wishes to reach the possible *Existenz* of man through indirect illumination of those *modes of existential actualization* which he envisages.[17]

Here, once again, we encounter Jaspers' use of *Existenz* as a hermeneutic model for the fundamental Being of man. It is time that we directly confront the problem of the adequacy of this model for interpreting Nietzsche.

One of the greatest difficulties about the term *"Existenz"* is its ambiguity and by some this ambiguity is regarded as a necessity with regard to Jaspers' radical experiment in communication.

All expressions in Existenz-philosophy are ambiguous *in principle*. All its essential terms may be taken not as the indicators which they are, but as literal descriptions. Its "propositions" may be taken as objective assertions

---

[15] Jaspers, *Nietzsche*, p. 125.
[16] *Ibid.*, p. 125.
[17] *Ibid.*, p. 149.

about a knowable object. Such a misinterpretation is always possible and cannot be prevented by further words, by warnings and instructions; for they too can all be misinterpreted. But Existenz-philosophy may have the effect of needling the reader to perform the same inner acts of transcending which Jaspers intends. This is neither mysticism nor simple incommunicability; it is a recognition that only Existenz can understand Existenz. Thus, for Jaspers, the most essential thing men have to say to one another cannot quite be said; or rather its comprehension cannot be forced, nor can its truth be objectively established. Nevertheless, it remains the most important thing, and it remains true. Such expressions are corrigible only in existential communication, by authentic Existenz. There is, as Jaspers insists, an *essential* risk in such matters.[18]

Such a defense is difficult to respond to, for one is always open to the charge that one has not understood authentically in terms of one's own *Existenz*. However, it is neither our purpose nor our intention here to criticize Jaspers' philosophy as such, for certainly even the most radical experiments in communication on the part of a philosopher with the stature of Jaspers are worth careful examination. What we are concerned with is only the adequacy of the model for interpreting Nietzsche. One strongly suspects that Nietzsche, while sympathizing with the immense problems of communication, would, nonetheless, probably dismiss the notion of essential ambiguity as *Schaumschlägerei*. One thing, however, is quite clear – Jaspers' "doctrine of ambiguity" leads him to find "ambiguities" in Nietzsche which are not really ambiguities at all when examined in the context of Nietzsche's total work.

More importantly, there is a second objection to the use of the model of *Existenz* and this objection might be said to come from Nietzsche himself. It is indubitable that Jaspers' notion of *Existenz* inherently contains a conception of a positive kind of transcendence, which is no way related to the TRANSCENDENCE of the cosmological perspective which we have elucidated. It is also clear that this transcendence, as thought by Jaspers, is in some sense "theological," thus, the repeated charge of "godlessness" against Nietzsche.[19] Clearly, Nietzsche would reject any such notion of transcendence which has overtones of the "super-sensible." A third difficulty with the notion of *Existenz* is that, in spite of all of Earle's "warnings," it suggests an inherent structure within the Being of man. Just the fact that Jaspers persists in speaking of the *"Being* of man" in connection with *Existenz* is already suspicious and, at least, suggests the sort of "categorization" which Nietzsche

---

[18] Earle, "Introduction" to Jaspers' *Reason and Existenz*, p. 13.
[19] See Jaspers, *Nietzsche*, pp. 139 f., p. 167, pp. 209 f., pp. 363 ff., p. 375, pp. 429 ff., pp. 437 f.

rejects. But what *is* man then, for Nietzsche? Man "is" Becoming as an individuation of the Will to Power. The authenticity of man Nietzsche conceives of in terms of self-overcoming. Thus, perhaps, the Will to self-overcoming is what Jaspers means by *Existenz* and certainly Nietzsche's notion of Will is enigmatic enough to qualify as an "essential ambiguity." It might be said of the notion of Will that it is a limiting case and no explication of it can be given other than in terms of its particular manifestations. The same might be said for Jaspers' *Existenz* with this difference, Nietzsche can point to concrete instances of Willing, but it is difficult to imagine instances of *"Existenz*-ing." Ultimately, as a model of interpretation, *Existenz* creates more problems than it solves. It imports a notion of transcendence which Nietzsche would reject and it tends to de-emphasize the process-character of human existence. The notion of self-overcoming is much closer to the spirit of Nietzsche and emphasizes the dynamic nature of Nietzsche's view of man.

Jaspers continues his discussion of Nietzsche's theory of man by examining Nietzsche's attitude toward the view that man is a rational animal. Nietzsche regards man as a special kind of animal that has a capacity for rationality and spirituality, but he adds that man must pay a high price for forgetting his animality, Nietzsche is very literal in his fusion of "rational" and "animal" as a designation for man. If man forgets his rationality, he becomes barbaric and bestial; if man forgets his animality he becomes weak and insipid. Man is, in the most radical and literal sense, a *spiritual* animal. Yet, there is another sense in which man is indeterminate, for he is in the process of defining what he is.

In contrast to the animals, every one of which behaves in accordance with the laws of his species, man is "the animal that is *still not fixated (das noch nicht festgestellte Tier)."* That is to say that man is indeed no longer merely an animal, but a being whose nature is still to be determined. The indeterminacy of his boundless possibilities carries with it the threat of disorder, with the result that he appears as a sickness with which existence is infected: "That which has brought man victory in his struggle with the brutes has also brought his perilous pathological development." Consequently "there is a basic flaw in man."[20]

Nietzsche plays on this notion of sickness in a variety of ways. Sometimes he speaks of man himself as a sickness, a disease. Other times he says that there is a sickness in the nature of man, that led him to distinguish himself from the other animals. It is this second sense of sickness which is especially interesting. Man was possible, not only due

[20] *Ibid.*, p. 130.

to his capacity for self-awareness and self-reflection, but also because of his capacity for self-deception. The animal in him demanded illusions, lies, and delusions of grandeur in order to survive.

> The errors that were indispensable to the development of humanity are reducible to the "basic view that man alone is free in a world of the unfree; that he is the eternal miracle-worker, the superanimal, the demi-god, the meaning of creation, the one whose nonexistence is unthinkable, and who furnished the key to the riddle of the cosmos."[21]

Here again we encounter the fundamental dualism. The sickness of man is his ego. It is his ego that tells him that "he is the meaning of creation" and that he is the one "whose non-existence is unthinkable." But, at the same time, man is the creature who can take up the cosmological perspective and TRANSCEND his existence as *anthropos*, as ego and thereby, apprehend himself as "meaningless." Jaspers sees all of this, but he does not go on to draw the conclusion: Nietzsche's theory of man asserts that there is a "basic flaw," a *fundamental dualism* at the very core of the nature of man. The cosmological perspective threatens the perspectives of life, but the anthropological perspective, without the cosmological one, leads to stagnation and an absurd self-satisfaction. Authenticity or self-overcoming is possible only in terms of the dialectic which takes place between the cosmological perspective and the anthropological perspectives and the possibility for this dialectic resides within the nature of man himself.

Heidegger's View

Incredible as it may seem, in the 1155 pages of his two volume *Nietzsche*, Heidegger does not directly address himself to Nietzsche's "critique" of man. He does discuss the critique of past values and the "essence" of man in relation to the problem of radical nihilism, but always and only in terms of the Will to Power, Eternal Recurrence, and Trans-valuation. In other words, Heidegger's approach is almost exclusively metaphysical, and he tends to deal with man and the anthropological perspectives only in the greatest generality and presupposes that they are subsumable under Nietzsche's metaphysics. However, in his essay, "Who is Nietzsche's Zarathustra?," Heidegger does have a brief discussion of the problem of revenge.[22]

Heidegger centers his discussion around the passage we have already

---

[21] *Ibid.*, p. 130.
[22] Martin Heidegger, "Who Is Nietzsche's Zarathustra?," in *The Review of Metaphysics*, vol. XX, no. 3. Translated by Bernard Magnus. (New York, 1967).

cited regarding the deliverance from revenge as the "bridge to the highest hope." This deliverance, says Heidegger, opens up a new kind of freedom. "In the same way the sphere of this freedom from revenge lies outside of pacifism, power politics, and calculating neutrality."[23] It is not to be understood as a new social or political freedom, but rather as an individual freedom which as self-overcoming is a self-commanding and a self-obeying. Heidegger correctly observes that, for Nietzsche, the highest individual expression of the Will to Power is self-mastery and the attempt to impose one's Will on another is that perversion of the Will to Power which Nietzsche calls revenge. However, Heidegger wishes to go on to "ground" this discussion of revenge in metaphysics. Heidegger argues that revenge as "Spirit" is the determinate of one form of relation between man and entities. Revenge, metaphysically speaking, manifests itself as ill Will and from this point on Heidegger makes his usual metaphysical "connections": Will as Will to Power is the totality of entities as Becoming.

> Revenge is here not a mere theme of morality, nor is deliverance from revenge the task of moral education. Nor is revenge and vengefulness an object of psychology. Nietzsche sees the nature and significance of revenge metaphysically.[24]

At this point Heidegger brings in Schelling, Leibniz, Fichte, Hegel, and Schopenhauer and draws some rather dubious connections with Nietzsche. However, the core of his analysis as to why revenge is foreign to the Will as such is interesting.

> The "spirit of vengeance" is foreign to Will as Will. Why? Because it implies that whatever it is to which violence is done somehow resists Will, hence, initially at least, would seem to lie beyond its power and need to be subdued. But it is repugnant to universal Will that anything resist it in any way. The reason is that willing in its purity implies a domination over what is willed. The only "subduing" is a self-subduing, as, for example, when Will poses and then overcomes the conditions of its own unfolding. In the process of willing *as such*, the Will wills itself and nothing outside of it can "resist" .... The "spirit of vengeance," then, is repugnant to Pure Will, hence no response to Being-as-Will that is marked by this spirit is authentic.[25]

However questionable this "metaphysicalization" of the notion of revenge may be, Heidegger has, nonetheless, presented a provocative characterization of the overcoming of the spirit of revenge. In Heidegger's *What is Thinking?*, there are also discussions of Nietzsche's

[23] *Ibid.*, p. 419.
[24] *Ibid.*, p. 420.
[25] Richardson, *Heidegger*, p. 378.

notion of revenge, but there is nothing essentially different from what we have discussed here. [26]

In "Who is Nietzsche's Zarathustra?," Heidegger raises one other point with regard to revenge that is worth taking note of. He quotes Zarathustra's statement: "This, indeed this alone, is what *revenge* is: the will's ill will against time and its 'it was.'" [27] This, of course, is an occasion for Heidegger to relate the notion of revenge as ill *Will* to the metaphysics of time and especially to the doctrine of Eternal Recurrence. Here Heidegger unconsciously slips into the perspective of philosophical anthropology and observes that Nietzsche conceives of the "redemption" of man from revenge in terms of the "eternalization" of each moment. This is to be understood as an appropriation of the past by the Will in such a way that for the first time it becomes genuinely mine. Thus the past is transformed from the simple "it was" into "it was, but thus I willed it." [28] This is, as we shall later see, an *anthropological* application of the doctrine of Eternal Recurrence as a principle for creating man's individual existence as the highest and noblest expression of the Will to Power. To treat the doctrine of Eternal Recurrence exclusively as a metaphysical principle, as Heidegger does, leads one into a blind alley, as we have already seen. Heidegger's treatment of Nietzsche's "critique" of man is interesting, but inadequate. His neglect of the anthropological aspects of Nietzsche's thought results in a very unbalanced conception of Nietzsche's philosophy and tends to ignore the fundamentally dialectical nature of his thinking.

THE DEATH OF GOD AND NIHILISM

Nietzsche's pronouncement that God is dead has long been a subject of controversy. Some critics have been so literal-minded as to point out that if God is dead, then he must have at some time been alive. And then they proceed to ask what God died from. But Nietzsche anticipates such critics and has an answer ready for them – God died out of his compassion for man.

"When he was young, this god out of the Orient, he was harsh and vengeful and he built himself a hell to amuse his favorites. Eventually, however, he became old and soft and mellow and pitying, more like a grandfather than a

[26] Martin Heidegger, *What Is Called Thinking?*, translated by Fred D. Wieck and J. Glenn Gray. (New York: Harper and Row Publishers, 1968).
[27] Nietzsche, *Zarathustra*, p. 252.
[28] *Ibid.*, p. 253.

father, but most like a shaky old grandmother. Then he sat in his nook by the hearth, wilted, grieving over his weak legs, weary of the world, weary of willing, and one day he choked on his all-too-great pity." [29]

In *Thus Spoke Zarathustra*, Nietzsche frequently uses the device of parable and often couples it with a mischievous sort of irony. In the same section from which the above passage is taken, the old pope says of the old God, "He was a concealed god, addicted to secrecy. Verily, even a son he got himself in a sneaky way. At the door of his faith stands adultery." [30] A bit later Zarathustra says to the old pope, "He offended the taste of my ear and eyes; I do not want to say anything worse about him now that he is dead," [31] Considering what Nietzsche is capable of, e.g. some of his polemical remarks against Schopenhauer, Luther, and Kant, this is, indeed, a gentle sort of irony. In fact, in this respect Zarathustra is quite remarkable in that most often there is an undercurrent of sympathy behind his irony. Yet, extraordinarily, Jaspers fails to find genuine humor in Nietzsche.

In fact humor is almost completely absent in Nietzsche's nature; he was capable of a grim sort of humor without the soul of humor; he uses irony as a keen weapon, but it has no role in the illumination of the source where it has its proper protective and impelling function. [32]

But what does all of this have to do with the death of God and Nihilism? Just this: Jaspers' dogmatic insistence on the necessity of transcendence is deadly serious; it is truly in "the spirit of gravity."

The final result of the sort of thinking that is intended to substitute for transcendence is indulgence in merely imaginary situations that leave the impression of being a future reality of the highest order; but being nothing but vain illusions, they do not constitute transcendence. [33]

Not only would Nietzsche reject this notion of transcendence as nihilistic, he would regard this seriousness, this humorlessness as nihilistic. In fact it is this "spirit of gravity" that is partly responsible for the death of God. Not only is Jaspers temperamentally at odds with Nietzsche, but Jaspers' conception of the "seriousness" of philosophy would be rejected by Nietzsche.

What a philosopher is, that is hard to learn because it cannot be taught: one must "know" it, from experience – or one should have the pride *not* to know it. But nowadays all the world talks of things of which it *cannot* have any ex-

---

[29] *Ibid.*, p. 373.
[30] *Ibid.*, p. 373.
[31] *Ibid.*, p. 373.
[32] Jaspers, *Nietzsche*, p. 348.
[33] *Ibid.*, p. 432.

perience, and this is most true, and in the worst way, concerning philosophers and philosophical states: exceedingly few know them, may know them, and all popular opinions about them are false.

That genuinely philosophical combination, for example, of a bold and exuberant spirituality that runs *presto* and is a dialectical severity and necessity that takes no false step is unknown to most thinkers and scholars from their own experience, and therefore would seem incredible to them if somebody should speak of it in their presence. They picture every necessity as a kind of need, as a painstaking having-to-follow and being-compelled. And thinking itself they consider something slow and hesitant, almost as toil, and often enough as "worthy of the *sweat* of the noble" – but not in the least as something light, divine, closely related to dancing and high spirits. "Thinking" and taking a matter "seriously," considering it "grave" – for them all this belongs together: that is the only way they have "experienced" it.[34]

This charge applies to Heidegger as well with his interminable "preliminaries" and ponderous "preparatory analyses." Also, Heidegger, especially in his early work, repeatedly insists that Being is "transcendence." Nietzsche sees nihilism as something deeply rooted in the entire history of Western thought and it is characterized by a kind of thinking in which man takes himself too seriously and in the wrong way. The first symptom of this disease of nihilism is the appearance of the notion of transcendence. The "death" of the idea of transcendence signals the arrival of radical nihilism, but this is the first step on the path toward self-overcoming and the Superman. Out of the despair and sense of "meaninglessness" of radical nihilism, there must arise a sense of joy and even ecstacy, which is a celebration of Life and its possibilities and which is characterized by a kind of cosmic laughter. Zarathustra is the perfect vehicle for the revelation of the path to the Superman, for, according to ancient Persian legend, Zarathustra was born laughing.[35]

Nietzsche's notion of the death of God is not a nihilistic device which he uses simply to attack Christianity, rather, it is an attack upon an entire tradition of thinking. For Nietzsche, transcendence is man's projection of his own highest qualities and noblest aspirations into an absolute subject or principle beyond himself. The result is that man himself is left in a state of spiritual poverty; he has impersonalized all of his own best attributes and kept for himself only the baser drives – guilt, revenge, and despair. In short, man brings about his own dehumanization. Nietzsche abhors this loss and believes that man must seize these "divine" attributes and re-integrate them into his own nature giving him the richness and profundity which truly constitute

[34] Nietzsche, *Beyond Good and Evil*, p. 139.
[35] James Hope Moulton, *Early Religious Poetry of Persia* (Cambridge, 1911), p. 51.

the meaning of being human. For Nietzsche, the elimination of the fictions of God and immortality, in fact, all forms of transcendence, is a call to the re-education and development of humanity in its fullest sense.

Nihilism is not a sudden event, rather it is deeply rooted in the historical development of mankind and the same is true of the death of God. The "critique" of transcendence is something which began already in the ancient world, but the age that can fully appropriate it and overcome it has not yet arrived. In *The Joyful Wisdom*, in his parable of the madman, who has come to announce the death of God, Nietzsche says:

At last he threw his lantern on the ground, so that it broke in pieces and was extinguished. "I come too early," he then said, "I am not yet at the right time. This prodigious event is still on its way, and is travelling, – it has not yet reached men's ears. Lightning and thunder need time, the light of the stars needs time, deeds need time, even after they are done, to be seen and heard. This deed is as yet further from them than the furthest star, – *and yet they have done it!*" [36]

Thus, history too must be grasped dialectically. Nietzsche's vision of man is not just a wish-projection, but, in part, arises out of a psychological and anthropological analysis of the historical development of human cultures. The Superman is not another escapist fiction – it is a vision of possibility based on Nietzsche's notion of dialectic and an analysis of man as he is now and as he was in the past. However, the great age of "joyful wisdom" still remains in the future. "Meanwhile however, it is quite otherwise, meanwhile the comedy of existence has not yet 'become conscious' of itself, meanwhile it is still the period of tragedy, the period of morals and religions." [37] But even the age of "joyful wisdom" is not the final goal. When it is achieved men will still have visions even beyond it. The dialectic of the human Will to Power is open-ended; it becomes static only at the cost of also becoming nihilistic. Every age will posit its "absolutes," which in the next age must be overcome.

Man has gradually become a visionary animal, who has to fulfill one more condition of existence than the other animals: man *must* from time to time believe that he knows *why* he exists; his species cannot flourish without periodically confiding in life! Without the belief in *reason in life!* And always from time to time will the human race decree anew that "there is something which erally may not be laughed at." [38]

[36] Nietzsche, *The Joyful Wisdom*, pp. 168–69.
[37] *Ibid.*, p. 33.
[38] *Ibid.*, p. 35.

The dialectic between the cosmological perspective and the anthropological perspective is the one thing that can never be finally overcome and thus, it and it alone can provide that motive force for man to create himself even higher and "beyond" himself.

Jaspers' View

Jaspers' discussion of the death of God and the anthropological significance of nihilism is quite brief, but his position is clear. Jaspers places great importance on the formulation of Nietzsche's proclamation. "Nietzsche does not say, 'There is no God,' or 'I do not believe in God,' but 'God is dead.' He believes that he is ascertaining a fact of present-day reality when he peers clairvoyantly into his age and his own nature."[39] Jaspers underscores the importance of understanding the death of God in relation to the historical unfolding of nihilism. This nihilism is not only a result of transcendence-projections, but is partly a consequence of man's faith in reason and logic.

> Nietzsche believes that, from a *logical* standpoint, the situation in which such nihilism arose can best be characterized as a result of erroneously believing that such categories as meaning and wholeness have absolute validity when applied to the world.[40]

Jaspers also points out that the dialectic of history is not an evolutionary development toward some *telos*. There is no *necessary* progress which human history must make; the Superman is not inevitable. Any given period in history will contain both advancement and regression. Nietzsche's historical dialectic does not dictate some supreme end state; man changes, but not necessarily for the better. However, Nietzsche hopes to help bring about the death of transcendence and an overcoming of radical nihilism.

With regard to the overcoming of the radical nihilism which results from "God is dead," Jaspers takes up a strange position concerning the "truth" of this utterance.

> Hence definitive knowledge of our age, which we would have to accept as universally valid, cannot be intended when he writes: "God is dead." Such a statement would be without meaning, in spite of the apodictic form which he employs here as elsewhere.[41]

There are two reasons why Jaspers arrives at this peculiar notion. The first is that he is not consistent with regard to the two forms of truth

---

[39] Jaspers, *Nietzsche*, p. 242.
[40] *Ibid.*, p. 243.
[41] *Ibid.*, p. 246.

which he earlier explicated. Here he denies that dimension which we have called TRUTH and, thereby, implicitly repudiates his earlier distinction which even at that point was treated equivocally. The second reason is that he wishes to leave open the possibility for the *re-instatement of God*. It is for this reason also that Jaspers here makes no connection between the sentence "God is dead," and Nietzsche's universal attack on all forms of traditional transcendence. Jaspers here charges Nietzsche with dogmatism.

Perhaps the actual content of this statement can be realized only by those who dogmatically believe in it (Nietzsche would then become the seducer who instills nihilism through suggestion, but he would agree that it befits this type of human being to succumb to this seduction). It may also be said that this statement initiates a new and higher human reality conceived as a way of thinking that impels man upward, or it may serve to arouse us to do all the more resolutely anything that will refute it and thus gain the assurance that God is *not* dead.[42]

The question is not what *Jaspers* believes, but what *Nietzsche* believes and Jaspers, with his continual insertion of a notion of transcendence which Nietzsche would unquestionably reject, subtly misdirects Nietzsche's whole discussion of radical nihilism and alters its significance. If there is still any doubt that Jaspers is trying to smuggle in a notion of transcendence, consider the following:

If the regnant directive in Nietzsche's thought is the attainment in actuality of the highest and best that is possible for man without God, nevertheless, Nietzsche, *in spite of himself and without being aware of it, shows decisively* that the limited existence of man cannot fulfill itself without transcendence. The negation of transcendence brings about its own reappearance. It appears to thought in falsifying constructions of substitutes and to the authentic self in a still uncomprehended shattering confrontation of true transcendence in opposition to false. Nietzsche's nobility and honesty, in a time of apparently universal godlessness, produce in him the restive form of godlessness that, so far as we are able to discover, issues in the most extreme falsity of thought as well as the most genuine confrontation with transcendence.[43] (My italics).

Certainly this is not the internal dialogue which Jaspers promised us in his introduction. However, the major problem here is that it is *not* the case that Nietzsche "shows decisively" that "the limited existence of man cannot fulfill itself without transcendence." Nor is it the case that Nietzsche's "substitutes" are necessarily "falsifying constructions." The "substitutes" to which Jaspers refers are, of course, the Superman and Eternal Recurrence. However, we have already seen that it is not necessary, in fact, not desirable, to interpret Eternal

[42] *Ibid.*, p. 246.
[43] *Ibid.*, p. 430.

Recurrence in the way in which Jaspers does. As for the Superman, within the context of Nietzsche's thought, the only way in which it could genuinely be considered as "falsifying construction," is by attempting to understand it *in terms of transcendence*. The attempt to keep open the possibility of re-instating transcendence within the context of Nietzsche's THOUGHT is to destroy the entire foundation for the dialectic which resides at the heart of Nietzsche's philosophy.

Heidegger's View

Once again we turn to a source other than the two volume *Nietzsche*. Heidegger has written an essay explicitly devoted to the two problems we are considering here. It is titled, "Nietzsche's Saying 'God is dead.'"[44] If one approaches this essay with the hope of finding a new perspective on Heidegger's interpretation of Nietzsche, he will be disappointed. In fact, most of the material in the essay has been worked into the *Nietzsche* volumes and in some cases passages have been incorporated almost word for word.[45] The essay does, however, have the advantage of being a more concentrated discussion, even though Heidegger does give a general outline of his whole approach to the interpretation of metaphysics.

Heidegger begins with his thesis about the historical unfolding of the history of metaphysics and here, as elsewhere, there is the suggestion that there is a certain kind of autonomy, as though metaphysics were itself a "force" which dictates its own course. There is also the suggestion that it contains as its *telos* its own overcoming as a preparation for the re-establishment of Being, which will reveal itself and create the possibility for fundamental ontology. Certainly such a conception of history is alien to Nietzsche, for even when he speaks of the history of nihilism, he does not incorporate into its development the notion of a *telos*. Nietzsche distinguishes three types of history – the monumental, the antiquarian, and the critical. Heidegger's version of the "history" of the unfolding of metaphysics probably comes closest to Nietzsche's conception of monumental history.

The great moments in the individual battle form a chain, a highroad for humanity through the ages, and the highest points of those vanished moments

---

[44] Martin Heidegger, "Nietzsches Wort 'Gott ist tot'" in *Holzwege* (Frankfurt am Main, 1957), pp. 193–247.
[45] Compare, for example, p. 101 of *Nietzsche* vol. II with p. 210 of *Holzwege* and pp. 638–39 of *Nietzsche* vol. I with pp. 227–28 of *Holzwege*.

are yet great and living for men; and this is the fundamental idea of the belief in humanity that finds a voice in the demand for a "monumental" history.[46]

The "chain" of which Nietzsche speaks here is a human chain, the "super-historical individual" and there is in Nietzsche's conception nothing of Heidegger's notion of the autonomy of Being behind this historical unfolding. Heidegger also makes a very dubious statement here about the nature of "thinking" for Nietzsche. "Thinking, however, also for Nietzsche means: to represent the entity as the entity. Every genuine thinking is onto-logy or otherwise it is nothing."[47] Clearly this is another aspect of Heidegger's program to "metaphysicalize" Nietzsche.

In his discussion of the "God is dead" saying of Nietzsche, Heidegger makes the interesting point, that this saying is not simply the expression of a particular belief-disposition which happens to belong to the individual person of Nietzsche. It is a metaphysical statement about a dialectical process rooted in the historical development of mankind. It cannot be understood simply as a personal expression of atheism. Heidegger also points out that as early as 1870, Nietzsche relates his view to that expressed in the ancient Teutonic legends and quotes Nietzsche's remark regarding this: "I believe in the primitive Germanic saying: all gods must die."[48] Thus, for Nietzsche, the historical roots of radical nihilism are very ancient.

Heidegger, unlike Jaspers, directly connects the notion of the death of God with the traditional forms of transcendence. "The names God and Christian God come, in Nietzsche's thinking, to be used as a designation for the super-sensible World in general. God is the name for the realm of Ideas and the Ideal."[49] Heidegger argues that Nietzsche regarded the history of Western philosophy as Platonism and once again cites Nietzsche's characterization of his own philosophy as an inversion of Platonism. This inversion is accomplished through the death of God. In this inversion nihilism is replaced by radical nihilism which reduces to nothing "the super-sensible World, Ideas, God, Moral Law, the authority of Reason, Progress, the happiness of the most, Culture, Civilization."[50] This is the "de-valuation of all previously highest values" and is a necessary step to Transvaluation. This radical nihilism

---

[46] Friedrich Nietzsche, *The Use and Abuse of History*, trans. Adrian Collins (New York, 1957), p. 13.
[47] Heidegger, *Holzwege*, p. 194.
[48] *Ibid.*, p. 197.
[49] *Ibid.*, p. 199.
[50] *Ibid.*, p. 204.

– Nietzsche's diagnosis of the "mood" of his age – he affirms, but only as something to be later overcome through Transvaluation. This, as Heidegger observes, is the basis for Nietzsche's distinction between the "pessimism of weakness" and the "pessimism of strength."[51] In his mature years, Nietzsche became a severe critic of the "pessimism of weakness," the chief representative of which is Schopenhauer. Radical nihilism is, however, a "pessimism of strength," precisely because it aims at overcoming itself. As Heidegger points out, Nietzsche's analysis of the forms of nihilism is very subtle. Nietzsche recognizes the danger that the inversion of Platonism may bring about an incomplete nihilism – one which, in terms of its rejection of "dogmatic Christianity," would posit new anti-Christian *absolute* values.

The ground of the principle for the positing of new values can no longer be situated in some super-sensible realm. It must be situated in the perspectival life of the individual Will to Power.[52] Heidegger concludes from this that the ultimate ground is, for Nietzsche, "subjectivity." From this it follows that all Willing is at the same time a valuing. This means, according to Heidegger, that Being, for Nietzsche, has become value.[53] But, for Heidegger, this does not permit Being to be as it is in itself and, thus, Nietzsche's so-called overcoming of metaphysics is not really an overcoming, but simply the fulfillment and consummation of metaphysics as nihilism.[54] Here we need to examine the adequacy of Heidegger's interpretive model of "subjectivity," just as we had to examine Jaspers' model of *Existenz*.

Let us remind ourselves of the outcome of that analysis of *Existenz*. In the end we decided that *Existenz* has to be rejected as an interpretive model for two major reasons: (1) *Existenz* tends to obscure the dynamic character of the Will to Power and (2) *Existenz* illegitimately introduces a notion of transcendence. However, we do not reject that aspect of *Existenz* which can stand for the dynamic ground of valuing as self-overcoming. That is to say, there is a certain over-lapping between *Existenz* and the Will to Power understood as self-overcoming and as names for the ultimate source of the individual Will to Power as Becoming, both are ambiguous. Here Jaspers and Nietzsche agree that, at this point, we encounter a limiting or "border-situation." However, Jaspers uses this as an excuse to posit a form of transcendence, whereas

51 *Ibid.*, p. 207.
52 *Ibid.*, p. 209.
53 *Ibid.*, p. 238.
54 *Ibid.*, p. 239.

Nietzsche would reject any such positing and simply say that this is a TRUTH which reveals man to himself as perspectival.

Now, as Heidegger would say, "How does it stand with 'subjectivity'?" First we must be clear concerning the nature of Heidegger's criticism. For Heidegger, the fundamental error of metaphysics produces a corresponding error in epistemology. This error is the subject-object dichotomy.

Whe Dasein directs itself towards something and grasps it, it does not somehow first get out of an inner sphere in which it has been proximally encapsulated, but its primary kind of Being is such that it is always 'outside' alongside entities which it encounters and which belong to a world already discovered. Nor is any inner sphere abandoned when Dasein dwells alongside the entity to be known, and determines its character; but even in this 'Being-outside' alongside the object, Dasein is still 'inside,' if we understand this in the correct sense; that is to say, it is itself 'inside' as a Being-in-the-world which knows. And furthermore, the perceiving of what is known is not a process of returning with one's booty to the 'cabinet' of consciousness after one has gone out and grasped it; even in perceiving, retaining, and preserving the Dasein which knows remains outside, and it does so as Dasein.[55]

But seemingly Nietzsche too rejects the subject-object dichotomy. "There is no question of 'subject and object,' but of a particular species of animal that can prosper only through a certain relative rightness."[56] In another passage it sounds as though Nietzsche anticipates Heidegger's criticism. "'Everything is subjective,' you say; but even this is interpretation. The 'subject' is not something given, it is something added and invented and projected behind what there is."[57] And again, "'Subject,' 'object,' 'attribute' – these distinctions are fabricated and are now imposed as a schematism upon all the apparent facts."[58] However, Heidegger is fully aware of these passages and, yet, he goes on to argue that Nietzsche is, nonetheless, rooted in the tradition of "subjectivism" initiated in modern times by Descartes. His argument regarding Descartes is peculiar. Heidegger tries to show that Descartes and Nietzsche are both philosophizing in terms of the same basic underlying position, namely, a grounding of knowledge and, therefore, Being, in the *body*. He quotes Nietzsche's remark: "The belief in the body is more fundamental than the belief in the soul."[59] From this Heidegger concludes that Nietzsche has presupposed the fundamental position of Descartes, in that Descartes presupposes that "we have

[55] Heidegger, *Being and Time*, p. 89.
[56] Nietzsche, *The Will to Power*, p. 266.
[57] *Ibid.*, p. 267.
[58] *Ibid.*, p. 294.
[59] Heidegger, *Nietzsche*, II, p. 186.

eyes to see." [60] Thus, in this way, according to Heidegger, Descartes methodologically pre-establishes the body. Heidegger goes on to suggest by implication, that the "nucleus" of Nietzsche's idea that knowledge is useful to life (as the Will to Power) is to be found in Descartes. The implication is established by quoting a passage from Descartes.

But as soon as I had acquired some general notions concerning physics, and when I began to test them in various particular problems and noticed where they could lead and how much they differed from the principles used up to the present, I believed that I could not keep them secret, without sinning gravely against the law which obliges us to procure, to the best of our ability, the general good of all men. For they made me see that it is possible to arrive at knowledge which is very useful in this life, and that instead of that speculative philosophy taught in the schools, we can discover a practical one through which, knowing the force and action of fire, water, air, the stars, the heavens, and all the other bodies which surround us, as distinctly as we know the different skills of our artisans, we can use them in the same way for all the purposes to which they are suited, and so make ourselves the masters and possessors, as it were, of nature.[61]

In spite of the tenuous character of these "connections," Heidegger asserts that both Descartes and Nietzsche grasp the meaning of truth as "correspondence." Thus, the word "body" as Nietzsche uses it is really just another name for Descartes' "subject," if we understand Descartes "properly." [62] Heidegger also objects to Nietzsche's notion of "objectivity," which Heidegger interprets as "collective subjectivity." All through this discussion Heidegger implies that there is some sort of "objectivity," beyond any that can be arrived at within the context of the anthropological perspective. [63] This other sort of "objectivity" is, of course, derived from Being as *"transcendens"* and we have already discussed the critical problems which this view presents. However, we are still faced with the question as to what Nietzsche's position is.

Heidegger and Jaspers are correct when they say that Nietzsche has not fully thought out all of the aspects of the grounding of the principle for positing new values. But, just as *Existenz* will not serve as a model for understanding this aspect of Nietzsche, neither will "subjectivity." Nietzsche's notion of the body includes within it the notion of "self"

---

[60] *Ibid.*, II, p· 186.
[61] René Descartes, *Discourse on Method* in *Discourse on Method, Optics, Geometry, and Meteorology*, trans. Paul J. Olscamp (Indianapolis, 1965), p. 50. This is the entire passage. Heidegger quotes only the last half.
[62] Heidegger, *Nietzsche*, II, pp. 189–91.
[63] *Ibid.*, II, p. 191.

as something to be overcome. Values are not to be found in nature, nor are they simply whims of an individual Will to Power. Values are conditions for the existence of the individual Will to Power as perspectival. Thus, nihilism, radical nihilism, and Transvaluation are not merely "subjective" processes, but are part of the development and adaptation of the human Will to Power as a species and are in that sense "objective." Without this sense of "objectivity" there would be no possibility for a hierarchy of values as Nietzsche conceives it.

Let us attempt a re-statement and clarification. The nihilism expressed in the traditional theories of transcendence is deeply rooted in the historical dialectic of Western culture. This nihilism is finally made explicit in Nietzsche's saying, "God is dead." This means that the old values have de-valued themselves and as this insight comes to cultural consciousness, radical nihilism sets in. However, this radical nihilism is something to be overcome through the principle for the positing of new values. Nietzsche grounds this principle in life and human life in particular, which is not to be understood merely in terms of a "subject," but as "body" – the fusion of rationality and animality. The life of this body (understood as this fusion) constitutes a world. The notion of world in the anthropological perspective is not separable from life. This means that values are not something "objective" and discoverable in nature and neither are they simply "subjective." The principle of positing new values and the general framework and hierarchy of values are dialectically determined through the interaction between the life of *anthropos* and its world. The life of *anthropos* is understood in terms of the dialectic between the anthropological perspective and the cosmological perspective. In other words, through the cosmological perspective man can achieve an understanding of himself in terms of those conditions which define and delimit his perspective *as anthropos*. "Put briefly: perhaps the entire evolution of the spirit is a question of the body; it is the history of the development of a higher body that emerges into our sensibility." [64] It is precisely this sensibility which grasps the conditions which define and delimit man *as* man and it is through this sensibility that the principle for the positing of new values is grounded in the dialectic between the cosmological and the anthropological perspectives which create the possibility for the Superman.

[64] Nietzsche, *The Will to Power*, p. 358.

THE SUPERMAN

Nietzsche's vision of the Superman is one of the most fascinating aspects of his philosophy, as well as one of the most misinterpreted. With the doctrine of the Superman we get the other half of Nietzsche's theory of man – man understood as possibility. It is extraordinarily difficult to unfold the inner workings of any single aspect of Nietzsche's dialectic in an expository fashion – difficult, even for Nietzsche! – so, as a result, the most coherent and cohesive account of the notion of the Superman is to be found in the parables and poetry of *Thus Spoke Zarathustra*. From the very beginning we must keep in mind that the Superman (or "overman" in Kaufmann's translation) is not to be conceived of as a *state* which man can achieve. One never *is* a Superman except in a relative sense. Relative to the rest of society, we might speak of Goethe as a Superman, but even Goethe had not fully overcome himself and so was, in terms of his possibilities, still on the path to the Superman. No matter how fully and richly a man lives, there is still always the possibility for future self-overcoming.

The first step on the path to the Superman is, as we have already seen, the overcoming of radical nihilism. This opens up the possibility for the creation of new values and Nietzsche often refers to the Superman as the creating ones – the ones on the path to self-overcoming. "And life itself confided this secret to me: 'Behold,' it said, 'I am that which must always overcome itself.'" [65] It becomes clear in terms of the doctrine of the Superman, that even though there is a general framework and hierarchy of values, particular values are to be determined dialectically with reference to the struggle for self-overcoming.

And you tell me, friends, that there is no disputing of taste and tasting? But all of life is a dispute over taste and tasting. Taste – that is at the same time weight and scales and weigher; and woe unto all the living that would live without disputes over weight and scales and weighers! [66]

Here is Nietzsche's ground of values – "weight and scales and weighers" – it is neither simply "objective" or simply "subjective," but rather a dialectical relationship.

Zarathustra is the teacher of the doctrine of the Superman, but at the same time he himself is on the path to the Superman. Here again we must be careful, for there is *no single* path to the Superman. Each

[65] Nietzsche, *Zarathustra*, p. 227.
[66] *Ibid.*, p. 229.

has his own path as a *self*-overcoming. "'This is *my* way; where is yours?' – thus I answered those who asked me 'the way.' For *the* way – that does not exist." [67] This new vision of man depends upon two forms of freedom. The first is the freedom *from* nihilism, that is, the belief in transcendence and the second is the freedom *to* create, for it is only in creating as a Willing and valuing that self-overcoming is possible.

The two great VIRTUES of the Superman are honesty and nobility. In terms of the notion of nobility we are presented with some very subtle distinctions which provide a partial clue to Transvaluation. The Superman can hate his enemy, but he should not despise him; on the contrary he would be proud of him. But even in despising there is the hope of overcoming. "That you despise, you higher men, that lets me hope. For the great despisers are the great reverers." [68] Also the Superman can have contempt for the herd, but not malicious scorn. In the end, even contempt is overcome through the struggle with one's greatest enemy – oneself. The Superman may feel concern and love for the other, but he cannot yield to compassion, the greatest of all temptations.

Nietzsche placed an extremely high value upon honesty. "Take good care there, you higher men! For nothing today is more precious to me and rarer than honesty." [69] Nietzsche's conception of honesty is inextricably bound up with strength. Self-overcoming is a Willing that is simultaneously a commanding and an obeying grounded in a strict, even severe, sense of honesty with oneself. This includes a merciless recognition of one's own weakness and limitations.

Will nothing beyond your capacity: there is a wicked falseness among those who will beyond their capacity. Especially if they will great things! For they arouse mistrust against great things, these subtle counterfeiters and actors – until finally they are false before themselves, squinters, whited worm-eaten decay, cloaked with strong words, with display-virtues, with splendid false deeds.[70]

Needless to say, this honesty also applies to one's relations with others.

Here there is something of a problem, for Nietzsche's descriptions are not always consistent and he himself sometimes forgets that the Superman is not a type. From these various descriptions one gets a picture of the Superman as a man with incredible sensitivity and yet a kind of hardness and strength that verges on insensitivity. In part

[67] *Ibid.*, p. 307.
[68] *Ibid.*, p. 399.
[69] *Ibid.*, p. 401.
[70] *Ibid.*, p. 401.

this is a result of Nietzsche's own extreme sensitivity coupled with his obsession concerning health and strength, both physical and spiritual. Nietzsche was aware of the immense difficulty of bringing about such a fusion.

Why the philosopher rarely turns out well. His requirements include qualities that usually destroy a man:
1. a tremendous multiplicity of qualities; he must be a brief abstract of man, of all man's higher and lower desires: danger from antitheses, also from disgust at himself;
2. he must be inquisitive in the most various directions: danger of going to pieces;
3. he must be just and fair in the highest sense, but profound in love, hate (and injustice), too;
4. he must be not only a spectator, but also a legislator: judge and judged (to the extent that he is a brief abstract of the world);
5. extremely multifarious, yet firm and hard. Supple.[71]

There is much that is autobiographical in this passage and it also reveals the keenness of Nietzsche's insight into himself. Yet only a year or two later he writes:

The sublime man has the highest value, even if he is terribly delicate and fragile, because an abundance of very difficult and rare things has been bred and preserved together through many generations.[72]

What is clear, however, and also most important, is that the path to the Superman is a self-overcoming, which cannot be determined in advance, but which must be accompanied by the VIRTUES of honesty and nobility.

Jaspers' View

Jaspers prepares the ground for the discussion of the Superman in a very interesting way. He argues that the notion of creation is absolutely fundamental in Nietzsche's philosophy. Jaspers' exposition is especially valuable in that he points out all the various meanings and levels of meaning contained in Nietzsche's notion of creation. Here more than anywhere else in his interpretation one can sense an affinity between Jaspers and Nietzsche.

Creation is the highest demand; it is authentic being, the ground of all essential activity:
Creation is *evaluation* .... Creation is *faith* .... Creation is *love* .... In creation is *annihilation* .... "All creation is *communication* (Mitteilen)" .... Still, all of creation is great pain and lack of knowledge .... In creation *authentic being is attained.*[73]

---

[71] Nietzsche, *The Will to Power*, pp. 517–18.
[72] *Ibid.*, p. 518.
[73] Jaspers, *Nietzsche*, pp. 151–52.

Here, as Jaspers rightly points out, we have the groundwork for the existentialist conception of authenticity. In fact, creation, authenticity, and self-overcoming are all attempts to describe the same fundamental process. Creation is the highest form of Willing and even in the latest fragments of the *Nachlass*, Nietzsche celebrates artistic creation. Nietzsche never really departs from his youthful aestheticism, although he does come to understand the notion of creation in a richer way. The highest form of artistic creation becomes the individual human life. Man himself becomes the block of marble out of which the highest expression of beauty is to reveal itself. Man ultimately becomes the highest work of art.

The statement that creation is faith tends to be misleading, for Nietzsche certainly did not mean anything connected with theological dogmatics. What Nietzsche really means is a faith in vision, in "prophetic dreams." [74] Imaginative vision, the plunge into possibilities, is inseparable from genuine creation. Creation is also a love which both brings forth that which is new and annihilates the old. Some critics have not been able to see beyond Nietzsche's "critiques" and, thus, they grasp only the first phase, the "destruction" phase of Nietzsche's philosophy. For Nietzsche, "destruction" is justified only in so far as one creates "beyond" that which is "destroyed." Nietzsche's "philosophizing with a hammer" is only a preparatory stage to authentic creation.

Nietzsche's insistence on the relationship between suffering and creating has frequently earned his philosophy the label of Romanticism. Kaufmann presents a good counter-argument to this view and presents the thesis that Nietzsche is fundamentally an anti-Romantic. [75] To Nietzsche a Romanticizing of suffering would be a form of decadence, for, though suffering is regarded as a necessary condition of creation, it is, nonetheless, something to be overcome through creation. He regards Beethoven as a great creative genius, not because of his suffering, but because of the way in which he "transcended" his suffering. Creation is also communication, because it is a self-revelation of the highest type.

In spite of all this Jaspers says that the notion of creation "remains *necessarily* indefinite."

It is one of those *signa* of Nietzsche's philosophizing that, like "life," "will to power," and "eternal recurrence," is never conceptualized .... Nietzsche

---

[74] *Ibid.*, p. 151.
[75] Kaufmann, *Nietzsche*, pp. 277–78.

always treats creation as though it were self-evident, but virtually never takes it directly as his theme. He does not develop and explain its nature. It is never a possible goal of the will. But his formulations have all the power of an as yet indefinite appeal to recall and to come to grips with authentic being.[76]

However, we should take careful note of the fact that Jaspers is *not* saying that we cannot understand Nietzsche's notion of creation. Rather, it is simply the case, that we cannot present a few verbal formulae which express the full richness of the idea of creation. Jaspers is extremely sensitive to the problems of communication and emphasizes again and again that it is not possible to attain a genuine understanding of Nietzsche by examining isolated statements. The notion of creation is perfectly intelligible, but only within the context of the *whole* of Nietzsche's philosophy.

Jaspers emphasizes the distinction between the superior man and the Superman. Superior men have already appeared in history, but the Superman has not yet arrived.

As Nietzsche sees it, superior men do actually exist, even though they are constantly threatened and are forever coming to grief. They are in extreme *danger*, both *from without* and from *within*. Being extraordinary, they come to ruin in a society that is in bondage to the ordinary; they are made submissive, melancholy, and sick. Only "those with iron constitutions, like Beethoven and Goethe," were able to stand firm. But "even they show the effect of the most fatiguing struggle and tension: they breathe more heavily and their manner easily becomes too violent." Society is the relentless enemy of these great ones.[77]

As a result of these conditions, even the noblest man falls prey to his own pettiness, which manifests itself as contempt, irritability, withdrawal, and impatience. This leads Nietzsche to ask whether or not the superior men are truly involved in the process of self-overcoming, since it frequently appears that it is merely discontent with pervading conditions that has *pushed* them to their superior level.[78] As an answer to this, Nietzsche arrives at the doctrine of the Superman, for the striving must have the fundamental positivity of self-overcoming, rather than being a negative *reaction* to conditions. However, this insight gradually leads Nietzsche to modify his conception of the "political" and social roles which the Superman must adopt. Initially, he was content with a situation which would "permit" the Superman to exist in his own context as a self-creating being in a relationship of

---

[76] Jaspers, *Nietzsche*, p. 152.
[77] *Ibid.*, pp. 163–64.
[78] *Ibid.*, p. 164.

mutual tolerance between the Superman and the herd. In his later thought, however, Nietzsche comes to believe more and more strongly that the Superman must achieve the power to transform the nature of social and "political" institutions. Thus, the possibility of the Superman comes to depend upon a concomitant alteration of the conditions of existence. Ultimately, the doctrine of the Superman brings with it the vision of a new kind of humanity and the Superman becomes the "legislator of the future."

After having tried in vain for a long time to attach a definite concept to the word "philosopher" – for I found many contradictory characteristics – I recognized at last that there are two distinct kinds of philosopher:

1. those who want to ascertain a complex fact of evaluations (logical or moral);

2. those who are *legislators* of such evaluations. The former try to master the world of the present or the past by concentrating and abridging the multiplicity of events through signs: their aim is to make previous events surveyable, comprehensible, graspable, and usable – they assist the task of man to employ all past things for the benefit of his future.

The latter, however, are *commanders;* they say: "thus it shall be!" They alone determine the "whither" and the "wherefore," what is useful and what constitutes utility for men; they dispose of the preparatory work of scientific men, and all knowledge is for them only a means for creation.[79]

Here we have an explicit statement of the link between creation and the role of the Superman. Nietzsche gradually comes to the conclusion that the Superman must also create the conditions for his own self-overcoming. The creation of these conditions becomes the theme for what Nietzsche calls "Great Politics".

This conception of Great Politics has been grossly misunderstood. Great Politics is a struggle for power, but not for the sake of some State. The conception of State power is anathema to Nietzsche and he calls the State, "the new idol".

State is the name of the coldest of all cold monsters. Coldly it tells lies too; and this lie crawls out of its mouth: "I, the state, am the people." That is a lie! .... It will give you everything if you will adore it, this new idol: thus it buys the splendor of your virtues and the look of your proud eyes .... State I call it where all drink poison, the good and the wicked; state, where all lose themselves, the good and the wicked; state, where the slow suicide of all is called life.[80]

Nietzsche's attitude toward the State could hardly be less unequivocal. The celebration of the State is one of the dangers of incomplete nihilism – it may attempt to replace the smashed idol of God with the idol of

---

[79] Nietzsche, *The Will to Power*, pp. 509–10.
[80] Nietzsche, *Zarathustra*, p. 160.

the State. There is the omnipresent danger that God-surrogates will be placed before men as an Ideal and, for Nietzsche, this is simply the replacement of one form of transcendence by another.

If the struggle is not for political power, then what is it for? Jaspers puts it very well.

From the standpoint of great politics it means fighting with the aid of the creative thoughts which invisibly shape and transform men. Truth attains actuality only in the struggle for power; here lies both its source and limit.

The new masters for whom Nietzsche longs will represent and bring forth the noble man in a world that has become godless; Nietzsche's great politics takes upon itself the task of providing the philosophical interpretation these masters need and of making them aware of themselves: "I am writing for a species of men who do not yet exist: the masters of the earth." [81]

Ultimately, the Great Politics becomes the struggle to attain the power for creative Transvaluation. Man as he is now is the "bridge" to the Superman, and in Nietzsche's mature thought the Superman becomes a model in a two-fold sense – a *psychological* or, better, an existential model and an *historical* model. The notion of the Superman has an existential immediacy for the individual in terms of self-overcoming and yet, at the same time, takes on a cultural significance as a model for a future humanity. If we conceive of man as a Becoming, in the form of Will to Power, then any genuine understanding of man's situation must grasp his social institutions as Becoming also. The stagnation and ossification of social institutions is a massive obstacle to self-overcoming and the Great Politics of the Superman is Nietzsche's solution to this problem.

Heidegger's View

As we would expect, Heidegger's explication of the doctrine of the Superman is primarily from within the perspective of metaphysics. Once again, Heidegger brings in the theme of "subjectivity" and insists that since metaphysics is nihilism, the Superman must be understood in terms of its "nihilistic-*historical* essence." [82] The Superman is a denial or disavowal of what has been previously regarded as the essence of man – reason. However, Heidegger adds, this denial is nihilistic, since it still thinks the essence of man as "rational animal." [83] This is one of Heidegger's favorite games and is a derivative and perverse application of Hegel's dialectic of negation. Heidegger argues

[81] Jaspers, *Nietzsche*, p. 273.
[82] Heidegger, *Nietzsche*, II, 292.
[83] *Ibid.*, II, 294.

that Nietzsche's philosophy is anti-metaphysics in the traditional sense of metaphysics and as such is an antithesis and not a "synthesis," from which it ostensibly follows that Nietzsche's philosophy is after all metaphysics. Structurally Heidegger applies the same argument to Nietzsche's anti-Christianity and anti-anthropomorphism. If Nietzsche's anti-metaphysics were nothing more than a "critique," then this conclusion might be justified. However, as it is, Heidegger can arrive at this conclusion only by virtually ignoring the fundamental character of the dialectic between the cosmological and anthropological perspectives. In terms of this dialectic, it would be little less than absurd to claim that Nietzsche remains rooted in metaphysics, i.e., traditional metaphysics.

It is in the discussion of the doctrine of the Superman and its relation to the rest of Nietzsche's philosophy that the weaknesses of Heidegger's interpretation are most evident. Here Heidegger forces his arguments and creates connections by making oracular pronouncements. "The consummated subjectivity of the Will to Power is the metaphysical origin of the essential necessity of the 'Superman'." [84] This charge of "subjectivity," while *formally* correct within the frame work of Heidegger's schemata, is, nonetheless, tautological in exactly the same manner in which his charge of anthropomorphism is. This means that the charge is irrelevant unless Heidegger can provide an adequate critical foil, which would be his fundamental ontology and this, as we have seen, he has not done. However, even more exasperating is Heidegger's egregious forcing of Nietzsche's text. He takes Nietzsche's remark that man is the *"not yet determined animal"* and "deduces" from this that man is now determined, namely, as "animal"! [85] "The metaphysical determining of man as animal signifies the nihilistic affirmation of the Superman." [86] Heidegger further asserts that the doctrine of the Superman can be brought to completion only "where the entity as such is the Will to Power and the totality of entities is the Eternal Recurrence of the same." [87] However, this statement is meaningless in light of Heidegger's "suspension" of the metaphysical significance of the doctrine of Eternal Recurrence. [88] Heidegger's refusal to recognize the anthropological dimension (in any but a reductive sense) of Nietzsche's philosophy results in an

[84] *Ibid.*, II, 302.
[85] *Ibid.*, II, 306–07.
[86] *Ibid.*, II, 307.
[87] *Ibid.*, II, 307.
[88] See the section on Eternal Recurrence in Chapter II.

interpretation which ignores the immense existential significance of the doctrine of Eternal Recurrence as a creative force.

NIETZSCHE'S ETHICS AND THE TRANSVALUATION OF ALL VALUES

In terms of the essentially dialectical character of Nietzsche's philosophy, ethics presents a set of special problems. We shall be primarily concerned here with explicating the general structures and the dialectical character of Nietzsche's ethics and doctrine of Transvaluation, rather then presenting a detailed exposition of the wealth of particulars which Nietzsche examines. [89]

Nietzsche himself characterizes his metaphysics as anti-anthropomorphic, however, his theories of ethics and Transvaluation might be characterized as "hyper-anthropomorphic." The hue and cry of the doctrine of Transvaluation is that man has not yet taken himself "seriously" in the right way. Man has taken himself seriously, but in the "spirit of gravity." For man to take himself seriously in the right way means, for Nietzsche, a "joyful wisdom," an ecstatic understanding of himself and a celebration of the limiting conditions which define his possibilities. Man can become truly man only insofar as he grasps himself as perspectival within the dialectic between the anthropological and cosmological perspectives. Only in this way can man "become what he is."

Nietzsche distinguishes two basic types of morality – the "slave" or herd morality and the "master" morality. Here we must proceed with great care, for the dialectical inter-relationships which characterize Nietzsche's ethics are quite complex. Nietzsche increases the complexity by playing with the fundamental oppositions. Here again we find operative, Nietzsche's implicit distinction between positive and negative manifestations of the Will to Power. Only by keeping this distinction constantly in mind, will we be able to unravel the intricacies of Nietzsche's ethics. At first glance it might appear that the master morality is that of the tyrant, who imposes his Will on the herd. But this is not the case; the Will to tyranny is characteristic of the herd morality, not the master morality. The "ascetic priestly-type" is the practitioner of the herd morality, even though he "rules." The herd

---

[89] For a thorough exposition of Nietzsche's ethics and doctrine of Transvaluation, see William Henry Werkmeister, "Nietzsche's Transvaluation of Values" in *Theories of Ethics* (Lincoln, Nebraska, 1961), pp. 168–241.

morality is characterized by resentment, which finally leads to the Will to revenge – a *negative* manifestation of the Will to Power. In the herd morality there is a strong desire to punish those who are superior. The basic foundation for moral judgment within the herd morality is the opposition of "good" and "evil". In the master morality the opposition is "good" and "bad." This "good" of the master morality, we shall hereafter write as "Good," for though the two have the same name, there is an important difference. [90]

In the herd morality, evil is the more fundamental of the two concepts and, for the man of resentment, good is secondary and by it this man means himself. Anything or anyone who is superior to him is automatically judged evil. The herd morality also uses the fiction of transcendence as a "justification" for its moral condemnations. This, for Nietzsche, is the most egregious manifestation of nihilism. In the master morality, the primary concept of the Good arises out of the VIRTUES of nobility and honesty which we have already discussed. The noble man respects and values superiority and does not attempt to suppress it, but rather accepts it and attempts through a dialectical struggle with it to raise himself to a higher level. The bad for the noble man is the "vulgar," the "ignoble," which is characterized by the man of resentment, the "last man." The noble man does not attempt to impose his Will, but rather attempts through dialectic to *create* conditions which will elevate himself and create the demand for self-overcoming on the part of others. The judgment "bad" is not a repressive judgment; it is more like a challenge. The master morality wishes to raise others to the level of creative dialogue and is thus a "selfish" benevolence. On the other hand, the judgment "evil" is motivated by a destructive impulse and refuses to acknowledge superiority; it is the demand for "equality." For the herd morality, opposition is evil, whereas, for the master morality, opposition is not only Good, but necessary. Opposition is a condition for growth, for creating "beyond" oneself. For Nietzsche, the notions of herd morality and master morality are interpretive models and Nietzsche is fully aware that in practice we often find a mixture of the two.

We have seen in what sense Nietzsche speaks of a "morality of masters" and a "morality of slaves." "In all higher and mixed cultures," Nietzsche finds, "attempts are made at reconciliation of these two moralities, still oftener there is an inter-mixture of the two, and a mutual misunderstanding, at times even

90 *Ibid.,* p. 223.

a solidified coexistence – even within the same man, with one soul" (XII: 227); and this is the very situation which bodes ill for the future.[91]

Why is it that this "bodes ill for the future."? It bodes ill precisely because Transvaluation depends upon the recognition of an "order of rank." For Nietzsche, *justice* teaches that men are *not* equal. To aspire to that which is utterly beyond one's capabilities is self-destructive and breeds resentment, which in turn leads to the desire for revenge upon those who are superior. However, Nietzsche warns that we must beware of modesty and humility, for there are false and genuine forms. False modesty and false humility can become repressive tools of a negative Will to Power. In fact, the whole herd morality is directed against the notion of an order of rank. At the most fundamental level there are two orders of rank and they are distinguished in terms of the way in which the Will to Power is directed.

I distinguish between a type of ascending life and another type of decay, disintegration, weakness. Is it credible that the question of the relative rank of these two types still needs to be posed?[92]

The "mastery" of the master morality is primarily "self-mastery." The highest positive expression of the Will to Power is the power of a "master," who feels no psychological need to impose this power, a strength which does not need recognition and adulation.

In the dialectic between the moralities of the slave and the master, the superior man is labeled the "immoralist." Nietzsche appropriates this label and it becomes a sign for the dialectic of Transvaluation. The immoralist as creator and legislator is the "lawbreaker," the one who threatens all the old values. It is the immoralist, who for the first time desires the creation of a *human* morality rather than a *transcendent* morality. The demands of self-creation are overwhelming and offer little security or comfort. As a result, this threat of insecurity causes most men to flee from the struggle of self-overcoming. The herd man prefers to have answers given to him, rather than having to wrest his own from the struggle with existence. This explains how it is that the priest-type gains dominance. The priest-type is the one who directs resentment outside of the herd toward the superior man.

The immensity of the conflict between the immoralist who is striving for self-overcoming and an essentially repressive social order leads Nietzsche into inconsistencies. At times he falls prey to the illusion that future "freedoms" will "justify" present extremes. In

[91] *Ibid.*, p. 229.
[92] Nietzsche, *The Will to Power*, p. 457.

some passages Nietzsche explicitly states a belief that the master morality must establish itself as a tyranny over the herd. [93] Yet at other times he strongly emphasizes the *necessarily* individual and existential struggle to achieve a self-overcoming, which by its very nature cannot impose its Will on the other. That Nietzsche does not "solve" all the intricacies of these extraordinarily complex problems is hardly surprising. In the end, however, Nietzsche does achieve his goal, for his position presents a set of possibilities which, if we enter into the dialectic, becomes an occasion for genuine philosophical dialogue. Werkmeister puts it very well.

Nietzsche, properly understood, is still the radical challenge to any complacency in moral matters. His extreme views require an answer – and now, in our times of positivism, emotivism, and persuasive definitions, more than ever; for how would the emotivists and the hedonists answer Nietzsche? To set dogma against dogma is hardly sufficient. And Nietzsche has already branded them "nihilists" and has pointed up the necessity of a positive reconstruction of morals. [94]

We need only recall Nietzsche's attitude toward disciples to recognize the call of Nietzsche's challenge.

Jaspers' View

Jaspers begins his discussion with Nietzsche's attack on morality. Nietzsche's severest criticisms are leveled at so-called *moral* judgments. In fact, one might even say that, for Nietzsche, these so-called moral judgments are immoral. What Nietzsche is attacking is the absoluticity claimed for such judgments. Not only are epistemological judgments perspectival, but moral ones as well. This means that often our moral judgments are nothing more than a revelation of the limitation of our own perspective. Nietzsche's analyses of the psychological foundations for specific moral judgments are extremely perceptive and incisive.

His psychological observations concerning the origin and development of such judgments are inexhaustible. Among other things, he unmasks the pleasure taken in causing pain, the release of impotent instincts for revenge, the habit of furtive self-aggrandizement, the joy in feelings of power, and the mendacity of all moral indignation and the presumptuous judgment in all moral pathos. His magnificent "ridicule of all the moralizing of the present day" is conclusive. [95]

The hatred of hypocrisy was undoubtedly one of Nietzsche's strongest emotions and his passion for honesty led him to penetrate very deeply

---

[93] *Ibid.*, pp. 457–93.
[94] Werkmeister, *Theories of Ethics*, p. 240.
[95] Jaspers, *Nietzsche*, p. 141.

into the human psyche. We have already had occasion to observe the great respect that both Jung and Freud had for Nietzsche's power of insight.

According to Jaspers, Nietzsche places the historical origins of absolutistic and repressive morality, i.e. slave morality, in "Socratism" and Judaeo-Christianity, but especially in Pauline Christianity.

The powerless, too, have their will to power: it is "the instinct of the *herd* opposed to the strong and independent, the instinct of the *sorrowful* and poorly endowed opposed to the fortunate, the instinct of the *mediocre* opposed to the exceptional." In spite of their impotence, all of them find in morality the means to mastery and to the creation of an internal (and eventually an external) power. For these moral values are fundamentally evaluations, by inferior people, of behavior patterns that afford them protection; and wherever these values prevail, the existence of their creators and bearers, namely the inferior people, attains increased value while that of the intrinsically powerful and radiant people is depreciated.[96]

Both Socratism and Christianity place the "highest values" in a transcendent realm and as a result both are Nihilistic. The above passage from Jaspers supports the distinction we have been making between positive and negative manifestations of the Will to Power and also underscores the fact that there is an implicit hierarchy of values in Nietzsche's philosophy. Perhaps, it would be more accurate if we were to say that there is an implicit hierarchy of meta-values, for Nietzsche rarely legislates particular concrete values. Particular values are, for Nietzsche, always to be determined dialectically within the context of specific situations. The meta-values which he expounds are dynamic, that is, they project a value "direction" without themselves dictating particular values in individual cases.

Specific values are dialectically determined, but meta-values are not. Nietzsche is quite clear on this point. These meta-values are a part of the essential delimitation and definition of *anthropos* as such in terms of his possibilities. The two highest meta-values, for Nietzsche, are the fulfillment and challenge of self-overcoming and the ecstacy of creation. It is these two meta-values that constitute Nietzsche's central conception of man as potential work of art. As we have already seen, Jaspers places great emphasis on self-overcoming and creation in his interpretation. "Thus Nietzsche's freedom without transcendence is by no means intent upon simply returning to mere life; it aspires to the life of authentic creation." [97] Other meta-values, for Nietzsche, are

[96] *Ibid.*, p. 141.
[97] *Ibid.*, pp. 156–67.

"spiritual companionship," strength (both physical and spiritual), and the satisfaction of physical and psychological needs. This last is also the "lowest." It is clear that these meta-values are a part of Nietzsche's "ontological autobiography," yet they are also more than that. Werkmeister, who has been influenced by Hegel and Kant (both of whom Nietzsche misunderstood), has derived independently, as a value theorist, a hierarchy of values which is in astonishing agreement with Nietzsche's. Werkmeister's hierarchy, from highest to lowest, is as follows: (1) the sense of self-fulfillment, (2) the joy of doing something, especially creative activity, (3) the satisfaction of affiliative needs, (4) the feeling of well-being, and (5) the gratification of appetites. [98] This parallelism strongly suggests that, although these hierarchies are certainly anthropological, they are by no means merely "subjective."

Jaspers, however, refuses to recognize anything like what we have called meta-values. Jaspers argues that:

Nietzsche, in seeking to reject any "unconditionality," [absoluticity] can do this only on the basis of a new unconditionality. He himself knows this to be unavoidable. Whenever we value something unconditionally our experience is moral, and contrariwise, whenever our experience is moral in nature, we are dealing with something unconditional. It is "simply not possible to relativize a moral experience; it is essentially unconditioned." Hence in unconditionally opposing the value accorded to "nature" to the unconditionality of morality, Nietzsche himself does precisely what he condemns: he pronounces an absolute value-judgment.[99]

Jaspers does not explicitly pronounce the charge of "subjectivity," but it is, nonetheless, present. Jaspers believes that, even though he grounds the source of value in man, he escapes the charge of "subjectivism" since this ground is *Existenz* as a form of transcendence. However, Nietzsche rejects this transcendence and, as a result, is guilty, in Jaspers' eyes, of producing another basic contradiction.

The unambiguous arguments against morality can thus all be robbed of their decisive effect by an appeal to certain of Nietzsche's other tenents. He has a new way of raising critical questions – more ambiguous ones – by moving in inescapable circles. First he asserts that morality is itself a product of immorality, and then he urges that the criticism of morality itself derives from the highest kind of morality.[100]

Here we must take very seriously our earlier warning that Nietzsche plays upon the notions of morality and immorality. In fact, when

---

[98] From seminar notes and also William Henry Werkmeister, *Man and His Values* (Lincoln, Nebraska, 1967), p. 117.

[99] Jaspers, *Nietzsche*, p. 146.

[100] *Ibid.*, p. 146.

discussing morality and immorality, Nietzsche's communicative device is frequently a kind of irony which depends upon equivocation. However, Jaspers takes these notions univocally and as result not only does he miss the ironic word play, but he is forced into the position of interpreting Nietzsche's remarks as an "inescapable *contradiction.*" What does Jaspers offer as evidence for his "contradiction"?

But if one retains these positions, they remain in inescapable *contradiction,* so that while one is being expressed the other has to be left out of consideration. We hear that "it is not possible to live outside of morality," as well as the contrary, that "one can live only with an absolutely immoral way of thinking." Or again, morality "is the only interpretative scheme with which man can endure" and, on the other hand, "the world, morally interpreted, is unbearable."[101]

However, this is not convincing. If we recall Nietzsche's distinctions between the good and the evil and the Good and the bad and also his play in the conception of the "immoralist," then the "inescapable contradiction" dissolves. From the point of view of Nietzsche's philosophical anthropology, Jaspers has not taken man seriously enough, that is, he is not yet truly anthropological, for he still wishes to retain the notion of a transcendence.

In his explication of Nietzsche's conception of the "new masters," Jaspers points out that the ultimate goal is based on an overcoming of democracy which eventually results in a fusion of the Wills of the ruler and the ruled.

Nietzsche's hope is for "an audacious ruling race resting on the broad expanse of an extremely intelligent herdlike mass."

Hence the fate of humanity rests with the future masters. Nietzsche is alert to both *their possibilities and their perils.* From a psychological point of view, the *sort of masses* which are to be ruled determines what the masters can be. For they are not dictators who command merely on the basis of some abstract truth or as a result of their own superhuman greatness; they must be men who first win the unconditional confidence of the masses in a godless world by being men of the people. There must be effective and intimate interaction between the masters and the people whom they rule .... On the one hand, the nature of the masses is determined *through the nature of the masters* .... On the other hand, however, the masters depend on the *nature of the masses.*[102]

From this it is clear that the highest goal of society is a kind of conditioned freedom which creates conditions which permit each to achieve his highest level. Such a goal is by no means a final one, but it is the farthest one that our present perspectives permit. Nietzsche was aware that the achievement of such a society would require a "new"

[101] *Ibid.,* p. 148.
[102] *Ibid.,* p. 270.

philosophy, only the dimmest outlines of which we can now discern. Transvaluation becomes a perpetual "obligation".

Heidegger's View

Heidegger's view of Nietzsche's ethics and the anthropological aspect of Transvaluation is conspicuous by its absence. Heidegger does discuss briefly the problem of technology, but once again this is subsumed under the perspective of metaphysics. Even the doctrine of the Superman really interests Heidegger only as a dimension of metaphysics and Heidegger repeatedly uses it to raise the questions about the nature of metaphysics and the thinking of Being. The two major reasons for this almost total ignoring of the anthropological dimension of Nietzsche's thought are to be found in Heidegger's book, *What is Thinking?* The first reason is to be found in the nature of Heidegger's conception of philosophy. Heidegger's belief that all genuine Thinkers think only a single thought gets transformed into an ultimate principle of philosophy. That is to say, Heidegger has taken this notion so seriously, that all of his own philosophizing and his interpretations of other philosophies have been cast into the framework of the single thought which Heidegger thinks – Being. For this reason Heidegger rejects the notion that Nietzsche can be interpreted from the point of view of an "existential anthropology." [103] He argues that any philosophy which inquires into the essence of man, necessarily inquires into the essence of Being as such, if it is to reach its fulfillment. In other words, for Heidegger, Nietzsche's anthropology is secondary or even tertiary and the genuine issues are to be found in his metaphysics.

The second reason has to do with Heidegger's conception of thinking itself. For him, the concerns of thinking are of necessity highly abstruse. He lists four propositions which he believes popularly characterize thinking.

1. Thinking does not bring knowledge as do the sciences.
2. Thinking does not produce usable practical wisdom.
3. Thinking solves no cosmic riddles.
4. Thinking does not endow us directly with the power to act.[104]

Heidegger warns that these views "overvalue" and "demand too much of" thinking. Heidegger does not mean that these views are wrong, only that they are misdirected. He makes this very clear in his book, *Introduction to Metaphysics.*

[103] Heidegger, *What is Called Thinking?*
[104] *Ibid.*, p. 159.

This might suggest that philosophy can and must provide a foundation on which a nation will build its historical life and culture. But this is beyond the power of philosophy. As a rule such excessive demands take the form of a belittling of philosophy. It is said, for example: Because metaphysics did nothing to pave the way for the revolution it should be rejected. This is no cleverer than saying that because the carpenter's bench is useless for flying it should be abolished. Philosophy can never *directly* supply the energies and create the opportunities and methods that bring about a historical change; for one thing, because philosophy is always the concern of the few. Which few? The creators, those who initiate profound transformations. It spreads only indirectly, by devious paths that never can be laid out in advance, until at last, at some future date, it sinks to the level of a commonplace; but by then it has long been forgotten as original philosophy.[105]

Whether we agree or disagree with this position is not important here. What is important is the contrast between Heidegger's conception of thinking and genuine philosophy and Nietzsche's conception. However abstruse Nietzsche's metaphysics may be, it is not for nothing that the existentialists claim Nietzsche as a forerunner. His philosophy is filled with a wealth of concrete analyses of, and insights into, the world of the ordinary concerns of man. The depth of Nietzsche's exploration of the psychological and value situation of man makes these insights at least as important as the visions contained in his metaphysics. In this respect, Heidegger's remarks on the essential nature of philosophy seem odd, for from these one would expect that the anthropological dimension of Nietzsche's thought would be of great significance to Heidegger.

What philosophy essentially can and must be is this: a thinking that breaks the paths and opens the perspectives of the knowledge that sets the norms and hierarchies, of the knowledge in which and by which a people fulfills itself historically and culturally, the knowledge that kindles and necessitates all inquiries and thereby threatens all values.[106]

This statement is an excellent description of Nietzsche's very intention with regard to his analyses of the anthropological perspective and yet Heidegger almost totally ignores this aspect. A further statement by Heidegger makes this ignoring seem even stranger.

It is absolutely correct and proper to say that "You can't do anything with philosophy." It is only wrong to suppose that this is the last word on philosophy. For the rejoinder imposes itself: granted that *we* cannot do anything with philosophy, might not philosophy, if we concern ourselves with it, do something *with us?*[107]

---

[105] Heidegger, *Introduction to Metaphysics*, p. 10.
[106] *Ibid.*, p. 10.
[107] *Ibid.*, p. 12.

This concerning oneself with philosophy might be taken to be a description of Nietzsche's notion of self-overcoming. Both Nietzsche and Heidegger take up aristocratic attitudes toward philosophy, but Nietzsche's philosophy with its concrete concern for man and his possible development is much more likely to be a force which "threatens all values" and permits philosophy to "do something *with us*," than is Heidegger's more abstruse and less immediate kind of philosophy.

ETERNAL RECURRENCE, **TRUTH**, AND TRUTHS

We have seen how in one respect the notion of self-overcoming may be said to be the central "thesis" of Nietzsche's philosophical anthropology. With the doctrine of Eternal Recurrence we arrive at the motivating force which stands behind self-overcoming and the dialectic which takes place between TRUTH and truths. Even though the doctrine of Eternal Recurrence as a *metaphysical* doctrine "shipwrecks," its importance as a doctrine in Nietzsche's philosophical anthropology is immense. If we think of Eternal Recurrence metaphysically as a *literal* doctrine, then anthropologically we might describe it as a *"metaphorical"* doctrine. This is in keeping with Nietzsche's notion of truths as "necessary fictions." Here again we are reminded of Vaihinger's theory of fictions; the philosophy of "as if." If his parallel is genuine, we would then be able to regard Eternal Recurrence as analogous to Kant's Categorical Imperative. However, we must proceed with great care here and examine Nietzsche's texts and attempt to answer a criticism by Kaufmann to the effect that such an analogy is a "misapprehension." Let us here quote at some length Nietzsche's most eloquent statement of the doctrine of Eternal Recurrence.

How, if some day or night, a demon were to sneak after you into your loneliest loneliness and say to you: "This life, as you now live it and have lived it, you will have to live once more and innumerable times more; and there will be nothing new in it, but every pain and every joy and every thought and sigh . . . . must return to you – all in the same succession and sequence – even this spider and this moonlight between the trees, and even this moment and I myself. The eternal hourglass of existence is turned over and over – and you with it, a dust grain of dust!" Would you not throw yourself down and gnash your teeth and curse the demon who spoke thus? Or have you once experienced a tremendous moment when you would have answered him: "You are a god, and never did I hear anything more godlike!" If this thought were to gain possession of you, it would change you as you are, or perhaps crush you. The question in each and everything "do you want this once more and innumerable times more?" would weigh upon your actions as the greatest stress. Or how well disposed would you have to become to yourself and to life to *crave nothing more fervently than this ultimate eternal confirmation* .... ? [108]

The conclusion of the passage would certainly seem to contain an imperative – Live in such a manner that you can say, "I want this once more and innumerable times more." Notice also that the question which Nietzsche says Eternal Recurrence poses, would be omnipresent and "would weigh upon your actions." This would seem to apply to the particular actions that comprise man's behavior, but Kaufmann rejects this idea.

It is easy to see how this aphorism [the passage quoted above] gave rise to the misapprehension that the recurrence represents an analogy to Kant's Categorical Imperative. This passage was taken to show that the doctrine was intended to require man to ask himself constantly: "Do you want this once more and innumerable times more?" That, however, is not the meaning of Nietzsche's conception of "the greatest stress." As ever, he is not concerned with particular actions but with the individual's state of being.[109]

However, this last remark by Kaufmann is only a half-truth. Nietzsche certainly did not mean that we affirm only the past and the present. What more can the "individual's state of being" be than the total set of particular actions that have defined him up to the present moment? We might say that the individual is more in the sense that he has possibilities and this immediately re-instates the temporal flow, for possibilities project into the future. What is here required is an affirmation of possibility, as well as past and present; and possibility is Becoming, a self-overcoming in terms of the affirmation. This self-overcoming is *not* a "state of being," but is rather a dialectical struggle which manifests itself in particular actions. Kaufmann seems to realize the connection between Eternal Recurrence and self-overcoming, for he says that Eternal Recurrence may provide the motive power for the individual still trapped in radical nihilism to go beyond this condition and affirm himself and life, yet his conclusion is still one which denies the analogy of Kant.

The problem is plainly not one of devising a criterion for particular acts, but, insofar as it concerns our behavior at all, to provide an incentive for man to raise his state of being (cf. FW 335), to cross the cleft from the animals to true humanity – or, in Nietzsche's word, to become an overman.[110]

The passage to which Kaufmann refers in the above quotation is section 335 of *The Joyful Wisdom*, in which Nietzsche attacks Kant's

---

[108] Nietzsche quoted in Kaufmann, *Nietzsche*, p. 280.
[109] Kaufmann, *Nietzsche*, p. 180.
[110] *Ibid.*, p. 281.

Categorical Imperative. However, what Nietzsche attacks there, namely the absoluticity of the Categorical Imperative as a foundation for *moral judgments*, is not what is at issue here. What is analogous between the Categorical Imperative and Eternal Recurrence is that both posit a goal for action. Nietzsche's imperative is dynamic; it is an imperative which indicates a direction. "We, however, *would seek to become what we are*, – the new, the unique, the incomparable, making laws for ourselves and creating ourselves." [111] Nietzsche does not legislate particular actions – these must be determined within the context of existential individuality – but, he does legislate the *direction* of those actions. Also Nietzsche does universalize his meta-values, but these too must be grasped as processes, as *directives*. This is especially clear with regard to self-overcoming and creation. Kaufmann is misled as to the nature of the analogy, for Eternal Recurrence as an existential imperative has nothing to do with moral judgments in the traditional sense. (Kaufmann, like Jaspers, seems to forget the manner in which Nietzsche plays with the notion of morality.) Nietzsche's imperative is: Create for yourself as many moments as possible that you would be willing to live again and again throughout eternity!

Here the weakness of the literal metaphysical interpretation of Eternal Recurrence comes to the fore. If the repetitions are identical, then the number of repetitions is irrelevant, for I would never know that it was a repetition and the situation would be the same as though it only occurred once. If, however, the repetitions were variable, I would then know that *all possible* variations would recur an infinite number of times, so there would be no incentive to Will one alternative over another. However, *if there were no repetitions at all*, if this is the "once and only" Life, *then* the imperative to create "eternal" moments could raise man's struggle to the greatest heights of nobility and tragedy. This is why Eternal Recurrence is at once the "greatest stress," or the "heaviest burden" and "the triumphant idea." Thus man raises himself to the level of a work of art, the highest expression of the Will to Power, by creating for himself as many "eternal" moments as is *humanly* possible, while at the same time confronting the terrible TRUTH, that he must die – forever a unique and unrepeatable event. This TRUTH is grounded in the very nature of man, for he is the creature who can TRANSCEND the perspectives of Life and view his own Nothingness from the cosmological perspective. This is the ultimate ground of

[111] Nietzsche, *The Joyful Wisdom*, p. 263.

man's possibility to achieve dignity and nobility, and Nietzsche, whose Being was so thoroughly permeated with Greek tragedy, pronounces his ultimate imperative in the most profoundly Greek fashion – *amor fati*, the love of fate. The highest self-overcoming becomes finally to Will one's own annihilation. Surely, there would be nothing of dignity in the endless repetition of such a struggle, for tragedy would then be transformed into a sardonic farce. This TRUTH of Nietzsche's about man's condition requires the greatest strength. In another passage in *The Joyful Wisdom* Nietzsche says, "'Who will give thee the strength to do so? *No one has yet had this strength!*'" [112] (My italics.) Even for Nietzsche this "heaviest burden" was sometimes too much to bear. It was at such times that he was led to try to bridge the unbridgeable dualism that lies at the heart of man's Being by transforming Becoming into eternal Being through a metaphysical version of the doctrine of Eternal Recurrence. Ultimately, Nietzsche has to reject the metaphysical version, for what it really amounts to is an attempt to smuggle back in the notion of a transcendence. Life is only once and we must affirm it *as unique*, thereby affirming (and loving) our own annihilation, for it is the condition of our uniqueness – this is Nietzsche's "heaviest burden" and "triumphant idea." A total confrontation with this TRUTH cannot help but transform one's existence. One's own temporality takes on a new significance and the contents of one's day-to-day existence take on a new significance. This dualism at the heart of man's Being presents a demand for the realization of those *most essential* and *most authentic* possibilities. Self-overcoming, as the highest realization of these possibilities, becomes the condition for all other values.

There is another dimension to the doctrine of Eternal Recurrence that we have not yet considered, namely, its social dimension. Here the multitude of problems is overwhelming. If an entire society lived and acted in terms of the doctrine of Eternal Recurrence as self-overcoming, then the problems would be minimal. However, Nietzsche is fully aware that only a very few have the necessary strength. The Superman must be able to create viable truths out of the context of the TRUTH of his finitude. These truths must be viable not only for him, but for the "intelligent masses of the herd" as well. But since few have the strength to fully encounter *and affirm* the TRUTH of their finitude, how is it possible to create viable truths without deception? Here we need to remind ourselves that, for Nietzsche, truths are per-

---

[112] *Ibid.*, p. 221.

spectival; they are *necessary* fictions. In a sense, even the Superman has his necessary fiction – Eternal Recurrence, for he must live "as if" each moment were eternal. This, however, is a different dimension of the dialectic. With regard to the herd, Nietzsche believes that to give them what is *necessary* is not a deception. For the man who cannot master algebra, tensor calculus holds no truths. But then why not leave the herd to live with their truths of Christianity and "Socratism"? For the simple reason that Nietzsche does *not* believe that fictions of transcendence are necessary – this is Nietzsche's great *faith* in the possibilities of the human Being. In one respect, this is perhaps the weakest part of Nietzsche's philosophy, but it is also one of the noblest. In spite of all of his contempt, rage, disgust, and mockery, Nietzsche is motivated by a profound humanism. In the face of this subterranean but, nonetheless, overwhelming faith in the human Being, one can forgive Nietzsche his excesses.

One other major problem yet remains and that is the problem of suffering. Here Nietzsche's ambivalence is at its most extreme. At times, especially when discussing the "Great Human Being," Nietzsche's arrogance is repugnant and he speaks as through the achievement of a future Good would justify causing great suffering.

> To gain that tremendous energy of greatness in order to shape the man of the future through breeding and, on the other hand, the annihilation of millions of failures, and not to perish of the suffering one creates, though nothing like it has ever existed! [113]

Even though we have already seen what Nietzsche means by "breeding" and "annihilation of millions of failures," this statement is, nonetheless, most extreme. However, this statement does not represent Nietzsche's considered opinion. What he is consistently critical of, is the Romanticizing of suffering.

> The preoccupation with suffering on the part of metaphysicians – is quite naive. "Eternal bliss": psychological nonsense. Brave and creative men *never* consider pleasure and pain as ultimate values – they are epiphenomena: one must *desire* both if one is to achieve anything –. That they see the problem of pleasure and pain in the foreground reveals something weary and sick in metaphysicians and religious people. Even morality is so important to them only because they see in it an essential condition for the abolition of suffering. [114]

It is clear from this passage that Nietzsche makes an implicit distinction between two kinds of suffering. The kind that he is most concerned with is the personal suffering of the individual in his struggle

---

[113] Nietzsche, *The Will to Power*, p. 506.
[114] *Ibid.*, p. 311.

to come to terms with his own existence. The second kind of suffering takes two forms: (1) the suffering caused by others imposing their Will and (2) the suffering which results from the particular circumstances of the individual existence. This latter, which results from poor health, emotional hypersensitivity, etc., Nietzsche regards as obstacles to be overcome. He insists on a kind of strength that will not permit the individual to indulge himself in misfortunes due to circumstance. In this respect Nietzsche is very close to Spinoza. The suffering caused by imposition of the Will, however, Nietzsche does not sanction even for the Superman. The nobility of the Superman, if he is genuinely superior, excludes the possibility of his imposing his Will upon the mediocrity of the herd in such a way as to make them suffer, for there must ultimately be a fusion of the Will of the Superman and the Will of the herd. In some places, Nietzsche even describes the role of the Superman as a protective one.

Hatred for mediocrity is unworthy of a philosopher: it is almost a question mark against his *"right"* to philosophy." Precisely because he is an exception he has to take the rule under his protection, he has to keep the mediocre in good heart.[115]

Thus there are really two problems concerning suffering. The first is individual and is involved with the individual attempt at self-overcoming. This kind of suffering, Nietzsche argues, one must appropriate and even affirm, for it becomes a condition for creating "beyond" oneself. The second kind of suffering – that produced by the Will of other men – must be eliminated by altering the social conditions of man's existence and this is the task of the Superman. Nietzsche is not a moral monster. Even the Superman cannot ultimately affirm the suffering and torture of innocent people, the exploitation and enslavement of the masses, nor the dissolution of the body and spirit brought about by debilitating diseases. It is for these reasons that the Dionysian affirmation, *amor fati*, remains finally an individual affirmation. Nietzsche could affirm his own suffering, but not the suffering of others and because of this, compassion becomes the greatest of all temptations for Zarathustra.

Jaspers' View

Jaspers' discussion of the anthropological significance of the doctrine of Eternal Recurrence centers around its transformation of the meaning of time and the existential ramifications of the transformation. He

[115] *Ibid.*, p. 276.

begins with a consideration of the actual moment of Nietzsche's epiphany on the mountain. Nietzsche describes this moment as follows:

> I would now like to tell you the history of my *Zarathustra*. Its fundamental conception, the idea of *Eternal Recurrence*, the highest formula of affirmation that can ever be attained, belongs to August, 1881. I made a hasty note of it on a sheet of paper, with the postscript: "Six thousand feet beyond man and time." That day I was walking through the woods beside Lake Silvaplana; I halted not far from Surlei, beside a huge, towering, pyramidal rock. It was there that the idea came to me.[116]

It is the character of the moment itself that leads Nietzsche to celebrate and affirm Eternal Recurrence. Jaspers points out that this moment became one of Nietzsche's "eternal" moments and the archetype for his imperative to create for oneself as many moments as possible which are "beyond man and time".

> Of decisive importance is only *that* significance which the moment attains through its philosophical substance. If the moment is at once *revelation of being* and, in this sense, eternity, then recurrence is merely a symbol for this eternity. Nietzsche knew, by way of transcending, of the eradication of time as the revelation of being in (the flash of) the moment: He has Zarathustra say "at the hour of full noon": "Quiet! Quiet! Did the world not become perfect just now? .... Did I not fall – hark! into the well of eternity?" This noon is "noon and eternity."[117]

From this it is clear, that Jaspers finds the "metaphorical" or anthropological interpretation of Eternal Recurrence to be of much greater significance than the metaphysical one. Jaspers argues that this "revelation of being" can be the condition for *Trans*valuing the whole significance of one's existence, by means of this "transcending" experience. However, this is not any traditional form of transcendence, rather, it is the TRANSCENDENCE to the cosmological perspective which is a revelation of Becoming, not Being, – a revelation both sublime and terrifying.

Jaspers also points out that Nietzsche's conception of noon or midday is a symbol for the midpoint of the path between man and the Superman. It is only through a full encounter with the TRUTH of Eternal Recurrence that man can begin to truly create "beyond" himself toward the Superman. Thus, the revelation of Becoming is the turning point in the struggle for self-overcoming. Eternal Recurrence is the supreme risk, for its impact may overwhelm and even destroy the one who experiences it. Nietzsche realized this and because of the magnificence of his vision of the possibilities of man, he preferred that man

---

[116] Nietzsche, *Ecce Homo* in *The Philosophy of Nietzsche*, p. 892.
[117] Jaspers, *Nietzsche*, p. 358.

succumb, if he did not have the necessary strength to create himself as the highest work of art.

He believes that the *effect* of this thought must be tremendous. The structure of Zarathustra was tacitly already oriented to it, so that its effect might be proclaimed symbolically: this thought, like no other, is dangerous for the one thinking it. Hence Zarathustra must first run the risk himself – he must have the courage to think what he already knows – and experience profound personal crises as he, under the impact of the thought, undergoes a complete transformation that will make him mature and ready to proclaim it and, consequently, be destroyed. Nietzsche communicated this thought, in soft whispers, with all the symptoms of terror, and like a secret, to Lou Salomé and Overbeck.[118]

The existential impact of the idea of Eternal Recurrence will produce a reaction of radical nihilism, but this must be transformed into an affirmation.

Earlier we arrived at the conclusion that the doctrine of Eternal Recurrence can be understood as a new kind of imperative. Jaspers too takes this view and regards Eternal Recurrence as that which can provide the motive force for the necessary transformation.

This is like a new ethical imperative, which demands that I measure everything I feel, will, do, and am by one standard: whether I accomplish it in such a way that I should like to do it repeatedly in the same way or, in other words, whether I can will that this same existence occur time and again. This imperative is a mere form, capable of receiving a limitless number of contents. Perhaps each one can experience the eternally desirable only in his own special way and never as something universally valid.[119]

What Jaspers here describes as "mere form" with regard to the imperative is what we have called a meta-value. Jaspers fully recognizes that Eternal Recurrence is only the general framework; it does not provide specific criteria for particular choice situations, but it does, nonetheless, come to condition all authentic valuations. Nietzsche rejects the validity of moral judgments outside of their particular perspective, but he does posit a higher, i.e., a creative, morality which shapes and defines the conditions of value. This is Nietzsche's morality of aesthetics and even in his very last writings he remains true to the position which he expounded in *The Birth of Tragedy* – that the only "justification" for existence is an aesthetic one. Here one is reminded of Wittgenstein's equating of ethics and aesthetics in some remarks toward the end of the *Notebooks*. As Jaspers shows, this aesthetic "justification" of existence is to be accomplished through the "eternalization" of particular moments.

[118] *Ibid.*, pp. 358–59.
[119] *Ibid.*, p. 359.

This imperative does not demand definite types of action, ways of behavior, and modes of living; it even leaves room for the most radical contrasts and for judgments that mutually exclude each other as contrary with respect to value. The imperative demands only this one thing: "Let us impress the image of eternity upon our lives!"[120]

In a sense, the affirmation of any single moment is an affirmation of the whole of life, for everything which has preceded has been a condition for that moment which is affirmed. Nietzsche says that one must live in such a manner that at the end of his life he can say, "I regret nothing!"

At this point, Jaspers shifts back for a moment to a literal interpretation of Eternal Recurrence.

But if "every moment of becoming is justified (*or escapes evaluation – and this amounts to the same thing*)," then it follows that "the present is not to be justified for the sake of the future nor the past for the sake of the present."[121]

If we interpret this literally, then the entire notion of value becomes meaningless. Nietzsche was fully aware that it was utterly impossible to transform every moment. What must be transformed is the significance of time in relation to value such that one seeks out only that which is essential and authentic insofar as that is possible.

Jaspers also discusses what he calls the "redeeming character" of the doctrine of Eternal Recurrence. Once again, Jaspers inadvertently demonstrates what an embarrassment the doctrine of Eternal Recurrence is, if one does not distinguish its two forms – metaphysical and anthropological. Jaspers says that this redemption "turns into knowledge of immortality."[122] Nietzsche's views on the nature of knowledge are, alone, enough to falsify this assertion. Furthermore, as Jaspers himself later points out, the notion of redemption applies primarily to the past. Zarathustra says, "To recreate all 'it was' into a 'thus I willed it' – *that alone should I call redemption.*"[123] (My italics.) A bit later he adds, "All 'it was' is a fragment, a riddle, a dreadful accident – until the creative will says to it, 'But thus I willed it.'"[124] However, Jaspers persists in interpreting Eternal Recurrence literally and understanding it in terms of the kind of immortality, i.e. endless repetition, which we discovered had to be rejected, since it would transform tragedy into farce. As a result, Jaspers "discovers" an antinomy here in Nietzsche.

[120] *Ibid.*, pp. 359–60.
[121] *Ibid.*, p. 360.
[122] *Ibid.*, p. 361.
[123] Nietzsche, *Zarathustra*, p. 251.
[124] *Ibid.*, p. 253.

But, without Nietzsche's being aware of it, an antinomy arises as always happens in the course of any thinking that transcends. It takes the form of asserting both that the will expresses the freedom to *bring forth what is yet to come*, and that the will itself is after all the cycle that *simply repeats what has been*. The result is that, if this type of philosophizing is genuine, the statements cannot but nullify each other.[125]

These statements 'nullify each other" only if they are on the same plane. However, this is not the case, for one is a statement from within the anthropological perspective and the other is a metaphysical statement which *illegitimately* attempts to establish a bridge between the anthropological perspective and the cosmological perspective.

In addition to this existential dimension of the doctrine of Eternal Recurrence, Jaspers shows that there is also an historical dimension. Nietzsche was very much afraid that Eternal Recurrence would become a catch-phrase and a fad for "the credulous and enthusiastic ones." In fact, there is the strong suggestion that Nietzsche almost wanted to treat Eternal Recurrence as a secret doctrine much in the fashion of the secret knowledge of the inner brotherhood of the *mathematici* in Pythagoreanism. He even comes to speak of his idea as a religion – a religion without transcendence, but nonetheless, a religion! "It is to be the religion of the freest, most serene, and most sublime souls – a lovely meadow-land between gilded ice and pure sky!"[126]

With regard to the problem of suffering, Jaspers shows that, for Nietzsche, there are two fundamental approaches to the problem. These are the Dionysian and the Christian attitudes. Nietzsche says,

Dionysus versus the "Crucified": there you have the antithesis. It is *not* a difference in regard to their martyrdom – it is a difference in the meaning of it .... One will see that the problem is that of the meaning of suffering: whether a Christian meaning or a tragic meaning. In the former case, it is supposed to be the path to a holy existence; in the latter case, being is counted as *holy enough* to justify even a monstrous amount of suffering. The tragic man affirms even the harshest suffering: he is sufficiently strong, rich, and capable of deifying to do so. The Christian denies even the happiest lot on earth: he is sufficiently weak, poor, disinherited to suffer from life in whatever form he meets it. The god on the cross is a curse on life, a signpost to seek redemption from life; Dionysus cut to pieces is a *promise* of life.[127]

Notice here how Nietzsche plays on the notion of redemption. Nietzsche does not wish to celebrate suffering; however, he believes that since

[125] Jaspers, *Nietzsche*, p. 362.
[126] Nietzsche quoted in Jaspers, *Nietzsche*, p. 363.
[127] Nietzsche, *The Will to Power*, pp. 542–43.

it is a necessary part of man's existence, it must be accepted and man must learn to create "out of and beyond" suffering.

We have already seen that Jaspers quite emphatically rejects Nietzsche's conception of the world as being without transcendence. In the end Jasper's rejection of Nietzsche's philosophy is almost total.

While the basis and language of modern philosophizing has been enriched, through imperceptible appropriation, by Nietzsche's original nature-mysticism, no one has adopted his Dionysus as a symbol or, for that matter, any of the affirmatively defined and *ipso facto* narrowly delimited, metaphysical hypostatizations that he formulated, including the superman and eternal recurrence.[128]

Ultimately, Jaspers cannot accept any view of the world which does not ground man's existence and his values in some form of transcendence, and this means that he must finally reject not only Nietzsche's metaphysics, but his philosophical antnropology as well.

Heidegger's View

Again we are faced with the problem that Heidegger offers no interpretation of Eternal Recurrence or truth from the perspective of philosophical anthropology. This is somewhat preplexing at first, since it would seem that the TRUTH revealed by Eternal Recurrence, namely, that man is finite and must fully confront his own death if he is to achieve self-overcoming or authenticity, would be embraced by Heidegger, since it parallels his own philosophy. Heidegger, as we have already pointed out, does recognize the distinction between truths and TRUTH, but he never elaborates it or examines its significance for Nietzsche's philosophy. If we think carefully about Heidegger's major interpretive thesis in connection with Nietzsche, the reason soon becomes apparent. For Heidegger, Nietzsche's philosophy, as the "consummation" of metaphysics, is still grounded in traditional metaphysics and thus he never achieves an "overcoming" by means of thinking the question of Being as such. However, if Heidegger admitted that the TRUTH of the cosmological perspective reveals man's finitude to himself, he would then also have to admit that Nietzsche is doing existential analysis in precisely the same sense in which he is in *Being and Time*. This, however, would bring Heidegger's thesis that Nietzsche has not "overcome" metaphysics to disaster!! This is by no means to say that this is a conscious project of obfuscation on the part of Heidegger.

---

[128] Jaspers, *Nietzsche*, p. 378.

Rather, it is simply the result of Heidegger's whole approach to the interpretation of the historical development of philosophy. As far as Nietzsche's philosophical anthropology is concerned, Heidegger not only rejects it, he refuses to recognize it at all.

NIETZSCHE'S ANTHROPOCENTRISM

Nietzsche's inversion of Platonism is an extremely interesting event in the history of Western philosophy. Nietzsche's theory of man contains a critique of the traditional ways of philosophizing about man and also a vision of what man can possibly become. For Nietzsche, traditional philosophies have not taken man seriously enough. Traditional views have almost always sought to ground man's existence and his values in some form of transcendence. Nietzsche argues that doctrines of transcendence lead man to project his action toward goals which are "outside" of himself and, as a result, there has never been the demand that man become what he is in the fullness of his Being *as human*. For Nietzsche, any manifestation of the Will to Power that seeks to direct man "outside" of himself is negative and in opposition to the meta-values of self-overcoming and creation. It is the case, however, that man cannot fully grasp his situation as man within the perspectives of life. Such an understanding is achievable only from a perspective outside of life, and this is possible in terms of the cosmological perspective. For Nietzsche, man's nature contains within itself an irreconcilable dualism – man is the creature who knows he must die, but he is also the creature whose non-existence is inconceivable to himself. From the standpoint of existence, the individual's non-existence is inconceivable. My non-existence from within the perspectives of life is an "ontological contradiction." Yet, at the same time, the individual knows that he is finite by means of adopting the perspective of cosmology. But how are these two insights reconcilable? They are not; they stand dialectically opposed to one another and provide the ground for man's self-overcoming.

From Nietzsche's point of view, the cosmological perspective, if its TRUTH is confronted, opens up the possibility for a new and genuine kind of anthropocentrism. From within the perspectives of life alone, man comes to believe that he is the measure of all things. He becomes immensely self-important and believes in himself as the creature who can discover the absolutes which forever govern the conditions of existence. He becomes the supreme dogmatist and comes to regard himself as the center of the universe, the special creature for whose sake the universe exists. From within the cosmological perspective alone, man discovers his Nothingness, his futility and uselessness. He realizes that he is not the center, that his existence has no special meaning which will earn him "Eternal Bliss." For Nietzsche, these are the two poles of the dualism that man is. There are three choices for man: (1) he can flee into the nihilism of transcendence, (2) he can flee into the radical nihilism of meaninglessness, or (3) he can enter into the dialectic of his existence and by accepting the conditions of his existence with dignity and honesty attempt to create himself as a work of art. Man cannot escape his condition and even his self-overcoming is of necessity tragic, but Nietzsche would say, that it is better for it to be transformed into a tragedy than for it to remain a farce. In terms of this tragedy, man does not become the center of the cosmos, but neither is his existence utterly meaningless. By entering into the dialectic of existence, man has the possibility, for the first time, of truly appropriating life and becoming the center of his own individual existence. This means that there is a new focus on man as man. He no longer projects himself into a principle or entity which stands outside of his existence; rather, he devotes his energies toward fully embracing his own existence in such a way that he can affirm himself as past, present and future. He is able to say, "Thus would I have it. Thus do I will it."

Nietzsche believes that doctrines of transcendence have enslaved man; they have made a prisoner of the Will. Man can realize his possibilities only insofar as he has the freedom to create his own values dialectically. This anthropocentrism is not egotism, for the dialectic necessarily includes an interaction with other human beings. This freedom is achievable only in an atmosphere in which one Will does not attempt to impose its values on another as though they were absolutes. The notion of dialectic, for Nietzsche, is not exclusively individual. One must create himself in relation to others. This is a profoundly Hegelian idea, for Hegel insists that self-creation is fully meaningful only in terms of a dialectic with other human beings. This idea is at the core of Nietzsche's application of his theory of man to the creation of a new social order. The individual *needs* the confrontation with perspectives other than his own. Perspectivism is the framework for Nietzsche's philosophical anthropology as well as for his metaphysics and epistemology. Within the context of an absolute system of meanings and values an individual is prevented from discovering the richness of the perspectives of existence. Absolutism leads to stagnation and

Nietzsche vehemently opposes anything which stifles man's creativity. By means of this creativity, man once more comes to occupy the center, but this time it is the center of life, the center between the *hybris* and arrogance of nihilism and the despair and meaninglessness of radical nihilism.

Jaspers' View

We have already observed that Jaspers rejects Nietzsche's philosophical anthropology, but we have not yet fully determined the reasons for this. Jaspers notes that Nietzsche regards the whole attitude of modern man's existence as a kind of *hybris*. Man is important, but not in the way in which he presently conceives of himself. Man's understanding of himself is diseased and he must cure himself. This can only be achieved through the self-overcoming which places man on the path to the Superman. Also Nietzsche says that this struggle will have to be accomplished through the "magic of extremes." Nietzsche firmly believes that if one is calm and moderate, no one will listen. Jaspers finds Nietzsche's extremism disturbing and charges him with a kind of qualified fanaticism. However, he goes even further and turns Nietzsche's own charge of *hybris* back upon Nietzsche himself.

Nietzsche appears as the representative of one kind of fanaticism after another, although his nature, his frame of mind, and his goal are far removed from fanaticism. He cannot attain the detached wisdom and steadfast circumspection possible to the nonrevolutionary spirit. Since he conceals nothing and gives of himself freely, his own profound wisdom – like that of Prometheus – becomes *hybris*.[129]

The question which confronts us here is that concerning the perspective from which it is possible for Jaspers to make this charge of *hybris*. While it is true that Jaspers finds Nietzsche's extremism distasteful, the reasons for the charge of *hybris* are to be found at a deeper level. For Jaspers, a world which is not in some way grounded in a form of transcendence is inconceivable. As a result, he even goes so far as to suggest that there is an "existential deficiency" in Nietzsche's Being which would permit him to recognize his own Existenz, even though he frequently, so Jaspers claims, speaks from that source.

When one examines such constructions as the above and then discovers how much Nietzsche really knows of just that of which the constructions, strictly applied, would show him to be ignorant – the fullness of historical *Existenz* – then paradoxical questions arise: Could it be that the existential deficiency of

129 *Ibid.*, p. 426.

his being gives rise to a new and to us, unfamiliar *Existenz* devoted to mankind as a whole? Is it possible that the standpoint to which he banished himself affords him a perspective and a medium for insights that are of incomparable value to the rest of us? Perhaps these insights touch so clearly and decisively upon existential possibilities precisely because they relate to an *Existenz* that is not granted to the one who illumines them – the existential exception whose awareness of this fact springs from another level. In this case, Nietzsche's greatness consists in an awareness of nothingness which enables him to speak more clearly and passionately of the other – of being – and to know it better than those who perhaps share in it without even being sure of it and consequently remain inarticulate.[130]

This kind of argument verges on sophistry. It is as though a Christian were to note that on the whole Nietzsche led a very moral life even by the standards of Christianity and from this went on to conclude that, even though Nietzsche did not recognize God, nevertheless his philosophy and his life enable him "to speak more clearly and passionately of the other" – of God – "and to know it better than those who perhaps share in it without even being sure of it and consequently remain inarticulate." Nietzsche himself would unquestionably brand Jaspers a nihilist.

The doctrine of the Superman when considered within the context of the whole of Nietzsche's philosophy is not in itself extremist. Nietzsche would deny that he is guilty of *hybris*, for the dialectic between the cosmological and the anthropological perspectives is meant to produce in man a balanced view of himself. He is neither the despicable, vile, weak creature who can never deserve grace and salvation, nor is he the lord of the universe by whose standards all things must be measured. He is the animal who is attempting to become lord of his own life and fulfill himself in his highest *and most human* way.

Heidegger's View

It will be remembered that Heidegger, from the very beginning, charges that Nietzsche's philosophy is anthropomorphic. Furthermore, anthropomorphism is, for Heidegger, nihilism. He argues that Nietzsche belongs to the tradition of philosophical "subjectivism" dating back in modern times to Descartes. In ancient times there was also a tradition of subjectivism," namely, Protagorean relativism, but this was a "subjectivism" of a different type in that it was grounded in a theory of truth (and, therefore, of Being also) which was fundamentally different from the one that manifests itself in modern times. None-

---

[130] *Ibid.*, p. 426.

theless, however, they stand related in that in both types man is made the center of truth, Being, and value.

For Heidegger, the history of Western philosophy from Descartes to Nietzsche is the onto-logical unfolding of metaphysics as "subjectivism" and, therefore, nihilism. Much that was implicit and simplistic in Descartes' philosophy is made explicit and is sophisticated in the philosophies of Leibniz, Kant, Fichte, Schelling, and Hegel. The "consummation" of this anthropomorphic kind of philosophy is achieved in Nietzsche with the elevation of the Will to the supreme principle in terms of which all else must be understood. However, now we are in a better position to examine more closely Heidegger's charge of anthropomorphism against Nietzsche.

Anthropomorphism and anthropocentrism are not identical. Anthropomorphism is the position which conceives of man as the absolute measure of all Being, meaning, truth, and value. Nietzsche's anthropocentrism, however, denies that man is the *absolute* measure of *anything*. This is due to the cosmological perspective, which Heidegger attempts to subsume under the categories of traditional metaphysics, thus ignoring the very real way in which Nietzsche does succeed in "overcoming" traditional metaphysics. From the cosmological perspective, man discovers that Being, meaning, truth, and value are all the result of particular perspectives which he adopts within the context of his existence as *anthropos*. What one man measures cannot even be a measure for mankind, let alone the entire cosmos. Thus, for Nietzsche, the cosmological point of view was to be a *corrective* to anthropomorphism. Futhermore, when Nietzsche speaks of perspectives as necessary *fictions*, he does not mean that these are fictions in the sense in which a unicorn is a fiction, nor does he mean that they are merely the arbitrary whims of the individual "subject." They are fictions *only from the standpoint of the cosmological perspective*. From within the context of the particular life situation, these perspectives are, within their limited range, *perfectly valid*. It is for this reason that Nietzsche calls them "necessary." The range of their validity may be strictly individual, in which case the values and meanings arising out of these perspectives would be "subjective." However, in a vast number of cases, the conditions which define and delimit the perspective are social and cultural applying to large groups of human beings and are, therefore, in Nietzsche's sense "objective." This sense is, of course, unacceptable to Heidegger, since he argues for an "objectivity" which is in itself a revelation of a transcendent Being. It is interesting to note in this respect that Nietzsche would turn Heidegger's charge of nihilism back upon Heidegger himself. From Nietzsche's point of view, both Jaspers and Heidegger are still rooted in traditional metaphysics, since both still want to retain some form of transcendence. Such a situation is one of the traditional ironies in the history of philosophy and one feels sure that Nietzsche, with his doctrine of perspectivism, would have enjoyed the irony.

We noted earlier that Nietzsche rejects traditional metaphysics on the grounds that *it* is anthropomorphic with its doctrines of transcendence and he regarded his own metaphysics as anti-anthropomorphic. Once again, Heidegger does not take Nietzsche's claim seriously. To do so, would again mean that Heidegger would be forced either to modify or even abandon his whole conception of the nature of the historical unfolding of metaphysics. Here Nietzsche's own conception of the conditioning of perspectives by their limitations applies very well. Heidegger seems so totally obsessed with the idea of Being as *transcendens*, that it is virtually impossible for him to adopt any other perspective. Unfortunately, however, we are not even in a position to explore fully the limitations of Heidegger's perspectives, for he has never published his "fundamental ontology." However, the outlines that are discernible, suggest that perhaps many of the roots of Heidegger's own philosophy are discoverable in Nietzsche. Heidegger has concerned himself with Nietzsche over a considerable number of years and his preoccupation with Nietzsche sometimes seems rather odd in light of his often sweeping and sometimes eccentric criticism. In the next chapter we shall consider some of the basic reasons for Heidegger's pre-occupation.

SOME CONCLUDING REMARKS

As we can now see, the elaboration of Nietzsche's theory of man requires an examination of all of the basic doctrines of Nietzsche's philosophy. This is not to say that Nietzsche's philosophy is a unified "system." There are certainly aspects of Nietzsche's philosophy which he does not completely think through, and there are genuine contradictions, such as the one between the literal and the "metaphorical" conceptions of Eternal Recurrence. However, we have throughout tried to show that, on the whole, the various doctrines which comprise Nietzsche's philosophy are coherent. His philosophy cannot be regarded as a collection of random remarks and aphorisms. Nietzsche's theory of man is interesting not only in terms of its general structure, which is primarily what we have been concerned with here, but also because of its wealth of concrete psychological and cultural insights. It is this latter which makes the reading of Nietzsche a constant delight, for, although the major outlines of the basic doctrines are fairly well fixed, Nietzsche fills these outlines with an almost endless number of ironical and incisive observations regarding situations and events which are encountered daily. This mass of particular observation lends great weight to many of Nietzsche's theses and, as is not the case in many philosophies, transforms the theory of man into something vital and immediate.

At the beginning of this chapter we said that there is a sense in which Nietzsche's philosophical anthropology is "metaphysical." We are now in a position to specify that sense. For Nietzsche, man's essence is fundamentally dualistic – man is the creature who, through the knowledge that he must die, can take up the cosmological perspective which stands opposed to his existence as *anthropos*. The dualism as such is irreconcilable; however, the two poles of the dualism create the possibility for a metaphysical dialectic. Even though the two poles are opposed, they stand in essential relation to each other in that they "reside" at the very heart of man's Being. In this sense we can say that man is the metaphysical creature and it is only because of his essentially dualistic nature that the dialectic of self-overcoming is possible at all.

This also means that Nietzsche's metaphysics is a thorough-going anthropology in the sense of anthropo*centrism* and not in the sense of anthropo*morphism*. Anthropocentrism, for Nietzsche, opens up for the first time the possibility for a truly profound and meaningful humanism. Man no longer de-values himself in the face of some abstract or emotional principle of transcendence. He is given the freedom to focus fully upon himself in a creative fashion. He becomes the fusion of his animal nature and his spiritual nature. Nietzsche firmly believes that any philosophy that permits and promotes the ascendancy of either the animal or the spiritual side of man without bringing them into a proper balance is a perversion. It is a mistake to understand Nietzsche's conception of the Superman single-mindedly in terms of his metaphor of the "blond beast." Nietzsche emphasizes repeatedly that the greatest and most difficult task which faces man on the path to the Superman is the overcoming of the desire for revenge. Nietzsche's conceptions of justice, honesty, dignity, and the overcoming of revenge must always be kept in mind in any evaluation of his doctrine of the Superman. Nietzsche's belief in the potentialities of man is so great that he thinks of the society comprised of the Supermen and the herd in terms of a fusion of their Wills in such a manner that they can live together creatively.

Nietzsche's doctrine of "immorality" is really the morality of his radical humanism. The severest criticism he can make against a view is that it is anti-human. This is the basis for his rejection of Christianity, "Socratism," and democracy, not to mention socialism and tyranny. To Nietzsche, conventional morality is a prison. It promises punishment for those who do not submit and, for Nietzsche, one of the most inhuman threats of all was the transcendently derived, that is, nihilistic, doctrine of eternal punishment. Nietzsche strongly believed that any "morality" that had to be enforced by the threat of punishment was degenerate. Nietzsche desires that man learn to live in this world and love life, rather than denying this life and projecting all of his energies into some fictitious "supersensible" realm. This is perhaps the most fundamental of all of Nietzsche's lessons: Learn to love life!

In the main, I agree more with the artists than with any philosopher hitherto: they have not lost the scent of life, they have loved the things of "this world" – they have loved their senses. To strive for "desensualization": that seems to me a misunderstanding or an illness or a cure, where it is not merely hypocrisy or self-deception. I desire for myself and for all who live, *may* live, without being tormented by a puritanical conscience, an ever-greater spiritualization and multiplication of the senses; indeed, we should be grateful to the senses for their subtlety, plenitude, and power and offer them in return the best we have in the way of spirit. What are priestly and metaphysical calumnies against the senses to us! We no longer need these calumnies: it is a sign that one has turned out well when, like Goethe, one clings with ever-greater pleasure and warmth to the "things of this world": – for in this way he holds firmly to the great conception of man, that man becomes the transfigurer of existence when he learns to transfigure himself.[131]

It is hard to imagine a profounder or more vital sense for the potentialities of the human being. For Nietzsche, this was the central vision which dominated his life and his thought.

[131] Nietzsche, *The Will to Power*, p. 434.

CHAPTER IV

AN EVALUATION OF HEIDEGGER'S AND JASPERS' INTERPRETATIONS

The task of critical evaluation carries with it an immense responsibility. Criticism is not simply dissection; it presupposes a genuine attempt to gain an internal understanding. Even if we finally decide that Jaspers failed in this attempt, there is little question about the authenticity of the attempt itself. With Heidegger the situation is somewhat different. It is clear from the beginning that Heidegger is not so much interested in Nietzsche for his own sake as he is in Nietzsche as an illustration of his thesis about the historical unfolding of the nature of metaphysics. Thus, part of our responsibility in attempting a critical evaluation of Heidegger and Jaspers is a recognition of the fundamental aims of their interpretations. This does not mean that we are compelled to accept their aims, but we must take these aims into account if we are to understand fully the nature of Heidegger's and Jaspers' interpretive projects.

There are three basic aspects involved in the project of presenting a Nietzsche interpretation: (1) a careful examination of the texts themselves, (2) an attempt to understand and explicate Nietzsche's ideas within the framework of his own philosophy, and (3) the presentation of a critical standpoint as the basis for an evaluation of Nietzsche's philosophy. A careful examination of the text is especially crucial in the case of Nietzsche, because of his non-systematic method of communicating. Also a random reading of Nietzsche can produce a very distorted view indeed. The attempt to understand and explicate Nietzsche presupposes a careful weighing of Nietzsche's remarks and the establishment of a certain rapport with Nietzsche's style of philosophizing. Finally, in attempting a critical evaluation it is important to examine one's own critical standpoint in order to avoid adopting a bias which falls subject to Nietzsche's own critical enterprise. This last is extremely important, for unless one can provide a justification for one's critical standpoint which will remove it from the realm of Nietzsche's own criticism, then such a bias must be rejected as dogmatic.

Two other considerations apply to Nietzsche interpretation. A genuine interpretation must take into account the development of Nietzsche's philosophical ideas and attempt to understand the patterns of this development. Secondly, genuine interpretation must grasp the essentially dialectical character of his philosophy. This is no easy task, and there is the omnipresent danger of interpreting one dialectical pole as the representative position, when in fact Nietzsche pursues the ramifications of the idea in terms of further and more complex dialectical convolutions.

Perhaps the greatest complication of all in dealing with the interpretations of Heidegger and Jaspers is the fact that neither of them make explicit the critical standpoint from which they make their own evaluations of Nietzsche. As a result, a certain familiarity with the philosophies of Jaspers and Heidegger becomes necessary in order to grasp the context out of which their evaluative enterprise arises. We have made some attempt to explicate the essential aspects as we proceeded. A full-scale investigation of these philosophies is, of course, impossible here; however, certain basic concepts in their philosophies will provide us with a sufficient understanding to see the direction of their critical and evaluative thought.

With regard to Heidegger, we must remember that his Nietzsche interpretation is part of a much larger critical project which extends from the pre-Socratics up to the present. Nonetheless, his work on Nietzsche holds a position of special prominence. Jaspers' interpretation is somewhat conditioned by the existential-psychological background which he has. In fact, one of Jaspers' first major publications was his *General Psychopathology* and, in European circles and more recently in America, his early works in the area of psychiatry are highly regarded. This background occasionally reveals itself in his Nietzsche interpretation when, in certain discussions, Jaspers seems on the verge of treating Nietzsche as a clinical case study. However, on the whole, this particular aspect of Jaspers' background rarely conditions his interpretation in any explicit way. A factor of background which Jaspers and Heidegger share is the discipline of a late nineteenth century and early twentieth century European education. This discipline manifests itself in two important ways. First of all, it produces a certain special sort of thoroughness which is grounded in an extensive cultural background and which is, on the whole, a valuable asset.

However, this discipline also breeds a rather unfortunate tendency toward dogmatism which often results in a certain narrowness of perspective. However, this discipline has served to make Jaspers and Heidegger philosophers of considerable stature and an examination of their thought about Nietzsche cannot help but be stimulating and enriching. In fact, a critical evaluation of their Nietzsche interpretations must also be undertaken in the spirit of dialogue, and in this way it is hoped that we may arrive at a better understanding of Jaspers and Heidegger as well as Nietzsche.

HOW JASPERS READS HIS OWN PHILOSOPHY INTO NIETZSCHE

There are two major concepts of Jaspers' own philosophy that appear very frequently in his Nietzsche interpretation. These, of course, are *Existenz* and transcendence. A third concept which appears much less frequently is Jaspers' idea of the Encompassing. These three concepts provide the basis for Jaspers' critical standpoint. We have already presented a descriptive outline of the essential meaning of *Existenz* and have made frequent reference to the notion of transcendence. However, here it is necessary that we take a somewhat closer look at the meaning of transcendence for Jaspers, and also provide a brief description of the concept of the Encompassing. Until now we have only made passing reference to the Encompassing, because this notion is more relevant to Jaspers' final criticisms of Nietzsche than it is to an explication of Nietzsche's philosophy.

The conception of transcendence which Jaspers attempts to explicate is essentially and consciously ambiguous. The attempt to understand it is further complicated by the fact that, according to Jaspers, transcendence can only be genuinely grasped through *Existenz*.

Only through Existenz can Transcendence become present without superstition, as the genuine reality which to itself never disappears.

Further, Existenz is like the counterpart to spirit. Spirit is the will to become whole; potential Existenz is the will to be authentic .... Spirit lets everything disappear and vanish into universality and totality. The individual as spirit is not himself but, so to speak, the unity of contingent individuals and of the necessary universal. Existenz however is irreducibly in another; it is the absolutely firm, the irreplaceable, and therefore, as against all mere empirical existence, consciousness as such, and spirit, it is authentic being before Transcendence to which alone it surrenders itself without reservation.[1]

---

[1] Jaspers, *Reason and Existenz*, p. 62.

If the notion of *Existenz* is ambiguous, then the notion of transcendence is doubly so. The sentence, "Spirit is the will to become whole," is especially interesting. When we consider the essential dualism which characterizes Nietzsche's theory of man, it immediately becomes clear that Jaspers and Nietzsche are philosophically opposed in terms of the most fundamental groundwork. It is true that in terms of the metaphysical doctrine of Eternal Recurrence, Nietzsche himself yielded to this "will to become whole." However, in the end Nietzsche insists that this "will" is a fundamental mistake which would produce a paralysis of the essential dialectic which creates the possibility for the highest development of man's existence. It also seems certain that Nietzsche would be puzzled by Jaspers' statement that "only through Existenz can Transcendence become present *without superstition.*" Nietzsche regards all appeals to traditional forms of transcendence as superstitious. But perhaps Jaspers' notion of transcendence is not a traditional form. Let us examine another passage.

The idea which grasps Transcendence from the unfulfillment of all communication and from the ship-wrecking of every form of truth in the world is like a proof of God: from the unfulfillment of every sense of truth and under the assumption that truth must be, thought touches upon Transcendence. Such an idea is valid only for Existenz which is an absolute concern for truth, and to whose honesty truth, as a single, unique, and static possession of timelessness, never shows itself in the world.[2]

Nietzsche and Jaspers are very close here with regard to the limitedness of truth, and out of this Nietzsche develops his doctrine of perspectivism. Jaspers, however, takes up a very traditional position, which can be found in many philosophies and theologies, and argues that this limitedness in some way implies that which is limitless. It is also clear that he follows tradition in continuing to accept the notion of some kind of absolute truth, and he admits that this truth "never shows itself in the world." The other traditional attributes of timelessness, singularity, uniqueness, and stasis are also present. Thus, in the end, there can be little question but that Jaspers does espouse a quite traditional form of the concept of transcendence.

The problem of communication is also important here. Jaspers wants to argue that, since all communication is somehow incomplete, this necessarily leads to the notion that somewhere there is the possibility for a *complete* perspective and this he variously calls Being, transcendence, and God. Nietzsche, however, rejects the idea that the

[2] *Ibid.*, p. 98.

notion of perspective implies some complete perspective that constitutes an absolute truth. The conceptions of unity and totality are, for Nietzsche, simply convenient fictions. As far as Nietzsche is concerned, incommunicability is no argument for absolute truth.

In one respect Jaspers' problem with Nietzsche is a very personal one which Jaspers translates into the realm of theology. When discussing Nietzsche's saying, "God is dead," Jaspers is careful to point out that this is not a declaration of atheism. Nonetheless, Jaspers comes to that very conclusion in *Reason and Existenz.*

Kierkegaard and Nietzsche are distinguished from the other great philosophers in that both consciously subverted philosophy itself: one in favor of faith in absurd paradox and martyrdom as the only true life, the other [Nietzsche] in order to arrive at atheism.[3]

Jaspers also makes it clear that he regards atheism as something which is antithetical to philosophy.

Or, philosophical thinking can seek its realization in atheism which presents itself as the conclusion of a philosophizing which opposes revealed religion; and then, retroactively, *philosophy as such tends to be annulled* in favor of its finite knowledge of the world. Atheism however applies philosophy, *now robbed of its essence,* as a disintegrating force *against everything permanent or authoritative,* so long as this is not the authority affirmed by atheism itself of dominance in empirical existence.[4] (My italics.)

It should now be very clear that the disagreement between Jaspers and Nietzsche is no mere verbal one. Jaspers regards Nietzsche as a genuine threat and a very dangerous one. If we push Jaspers' remarks to their logical conclusions, then, in effect, Jaspers accuses Nietzsche of having robbed philosophy of its essence. Jaspers also takes it for granted that there is something more than the "finite knowledge of the world," but he argues that he cannot say what this is, since by its very nature it is incommunicable. To say on the one hand, that empirical truth is deficient and on the other hand, that there is an absolute truth, but it is incommunicable and then to assert further that one must recognize the authority of this uncommunicable truth is an example of the dogmatism of which we spoke earlier. Certainly, such an argument would have enraged Nietzsche.

With regard to the Encompassing, Jaspers distinguishes two major modes.

---

[3] *Ibid.*, p. 137.
[4] *Ibid.*, p. 139

The Encompassing appears and disappears for us in two opposed perspectives: either as Being itself, in and through which we are – or else as the Encompassing which we ourselves are, and in which every mode of Being appears to us. The latter would be as the medium or condition under which all Being appears as Being for us. In neither case is the Encompassing the sum of some provisional kinds of being, a part of whose contents we know, but rather it is the whole as the most extreme, self-supporting ground of Being whether it is Being in itself, or Being as it is for us.[5]

For sheer opacity this passage rivals Heidegger. However, this much is clear: Jaspers is distinguishing between the world as we experience it and a "super-sensible" realm of Being in itself. Jaspers uses this notion of Being in itself to make the move to God as absolute transcendence. With regard to this move, Nietzsche makes some very interesting remarks in the *Twilight of the Idols*. He suggests that this metaphysical move from beings to Being (subsequently interpreted as absolute ground or God) is nothing more than a mistake in grammar.

Formerly, alteration, change, any becoming at all, were taken as proof of mere appearance, as an indication that there must be something which led us astray. Today, conversely, precisely insofar as the prejudice of reason forces us to posit unity, identity, permanence, substance, cause, thinghood, being, we see ourselves somehow caught in error, compelled into error .... Everywhere "being" is projected by thought, pushed underneath, as the cause; the concept of being follows, and is a derivative of, the concept of ego .... I am afraid we are not rid of God because we still have faith in grammar.[6]

Thus, Jaspers' notion of Encompassing would be regarded by Nietzsche as simply another in the development of dogmatic metaphysics to which he hoped that his own philosophy would provide a corrective.

We now need to consider explicitly the problem of the vulnerability of Jaspers' critical standpoint to Nietzsche's own criticisms. Certainly Jaspers has the advantage of knowing beforehand the precise nature of the criticisms which Nietzsche could direct against his critical standpoint. Yet apparently Jaspers does not take such possible criticisms very seriously, and judging from his almost total silence on this issue, he regards these criticisms as self-refuting. Considering the antithesis that Nietzsche represents in relation to Jaspers, it is interesting that Jaspers should undertake to write a book on Nietzsche's philosophy, for in many ways Jaspers' book is a very sympathetic and understanding examination. His book is by no means a mere diatribe or polemic. That Jaspers undertook such an enterprise is a tribute to the strength of Nietzsche's fascination.

[5] *Ibid.*, p. 52.
[6] Nietzsche, *Twilight of the Idols* in *The Portable Nietzsche*, pp. 482–83.

Again and again Jaspers introduces the concepts which constitute the foundation of his own philosophy into his Nietzsche interpretation. However, he provides virtually no defense for these notions as an adequate standpoint for a criticism and evaluation of Nietzsche. Perhaps the reasons for this are to be discovered within the context of the interpretation. With this in mind, let us review some of the more important aspects of Jaspers' interpretation. At the same time, we shall attempt to bring into closer relation the two major facets of the interpretation, namely, metaphysics and philosophical anthropology.

From the beginning it is clear that Jaspers regards Nietzsche's metaphysics as in some way deficient. The first indication of this we found in Jaspers' attitude toward Nietzsche's doctrine of Being as Becoming. Jaspers does very definitely appreciate the essentially dialectical character of Nietzsche's philosophy and places much more importance on the process of Nietzsche's philosophizing than on Nietzsche's doctrines. Nonetheless, there are very real indications of reservation on Jaspers' part regarding any metaphysics that so radically and thoroughly rejects every notion of Being as permanence, unity, and transcendence. As a result, Jaspers concludes that Nietzsche's thought is repeatedly forced into inescapable circles and finally undermines itself. It does this, Jaspers argues, by attacking the very conditions for philosophizing as such. Jaspers arrives at this conclusion because he fails to distinguish adequately the two levels which constitute the radically opposed perspectives of cosmology and philosophical anthropology. The TRANSCENDENCE of the cosmological perspective is unsatisfactory as far as Jaspers is concerned, for the very reason that it does not have the characteristics of the traditional forms of transcendence.

The key to this opposition is to be found in the theory of truth. For Jaspers, truth and communication are inextricably bound up with one another.

Truth therefore cannot be separated from communicability. It only appears in time as a reality-through-communication. Abstracted from communication, truth hardens into an unreality. The movement of communication is at one and the same time the preservation of, and the search for, the truth.[7]

Jaspers distinguishes three basic types of communication. The first is a practical sort which has to do with the preservation and functioning of the individual and the community. The second type involves

---

[7] Jaspers, *Reason and Existenz*, pp. 79–80.

consciousness as such and deals primarily with the abstractions and logical categories which characterize the relationships of individual and social consciousness to what is knowable. The third type Jaspers defines as follows:

The communication of spirit is the emergence of the Idea of a whole out of the communal substance. The individual is conscious of standing in a place which has its proper meaning only in that whole. His communication is that of a member with its organism. He is different, as all the others are, but agrees with them *in the order which comprehends all*. They communicate with one another out of the common presence of the Idea. In this communication, it is as though some whole not clearly knowable by consciousness as such spoke, limited itself, and gave indications of whence it came. When the communication is not enlivened with the actual content of this whole, to that extent it slips into the indifferent and trivial.[8] (My italics.)

It is this third form which is of interest to us here.

This notion, insofar as it is conceived dialectically, comes very close to being the cultural "Idea" of a destiny. Jaspers universalizes the "Idea," but within a limited range and tries to preserve the notion of perspective.

As a community of spirit, the members are united through the knowledge of a whole into the community of its Idea. It is always *a* whole, never *the* whole, and it must as a whole relate itself to other wholes and always remain uncompleted in its own actual existence.[9]

However, as a cultural idea, this "whole" is a cultural phenomenon and, from Nietzsche's point of view, a fiction. The fact that an idea is central to a culture does not justify its transformation into an absolute. Nietzsche would never deny the utility of such ideas; however, he would insist on grasping them in terms of their limitations. Furthermore, Nietzsche is very suspicious of an "Idea" which is so established that it can be appealed to as "authority." Even cultural "Ideas" must be dynamic, if the culture is not to stagnate. For Nietzsche, these "wholes" of which Jaspers speaks can be dealt with as manifestations of "group fictions" within the realm of philosophical anthropology. The fact that they are collective in no way justifies a leap into transcendence.

Later in his discussion, Jaspers approaches the problem of communication in another way. He makes the distinction between rational and existential communication. Rational communication refers primarily to the first two forms which we mentioned above. Existential communication, however, is of a very special nature and comes very close to

---

[8] *Ibid.*, p. 82.
[9] *Ibid.*, p. 85.

the religious notion of communion. Jaspers admits that every real attempt at communication is limited, even this existential one which is the communication of *Existenz* with another *Existenz*. Thus, in this one respect at least, he agrees with Nietzsche that truth is always particular and limited in such a way as to be perspectival. However, behind this perspective Jaspers posits an absolute truth which in and of itself and for the particular *Existenz* which apprehends it, is unconditional.

Since it is impossible for man to have Transcendence in time as a knowable object, identical for everybody like something in the world, every mode of the *One Truth as absolute in the world* can in fact only be historical: *unconditional for this Existenz* but, precisely for this reason, not universally valid.[10]

From this we can see that, for Nietzsche, Jaspers has to be regarded as a Platonist. Nietzsche's inversion of Platonism stands in direct opposition to Jaspers' position with regard to the most fundamental issues. For Jaspers, metaphysics without transcendence is simply not metaphysics or, at least, deficient metaphysics. Jaspers has, of course, the weight of an immense historical tradition behind his position and it would seem that this is his ultimate justification for neither explicitly stating his critical standpoint nor defending his position against Nietzsche's criticisms of transcendence. However, such a position does not really face Nietzsche's criticisms and the appeal to the authority of tradition is, in this case, not convincing.

A methodological problem in relation to Jaspers' interpretation is his notion of Nietzsche's dialectic of contradiction. Again this arises from Jaspers' dissatisfaction with the idea that there are "doctrines" in Nietzsche's philosophy. The weakness of this approach is that it tends to obscure the very interesting cases in which there genuinely is contradiction. In other words, Jaspers' view creates a kind of leveling and leads him to attribute all contradictions to the working of Nietzsche's dialectic. However, as we have already discovered many of these contradictions which Jaspers elaborates are only apparent contradictions, e.g., Nietzsche's play upon the words 'morality' and 'immorality.' As a result, the genuine cases of contradiction, such as the metaphysical version of the doctrine of Eternal Recurrence, are not pursued by Jaspers to their source. This is a partial explanation for Jaspers' virtual dismissal of Eternal Recurrence as a metaphysical position.

[10] *Ibid.*, p. 100.

Jaspers regards Eternal Recurrence as Nietzsche's attempt and failure to provide a doctrine of transcendence. This is, of course, the case. However, Jaspers does not go on to explore the reasons for Nietzsche's extraordinary attempt. It is extraordinary, because Nietzsche is so severe in criticisms of all forms of transcendence. The reasons for this metaphysical aberration, which we have already discussed, provide a glimpse into the existential depths of Nietzsche's humanness. The judgment that it is an aberration is, as we have developed it, an internal one derived from Nietzsche's own criteria for metaphysics and not an external judgment imposed from a context outside of Nietzsche's philosophy. Jaspers' rejection of the metaphysics of Eternal Recurrence is, however, grounded in reasons external to Nietzsche's philosophy. However, when Nietzsche does outline a more or less traditional doctrine of transcendence in his metaphysical version of Eternal Recurrence, Jaspers cannot accept it, because it is impersonal and non-teleological. In this respect, Jaspers is very deeply rooted in the Platonic and Christian traditions, and his criticism suggests at times that he considers Eternal Recurrence to be a rather pagan notion.

Jaspers also has difficulty in his interpretation of the Will to Power, and some of his reservations are psychological ones. Jaspers seems to fear that Nietzsche's attempt to liberate man from the restrictives implied by transcendence will result in a violent eruption of man's unconscious drives.[11] The phrase, "Will to Power," is highly emotive and can be easily misinterpreted, but even when interpreted correctly the phrase itself tends to exert an almost magical influence. However, Nietzsche sharply distinguishes positive and negative manifestations of the Will to Power. Permissiveness and self-indulgence are not part of Nietzsche's notion of the positive Will to Power of the Superman. Jaspers' criticisms of the anthropological aspect of Will to Power indicate that he does not always recognize the distinction between the positive and the negative forms. Furthermore, Jaspers is in many ways committed to a more traditional morality. He acknowledges the depth and correctness of many aspects of Nietzsche's critique of traditional morality, but he is reluctant to abandon entirely some trans-human source of authority. There is a certain irony here, for Nietzsche's conception of morality has frequently been attacked as being inhuman, yet it is his extraordinary faith in the possibilities of the human being

---

[11] Jaspers' fear was, of course, well-founded. His Nietzsche book was published in 1936 after he had observed the rise of Hitler and the outrageous persecutions which followed the election of a National Socialist Majority.

that leads him to be willing to risk breaking the fetters of transcendent authority thus providing man with a new kind of creative freedom. On the other hand, Jaspers, who is frequently regarded as a great humanist, is incapable of sharing Nietzsche's faith in man and believes that certain forms of trans-human authority must be preserved to restrain man and protect him from himself. There are good arguments for both positions and in terms of our dominant contemporary pragmatism, many might regard Nietzsche's faith as somewhat naive and unrealistic, but nonetheless one has to admit that it is rather a magnificent kind of faith.

Jaspers is also afraid that the creative morality of the Superman will lead from anthropocentrism to egoism. However, Nietzsche understood very well the subtleties of the relationship which would have to exist between the Superman and the herd and his conception of the Superman of necessity rules out any kind of willful egoism. Whether in actual fact such a relationship is achievable and workable cannot be determined in advance. Jaspers' reservations are certainly to be respected in terms of his extensive background in humanistic psychology, but we also need to remember that for Nietzsche the achievement of such a sophisticated society was a far from immediate goal. He explicitly states that thousands of years would be required for man even to begin to actualize such a society. Even if we wish to regard this notion as Utopian, it is certainly different from the classical Utopias in that it is always dynamic; there is no final perfect state posited as a goal. Thus, even his concept of Utopia remains true to his inversion of Platonism.

In his criticisms of Nietzsche, Jaspers refers to what he calls the "thought experiments" of Nietzsche. This notion is derivative from Jaspers' interpretation of the "dialectic of contradiction", and must be rejected for reasons similar to those for rejecting this dialectic. Two major examples of what Jaspers considers to be thought experiments are Nietzsche's notions of Being as Becoming and truth as fictions. Here again we encounter Jaspers' charge of dialectical circularity and again it is a result of the fact that he regards this dialectic as operative only on one level. The two examples are related in that Nietzsche regards Being as one of the fictions that we need in order to explain the world to ourselves from within the anthropological perspective. However, for there to be any dialectic at all Nietzsche realized that there must be a perspective which provided a kind of TRUTH which is not a life-preserving fiction. This is the cosmological perspective and the judgment derived from it that all Being is Becoming is not a relative truth of the anthropological perspective, for it does nothing to preserve life, but rather threatens it. The very judgment that truths are fictions designed to meet the needs of *anthropos* collapses into utter nonsense, if there is no perspective "outside" of life from which to make this judgment. Certainly Nietzsche was much too subtle a dialectician to fall into such an obvious trap. This perspective "outside" of life is what we have called the TRANSCENDENCE of the cosmological perspective, precisely because it is "beyond" and opposed to the perspectives of life and forms one pole of the essential dualism which resides at the center of man's Being (or nature). Jaspers, however, argues that these thought experiments lead to a "dissolution of reason." Nietzsche's critique of reason is certainly thorough, but it is by no means a total abandonment of reason. Nietzsche can hardly be fairly represented as a philosopher of "irrationalism." Even Nietzsche's most ecstatic Dionysian flights are eventually tempered by the Apollonian counter-balances of harmony and form. In fact, Nietzsche's later and more mature conception of the Dionysian is really a synthesis of Dionysian and Apollonian elements. Nietzsche does not want to discard reason; he wants to fuse it harmoniously with man's "animality," thus creating the possibility for it to achieve its highest estate through man's fullest and richest development of all of his aspects. Jaspers' failure to explicate fully the two distinct levels that are the ground of Nietzsche's dialectic leads him to an interpretation that makes Nietzsche's philosophy seem highly ambiguous and rather mysterious, if not mystical. This is perhaps one of the most explicit examples of a case where Jaspers reads his own philosophy into Nietzsche's. Jaspers, in terms of his own philosophy, not only regards ambiguity as necessary, he comes to regard it as a virtue. As we have already seen, his theory of communication suggests that anything which is not essentially ambiguous, in that it relates to a whole not fully known, "slips into the indifferent and trivial." This is an unnecessary complication, for there is a great abundance of problems in Nietzsche, the interpretation of which fully challenges one's best capabilities, and there is no reason to augment that challenge.

The confusion which results from this imposed ambiguity is also visible in Jaspers' discussion of nihilism. Jaspers' reluctance to interpret Nietzsche in terms of "doctrines" tends to obscure the full development of Nietzsche's thought and also makes it extremely difficult to deal with the juxtapositions of various sets of ideas within Nietzsche's philosophy. As a result Jaspers sometimes reacts to Nietzsche's doctrine of nihilism as though Nietzsche were advocating total anarchy. Jaspers' search for contradictions makes it difficult for him to view Nietzsche's doctrine of nihilism within the context of Nietzsche's humanism. Without this context as a background Nietzsche's radical nihilism certainly would be alarming, but within this context it may be properly viewed as a necessary step in the process of self-overcoming. This self-overcoming is, of course, the key to Nietzsche's humanism.

From the foregoing it seems quite clear that Jaspers very persistently reads his own philosophy into his interpretation of Nietzsche. He continually seeks to link up various aspects of Nietzsche's thought with his own notions of *Existenz*, transcendence, and Encompassing. Furthermore, he uses his own philosophy as a critical foil in such a way that his own critical standpoint is still subject to Nietzsche's criticisms. Jaspers' interpretation also reveals that his own temperament is in many ways radically opposed to Nietzsche's. Perhaps the greatest objection to Jaspers' interpretation is that as a *Nietzsche* interpretation it is not really intelligible without a knowledge of Jaspers' own philosophy. Nonetheless, Jaspers' interpretation is an exciting challenge and succeeds in laying open many critical questions which must be thoroughly investigated, if one is to understand Nietzsche at all. What is most remarkable of all is the genuineness of the attempt at dialogue with a thinker who so radically opposes so much in Jaspers' own thinking. Nietzsche did not demand agreement, in fact, he was suspicious of it. The dialogue which he envisioned as a part of the movement along the path to the Superman was of necessity characterized by opposition. At times such dialogue takes place here between Jaspers and Nietzsche.

HOW HEIDEGGER READS HIS OWN PHILOSOPHY INTO NIETZSCHE

We have already taken note of the fact that Heidegger's relation to Nietzsche is different from that of Jaspers' in that Heidegger's interpretation is an explicit attempt to illustrate a thesis which extends beyond the context of Nietzsche's philosophy. Nonetheless, one can fairly expect an interpretation which remains true to the spirit of Nietzsche's philosophy. Heidegger's interest in and emphasis on Nietzsche's metaphysics is understandable, however, his attempt to subsume Nietzsche's philosophical anthropology under metaphysics must be rejected. This attempted subsumption is one of the major ways in which Heidegger reads his own philosophy into Nietzsche's. Heidegger's critical standpoint, like Jaspers', is subject to Nietzsche's own criticisms. Heidegger also seems to take it for granted that these possible criticisms by Nietzsche are either self-refuting or else he believes that his own critical standpoint is self-justifying.

Heidegger's major thesis is that Nietzsche's philosophy, far from being an "overcoming" of metaphysics, is in many respects the acme of metaphysics. What is metaphysics in Heidegger's sense? We have already discussed what Heidegger calls the fundamental "mistake" of metaphysics and discovered that it consisted of the concern with the question of the Being of entities rather than the genuine question of ontology which seeks the essence of Being as such. However, much more is involved here. This "mistake" resulted in a gradual separation of ontology (which "degenerates" into metaphysics) and epistemology. Heidegger's conception of fundamental ontology involves an "overcoming" of metaphysics which is partially achieved through a reuniting of ontology and epistemology. The root of the "mistake" which led to this separation is, for Heidegger, to be found in the basic metaphysical distinction between subject and object. For Heidegger, this is the "original sin" of metaphysics and one which all traditional philosophy up until the present has inherited. We have already seen how Heidegger places Nietzsche in the epistemological tradition of "subjectivism" which in its modern version dates from Descartes. We have also remarked that this historical analysis of Heidegger's is rather dubious. However, more importantly, Heidegger's criterion for metaphysics can be viewed in another way. Heidegger regards every system of philosophy as "metaphysical," if it does not grasp Being as *transcendence*. He argues that the only philosophers who have even begun to approximate genuine ontology are Heraclitus and Parmenides. The subsequent development of the history of Western philosophy as metaphysics was a necessary stage in the history of the unfolding of Being – according to Heidegger's view – and Nietzsche simultaneously brings metaphysics to its highest development and also to its conclusive end as a dead-end. This event opens up the possibility for genuine ontology once more and Heidegger sees his own work on the problem of Being as such as the foundation for this new tradition.

Heidegger's concern with the problem of Being dates back to his earliest concern with philosophy.

From the very beginning, Heidegger's exclusive preoccupation, hence the unique sense of his way, has been to lay a foundation for metaphysics. By his own account, it all began on a summer day in 1907 when, as an eighteen-year-old gymnasiast in Constance, he received from Dr. Conrad Gröber, later archbishop of Freiburg (1932–48) but at that time pastor of Trinity Church in Constance, a book that was only gathering dust on Dr. Gröber's shelf. It was Franz Brentano's dissertation, *On the Manifold Sense of Being According to Aristotle* (1862), and it served not only to open Heidegger's eyes to the problem of Being, but to introduce him into the philosophical world of the Greeks.[12]

Also Heidegger's first major philosophical work was in the area of Scholastic philosophy and was titled, *The Doctrine of Categories and Signification in Duns Scotus* (the texts were at that time attributed to Scotus, but were later discovered to be the work of Thomas of Erfurt). Heidegger has an almost mystical attitude about the beginnings of philosophical thought (both historical and individual) dictating the subsequent course of that thinking toward what he calls its "destiny." In any case, Heidegger has unswervingly pursued the question of Being and none of his work is untouched by this concern. To many Heidegger's concern with Being is anachronistic in an age characterized by scientific technology, linguistic analysis, and logical positivism, yet in Heidegger's writing there is often a kind of urgency, since Heidegger is totally convinced that unless this modern era does concern itself with the question of Being, all of its other achievements will be vacuous. It is clear that this question of Being is, for Heidegger, no mere intellectual game. His total involvement with Being and its destiny is strongly reminiscent of the Aristotelian Scholastics who were an early and lasting influence on his thinking. It is precisely this quality in his thinking that creates an ambivalence. On the one hand, his particular analyses of *Dasein* and of contemporary society are often penetrating and precise. On the other hand, his concern with Being often seems as nebulous and distant as the more abstruse parts of the philosophizing of the Scholastics.

One can readily react with precisely this ambivalence to Heidegger's interpretation of Nietzsche. There are aspects of his interpretation that are highly stimulating and lead to new insights regarding the nature of Nietzsche's metaphysical enterprise. However, all to often, Nietzsche gets buried under Heidegger's attempt to demonstrate his thesis. Heidegger's commitment to a doctrine of transcendence also strongly conditions the nature of his interpretive investigation and criticism of Nietzsche. The ways in which Heidegger reads his own

---

[12] Richardson, *Heidegger*, pp. 3–4.

position into Nietzsche can best be seen by a brief re-examination of the general outlines and movement of his interpretation.

One of Heidegger's main interpretive aims is to explicate the "essential unity" of Nietzsche's philosophy. He argues that the notion of Being as Becoming is equivalent to the Will to Power which is in turn equivalent to Eternal Recurrence. Furthermore, Heidegger derives the notion of truth from Becoming and the doctrine of Transvaluation from Eternal Recurrence. The doctrine of the Superman is, for Heidegger, also derivative from the Will to Power and we have already examined the very peculiar nature of this argument, which fuses cosmology and "psychology" (philosophical anthropology) and "concludes" from this that, since cosmology centers around the Will to Power, Nietzsche's metaphysics as a kind of "psychology" is a "subjectivism" which "necessarily" leads to the Superman as a manifestation of the metaphysics of the Will to Power.

If we accept the notion that there is an essential dualism at the core of Nietzsche's philosophy characterized by the opposition of the cosmological and anthropological perspectives, then Heidegger's attempt to unify Nietzsche is contrary to the essential nature of Nietzsche's philosophy. However, even if one does not accept the thesis of a dualism in Nietzsche, Heidegger's arguments can hardly be regarded as convincing. Certainly his fusion of cosmology and "psychology" is very tenuous indeed. Furthermore, if we reject the notion of dualism, we are left with Heidegger's difficulty of not being able to make sense of the doctrine of Eternal Recurrence.

We have already mentioned Heidegger's fondness for playing on the relationships which exist between thesis and antithesis. He uses this device in his critical rejections of Nietzsche's claim that his philosophy is a reversal or inversion of Platonism. Heidegger takes Platonism to be a characterization of all philosophy since Plato and prior to Nietzsche and thereby regards it as also being a characterization of metaphysics as such. From this Heidegger argues that Nietzsche's inversion is also still metaphysics because it is the antithesis of the thesis of Platonism. However, Heidegger arrives at this conclusion only by already assuming in advance that Nietzsche's attempt to "overcome" metaphysics is not successful.

Heidegger characterizes Nietzsche's inversion of Platonism in terms of the relationship between art and truth. For Plato, truth is higher than art, but for Nietzsche art is higher than truth. Heidegger argues that Plato and Nietzsche both have essentially the same basic notion of truth as "representation." This alone, for Heidegger, places Nietzsche in the tradition of metaphysics as Platonism. Heidegger regards the only genuine notion of truth to be that of *aletheia* or "unhiddenness" and argues that only by means of this notion of Truth is the "overcoming" of metaphysics to be accomplished. Heidegger argues that Nietzsche's conception of truth is that presented by the tradition of classical metaphysics by means of his interpretation of Nietzsche's notion of truth as *homoiosis*. As we have already seen this argument is certainly questionable and illustrates very well Heidegger's penchant for imposing the structure of his own philosophizing on that of Nietzsche.

Heidegger's charge of anthropomorphism or "humanization" with regard to Nietzsche's metaphysics is also questionable, for it requires some highly dubious "interpretations" of some of Nietzsche's remarks, in which he clearly and explicitly states an anti-anthropomorphic view of metaphysics. Here, as in a number of other cases, Heidegger establishes the connections he wants by means of metaphysical puns. He plays on the notion of anthropomorphism in such a way that sometimes he uses it in a tautological sense, when he is criticizing Nietzsche, and other times he uses it in a restricted sense such that it can be "overcome" and it is this sense which he uses in defending his own analytic of *Dasein*.

This punning also extends to his discussion of nihilism, for he finally comes to regard metaphysics as equivalent to nihilism. From his previous "conclusion" that Nietzsche is still rooted in traditional metaphysics, it is an easy step to the charge that Nietzsche's philosophy is nihilistic. This, of course, has virtually nothing to do with Nietzsche's discussions of nihilism. Heidegger's charge rests on a critical basis which is external to Nietzsche's own philosophy. This basis is, of course, his doctrine of Being as *transcendence* and from our discussion of Jaspers, it is already apparent what criticisms could be advanced against this view from Nietzsche's standpoint.

Heidegger's interpretation suffers from several major weaknesses. (1) Heidegger reads his own special concern with the problem of Being into Nietzsche. (2) Heidegger attempts to unify Nietzsche's philosophy in such a way that he virtually discounts the entire dimension of philosophical anthropology. (3) Some of Heidegger's arguments rest on what can only be regarded as a "forcing" of Nietzsche's texts. (4) Heidegger leaves certain central issues in "suspension", especially the problem of the metaphysical meaning of the doctrine of Eternal

Recurrence. Strictly speaking, this "suspension" has disastrous consequences. Heidegger virtually admits that his interpretation of Eternal Recurrence comes to a dead-end when he says that it may require decades before this thought can be fully thought, but if this is true and if, as Heidegger claims, Eternal Recurrence is equivalent to the doctrine of Being as Becoming, then Nietzsche's entire metaphysics is in "suspension" and Heidegger has, in effect, said that at this time no interpretation of Nietzsche is possible!

Heidegger's Nietzsche interpretation reveals much more about Heidegger's own philosophy than it does about Nietzsche's. We have seen that Jaspers' interpretation presupposes a certain familiarity with his philosophy and this is even more true in the case of Heidegger's interpretation. On the whole, Heidegger's interpretation, as an interpretation of *Nietzsche* is a failure. It does force one to examine more deeply certain aspects of Nietzsche's philosophy, especially metaphysical ones, but in general the contexts in which Nietzsche's ideas are presented are misleading. There are some interesting and sometimes penetrating insights into Nietzsche, but one could hardly recommend Heidegger's interpretation as an explication of Nietzsche's thought. There is much here of interest to the Heidegger specialist, some of which is not to be found in any of Heidegger's other writings, but unfortunately Heidegger reads his own philosophy into his interpretations in such a way that it tends to dominate and thereby obscure Nietzsche's philosophy.

PARALLELS – NIETZSCHE AND JASPERS: AN EXPANDED VIEW

In order to fulfill the conditions regarding interpretation which we stated at the beginning of this chapter, we shall at this point examine Jaspers' and Heidegger's views from an additional perspective. In this section and the one following, we shall take a more explicit look at the parallels between the philosophies of the interpreters and Nietzsche's own philosophy. Hopefully by this means we shall be able to attain an expanded point of view in an attempt to see more clearly how their work on Nietzsche fits into the programmatic of their philosophies as a whole.

One of the most significant parallels between Jaspers and Nietzsche and the one which comes most immediately to mind is their strong emphasis on philosophy as process, i.e., as philosophizing. For both philosophers this emphasis involves a theory of communication and a theory of man in relation to the cosmos. A peculiarity arises here from Jaspers' refusal to recognize doctrines in Nietzsche's philosophy, for existentially Jaspers and Nietzsche both point to man as an absolutely fundamental locus of meaning. As we have noted before Jaspers' conception of *Existenz* is one which is compatible with Nietzsche's theory of man insofar as it is not used as a means to establish a transcendence beyond man himself. Thus even Nietzsche might admit to the doctrine of *Existenz* as a transcendent-*immanence*, although he would almost certainly not wish to formulate it in that way. Nietzsche and Jaspers agree that there is in man an inexplicable fundament which is the focal point for the revelation of the mystery of existence. Nietzsche sees the very transitoriness of man and his world as a haunting part of this mystery and the temptation of a doctrine of transcendence always lurks in the background of his thought and even becomes explicit for brief periods when Nietzsche tries to defend a literal version of the doctrine of Eternal Recurrence. On the other hand, Jaspers, as critical as he is of Nietzsche's notion of Eternal Recurrence, for reasons we have already discussed, moves directly and immediately to a doctrine of transcendence and regards such a doctrine as absolutely necessary for a theory of value.

Here we see two positions which are parallel in one sense and yet opposed in another. Jaspers and Nietzsche agree that value is radically grounded in the manner in which man exists in relation to his world. However, the opposition arises out of Jaspers' conviction that man himself must be grounded in something "beyond" man and his world. This same division occurs with Jaspers' notion of the "limit" or "border" situation. Nietzsche describes confrontations which man has with his own limits that parallel precisely the substance of Jaspers' view. However, for Jaspers, this confrontation leads further and further "beyond" man, whereas, for Nietzsche, such encounters are parabolic and throw man once again back upon himself as a problem and a mystery.

A further parallel is the view that communication is essentially ambiguous. However, this "position" allows for a rather wide latitude of viewpoint. Both Nietzsche and Jaspers recognize the necessity for an intuitive leap which appeals to that which is "personal" in the most radical sense and is yet not to be construed as merely and idiosyncratically individual. To philosophize out of one's "person" or *Existenz* is for both thinkers the basis of authentic thought and is universal, but for Nietzsche this universality is conditioned. For Jaspers, however, through his appeal to transcendence, this universality must finally be viewed as unconditioned. Thus, in Jaspers' view, ambiguity is saved from collapsing into chaos by an appeal to a ground "outside" of man, whereas for Nietzsche ambiguity is always present to goad man into a more profound inquiry and in this way ambiguity becomes a part of the motive force of dialectic. This is not nihilism nor does it mean that we can find no footholds at all in Nietzsche's philosophy. However, it does seem that this is Jaspers' conclusion. In a discussion of ambiguity, after speaking of Kierkegaard, Jaspers says the following about Nietzsche.

The significance of Nietzsche is no clearer. His effect in Germany was like that of no other philosopher. But it seems as though every attitude, every world-view, every conviction claims him as authority. It might be that none of us really knows what his thought includes and does.[13]

Surely this description and this judgment are too extreme. Jaspers himself would admit that many of these claims to Nietzsche's authority are illegitimate and if this is so, then there are viewpoints, perspectives, and positions which properly belong to the philosophy of Nietzsche and others which do not. Furthermore, Jaspers' criticisms of both Nietzsche and his critics presuppose that he has some rather distinct sense of what Nietzsche's thought "includes and does."

Finally both Nietzsche and Jaspers raise serious questions about the supremacy of reason. Both are suspicious of the extravagant claims put forth for reason either in the name of empirical science or in the systems of metaphysics and epistemology ostensibly grounded on innate truths grasped by the "clear light of reason." In the nineteenth century the faith in reason was profoundly challenged. "After the questioning of Kierkegaard and Nietzsche, reason is no longer self-evident to us."[14] This suspicion of reason on Jaspers' part is inseparably linked to his belief in the incommunicability of transcendence and he in no way suggests that reason should be abandoned, but much more moderately advocates a recognition of the limits of reason and a use of reason in the service of *Existenz* which is not itself graspable in terms of reason. Nietzsche's position is much more radical and if taken out of context and pushed to its extreme, is self-defeating. Nietzsche is concerned with the very nature of conceptualization. He believes that every conceptualization, no matter how basic, is useful

13 Jaspers, *Reason and Existenz*, p. 46.
14 *Ibid.*, p. 130.

only with regard to certain ends. The notion of utility here is important, for Nietzsche insists that a truth is always a means to a certain end and that it must be understood within that context.

The inventive force that invented categories labored in the service of our needs, namely of our need for security for quick understanding on the basis of signs and sounds, for means of abbreviation: − "substance," "subject," "object," "being," "becoming" have nothing to do with metaphysical truths.[15]

Even the "law of non-contradiction" is not sacred as Kierkegaard, along with Nietzsche, so eloquently demonstrates. Not only the "Laws" of logic, but all concepts, are static renderings of what is in constant flux and so, "paradoxes" are commonplaces in human experience and the fact that we can produce no formal calculus that encompasses them is no argument against their occurrence.

Perhaps the clearest and most explicit statements of Nietzsche's attack on reason and its categories are to be found in *The Will to Power*. From his discussions there, it becomes clear how radical Nietzsche's position really is. Not only does he insist that truths must be understood within a certain context and in terms of their "function," but he argues that certain concepts, transcendence among them, have no meaning and function precisely because they have no limit or "range." In other words, any concept which a thinker tries to employ with *absolute* generality without regard to context and function is meaningless.

We believe in reason: this, however, is the philosophy of gray *concepts*. Language depends on the most naive prejudices.
Now we read disharmonies and problems into things because we think *only* in the form of language – and thus believe in the "eternal truth" of "reason." (e.g., subject, attribute, etc.)
We cease to think when we refuse to do so under the constraint of language: we barely reach the doubt that sees this limitation as a limitation.
Rational thought is interpretation according to a scheme that we cannot throw off.[16]

These remarks are especially interesting in that they comprise not only an attack, but a description and a protest as well. This passage also helps us understand Nietzsche's description of his metaphysics as "an inversion of Platonism." Furthermore, it helps us understand Nietzsche's return to myth which we will examine in the next chapter. For Nietzsche, the further away we move from concrete experience, the less adequately language serves as a means of rational communication.

---

[15] Nietzsche, *The Will to Power*, p. 277.
[16] *Ibid.*, p. 283.

Nietzsche's remarks above and, of course, many others in *The Will to Power* point to a view of conceptualization which has immense importance with regard to Heidegger and we shall examine this issue more closely in the next section. It is sufficient to note here that Jaspers cannot accept such an extreme position, since it threatens the foundations of traditional Western philosophy.

It would seem then that we are justified in saying that most of the parallels between Nietzsche and Jaspers are superficial. Jaspers is very much afraid of the extremes which Nietzsche pushes his thinking toward. It is as though Jaspers feels that the Dionysian element in Nietzsche's philosophy is always on the point of gaining dominance and whirling off into chaos. It is certainly true that in many respects Jaspers' philosophy is much more comfortable and hopeful and in this regard perhaps even bourgeois. Jaspers has an undeniable propensity to moderate and qualify Nietzsche's remarks and this propensity goes beyond any enterprise directed toward achieving an interpretive balance. One cannot help feeling that Jaspers has a deep-rooted distrust of Nietzsche's aestheticism. Finally, although Jaspers insists upon the limitations of reason, he creates a distinct impression that that which is beyond those limits is supra-rational rather than unintelligible or irrational. In other words, for Jaspers, whatever transcendence is, it has the distinct aura of benevolence.

In light of these conclusions we must now inquire into the relationship between Jaspers' critical work on Nietzsche and Jaspers' philosophy as a whole. It would seem that Nietzsche is a recurring problem for Jaspers; a problem which must be solved. It is as though Jaspers' own thought keeps colliding with Nietzsche's and so he becomes a figure whom Jaspers must finally come to terms with. Nietzsche becomes Jaspers' gadfly. *Reason and Existenz* uses both Kierkegaard's and Nietzsche's philosophies as springboards for Jaspers' own ideas, but is also in part an attempt to answer their positions. *Nietzsche and Christianity* is an exposition of Nietzsche's attack and yet simultaneously an attempt to salvage something from Christianity. Jaspers' *Nietzsche: An Introduction to the Understanding of His Philosophical Activity* can be seen as a contest between two giants, for in many respects this book is a profoundly personal one and Nietzsche becomes not only a protagonist, but an antagonist as well. For Jaspers theer was no way around Nietzsche; he had to be confronted directly even though Jaspers' deepest philosophical dispositions ran counter to the direction of Nietzsche's thought. This context produced two results of great importance: a new and provocative perspective on the thought of Nietzsche and an enrichment of Jaspers' own philosophical thinking. That this context did not result in agreement is of no consequence, for as Nietzsche himself affirmed when he quoted Galiani:

Philosophers are not made to love one another. Eagles do not fly in company. One must leave that to partridges and starlings .... Soaring on high and having talons, that is the lot of great geniuses.[17]

PARALLELS – NIETZSCHE AND HEIDEGGER: AN EXPANDED VIEW

In view of Heidegger's tendency to use Nietzsche's thought for his own ends, rather than providing an interpretation in the sense we have been discussing here, it might seem strange to assert that the parallels between Nietzsche and Heidegger are more numerous and more profound than are the parallels between Nietzsche and Jaspers, yet such is the case. Let us begin with a point we raised in the previous section, namely, Nietzsche's attack on conceptualization. This attack must be considered within the context of Nietzsche's theory of perspectivism and his conclusion that truths are necessary fictions. We should here remind ourselves that a consequence of this view is that truth is not only a matter of utility, but a matter of aesthetics as well. Nietzsche's latest work returns to a position which gives an explicit priority to aesthetics. Thus it is no mere poetic flight that leads him toward the very end of his creative period to return to the Dionysian theme as is evidenced in the Dithyrambs and a section titled "Dionysus" in *The Will to Power*, as well as many of the general comments on art as a justification for existence in the same book. In fact, Nietzsche goes even further to suggest that without artistic creation, life would be unbearable. That this Dionysian theme had again become a preoccupation is also evident from the postcards and letters written immediately after his breakdown.

This explicit return to aestheticism is inextricably bound up with his attack on conceptualization, for here Nietzsche is moving beyond the realm of traditional philosophy and wrestling with limits of language and rationality. He, like the later Heidegger, in his attempt to "overcome" the limits of traditional philosophical thinking, turns to the poetic. Heidegger becomes progressively more radical in his attempts

---

[17] *Ibid.*, p. 516.

to "overcome" dualistic thought and attempts to "destroy" the metaphysical thinking that leads to bifurcations such as "subject-object," "real-ideal," and even "transcendence-immanence." In his most recent work we even find the idea of "overcoming" the notion of "overcoming."[18] In fact, the clearest sign of Heidegger's much discussed *Kehre* or "turning point" is his movement towards not only a "poetic" language, but a progressively more radical employment of language as a means of communicating within a realm where every dualism is seen as a misapprehension and, as a consequence, a distortion. The roots of this project are indeed to be found in *Being and Time* as Heidegger claims, but the significance which this enterprise takes on becomes clearer as one moves up to Heidegger's most recent writings. Heidegger and Nietzsche move to a point where language threatens to explode in the sense that rationalistic conceptualization is no longer accepted as an adequate vehicle for THOUGHT. The importance of this parallelism we shall consider in the next chapter.

One immediate ramification of this view is that language itself becomes problematic, somewhat in the sense in which it does for Wittgenstein. Wittgenstein feels that ultimately the most profound and personally meaningful experiences which human beings can have are forever beyond the reach of language, most particularly, philosophical language which he tends to regard more often as a hindrance than a help in moving closer to those most existentially significant experiences. Nietzsche and Heidegger recognize these limitations and even protest against them, but neither is willing to let the issue stand there. Both believe that radical communication is still possible and both are willing to "destroy" the traditional modes of conceptualization in order to achieve it.

Another parallel which develops out of the later work of Heidegger is a result of the increasing emphasis which Heidegger places on art. His highly provocative essay in *Holzwege* on the origin of the work of art opens up new dimensions in Heidegger's philosophy. Also Heidegger, through his concern with poetry, implicitly elaborates a new use of language for THOUGHT. Heidegger's essays on Trakl, Rilke, Hölderlin, Hebbel, and his own poetizing-thinking as found in *Der Feldweg* create new perspectives and new possibilities of direction for the enterprise of "approaching Being" and "allowing Being to approach us." This

---

[18] See Martin Heidegger, "Zeit und Sein," in *L'Endurance de la pensée. Pour saluer Jean Beaufret*. Edited by René Char. Paris: Edition Plon, 1968.

path is pursued even further in his "return" to the Greeks and the elaboration of the Quadrate or "foursome" – earth, sky, gods, and mortals. These themes are brought together in Heidegger's development of the view that the most fundamental mode of THOUGHT is "primordial poetizing."

It is interesting and significant that in 1888 Nietzsche turns again to poetry and in the *Dionysian Dithyrambs* speaks once more of necessity, of the longing for eternity, and of the sign or shield (*Schild*) of Being. Through their mutual concern with art and its essential relationship to philosophy, Heidegger and Nietzsche are closer than one might suspect at first glance. This parallelism has some especially interesting ramifications as we shall see in the next chapter.

One large problem remains in examining the relationship between the philosophies of Heidegger and Nietzsche and that is the concept of transcendence. Some critics have argued that in his radical attempt to "overcome" conceptual dualisms, Heidegger attempts to "overcome" the transcendence-immanence dichotomy and that, in spite of his discussion of Being as *transcendence* in *Being and Time*, the roots for this "overcoming" are already to be found in that work. There are, without question, justifications for such an interpretation in light of Heidegger's later writings, but the problem of explicating and understanding Heidegger on this point is by no means easy. In the later essays Heidegger attempts to speak from the perspective of Being itself or perhaps more accurately he attempts to let Being itself speak and *Da-sein* still remains the "place" at which and through which Being reveals itself. Thus, if Being were understood as strictly transcendent, then human *Da-sein* could not take up such a positionality.

We should then take careful note of the fact that Heidegger's "conception" of Being is not a reification or, more simply, Being is not a thing. Already in the first chapter of *Introduction to Metaphysics*, Heidegger suggests that the Being-question involves a certain way of living in the world. The ontological is always accessible to us through the ontic, but only if we "resolve" to undertake the task of its elucidation explicitly. Thus while Being may, on the whole, remain hidden within the context of our day-to-day pursuits, it is by no means inaccessible if we let things be what they genuinely are. The programmatics of this "letting-be" are extremely involved and need not concern us here, except to observe that Heidegger provides few guidelines for proceeding. Indeed he suggests that it must be an individual exploration, without a map, of the many *Holzwege* that are encountered in the acts of THOUGHT.

In view of this attempt to "overcome" this dualism between transcendence and immanence, one is tempted to create the rather unfelicitous neologism "trans-immanence." However, no matter how suggestive such a term might be, it in no way brings us to a truly clearer understanding of Heidegger's view. When Heidegger says that "the thing things" or that "the appropriating event events by appropriating," (*Das Ereignis ereignet*), we cannot help but feel here a sense of a "something" which has a kind of autonomy and this conveys the overtones of some kind of "transcendence." [19] However, these feelings may be a consequence of that encounter with the limits of language which we spoke of earlier and Kisiel quotes Heidegger on this very point, "'Every incipient and authentic naming utters the unspoken, and indeed in such a way that it remains unspoken,'" Kisiel than adds, "The unsayable is somehow said!" [20] The difficulty with this is that one is made to feel absurd if he goes on to ask what it is that has been said which is unsayable. We are further led into difficulty when it is implied that we must accept such enigmas as "non-assertive assertions." Let us here consider another passage from Kisiel, part of which is a quotation from Heidegger's essay *Plato's Doctrine of Truth*.

Generally speaking, it can be prefatorily stated that Heidegger's resorting to these peculiarly non-assertive assertions arises from his attempt to think Being *itself*, Being *as such*. The following quotation strikes the pervasive keynote: "Yet Being – what is Being? It is itself. This is what future thinking must learn to experience and to say. 'Being' – it is not God nor a world-ground. For being is further than any being, be it a rock or an animal, a work of art or a machine, an angel or God. Being is the nearest. Yet the near is farthest for man." [21]

Here we should take careful note of three things: Being is itself, i.e., it is *sui generis*; Being is not any particular entity or collection of entities; and finally "Being is the nearest." It is statements of this last sort that lead one to think that Heidegger cannot mean that Being is transcendent, yet the first two statements are certainly traditionally regarded as concepts of transcendence. Thus the claim that Heidegger has "overcome" the notion of Being as transcendence, is, to say the least, unclear. There is a strong impression created by some of Heidegger's commentators that the only way to understand

---

[19] Theodore Kisiel, "The Language of the Event: The Event of Language" in *Heidegger and the Path of Thinking*, ed. John Sallis, 1970, p. 99.

[20] *Ibid.*, p. 96.

[21] *Ibid.*, p. 97.

and overcome such difficulties is to philosophize as Heidegger philosophizes and to enter the path of poetizing-thinking. J. Glenn Gray states the difficulty with such a demand very incisively.

But there are strong negative aspects to this so-called rigorous thinking of Heidegger and to the whole program of simplicity in thought. It is indeed difficult for philosophic criticism to evaluate the poetic thinking of the later Heidegger. The implicit command here is: take it or leave it untouched – that is, think in this way or think conceptually and representationally. If you choose the second alternative, you will never be able to understand poetic thinking. There is a severe weakness in any method or path on the way to truth which makes such a presupposition as this. Let us make no mistake about it. No thinking, poetic or logical, ought to lay claim to immunity from criticism when that criticism is equally involved and impartial.[22]

Thus, to return to the charge that from Nietzsche's point of view, Heidegger's position involves a doctrine of transcendence, we can see that there are reasons for still accepting the validity of the charge in light of the passages which we considered above. On the other hand, if Heidegger has "overcome" the transcendence-immanence dualism, then we must have some framework for understanding this "overcoming" which as yet Heidegger has not provided. However, another possibility remains and that is that the charge is not applicable precisely because Heidegger's THOUGHT has moved into a dimension where the attempt to make such a charge would be a kind of "category mistake." We shall examine this possibility in the next chapter.

DOCTRINES VERSUS CONTRADICTIONS

One way of characterizing Jaspers' method of interpreting Nietzsche might be as a "radicalization" of dialectic. At every point Jaspers is interested in discovering oppositions to Nietzsche's theses and attempts to map out the often complex paths in Nietzsche's thinking. Jaspers succeeds in showing the intricate convolutions of Nietzsche's highly associative style of thinking. Nietzsche's thinking is often exploratory, investigative, tentative and he returns again and again to the same problems to examine them from new perspectives. His usual method of dividing his works into many short sections can be misleading, for these short sections are by no means random jottings. It is well known that Nietzsche spent much time polishing and re-working these sections before he would publish them as a book. Furthermore, the

---

[22] J. Glenn Gray, "Splendor of the Simple" in *On Understanding Violence Philosophically and Other Essays*, New York, 1970, pp. 63–64.

relations between the various sections are not as random as they might appear on a casual reading. One can often discern a flow of associated ideas moving in a rather well-defined direction. Sometimes, Jaspers' discussions show this inner movement very well, though at other times his dissection of the text in his search for contradictions tends to obscure this movement. On the whole, Jaspers' method succeeds in bringing to the foreground the essentially dynamic character of Nietzsche's thought. However, an interpretation which so strongly emphasizes this "dialectic of contradiction" tends to obscure the internal coherence of Nietzsche's thought.

Heidegger's interpretation, on the other hand, centers around an investigation of Nietzsche's doctrines. Heidegger succeeds in demonstrating that Nietzsche's philosophy contains definite sets of concepts that are essentially interrelated. Heidegger shows quite convincingly that Nietzsche does take up definite positions which come to define the framework within which the dialectic is possible. However, Heidegger's interpretation focuses so exclusively on the doctrines that one gets little sense of Nietzsche's dialectic.

The obvious conclusion to be drawn is that any adequate interpretation of Nietzsche must take into account both his dialectic and his doctrines. In fact, a careful study of Nietzsche will show that Nietzsche uses his dialectical method of philosophizing as a means of explicating the central doctrines of his philosophy. Here, however, we need to be careful how we understand the notion of doctrine. Nietzsche's doctrines are essentially frameworks within which he philosophizes dialectically. The doctrine of the Superman is a good illustration of this. For Nietzsche, the "nature" of the Superman is to be indicated in two ways. The first involves a presentation of certain defining characteristics, which is essential, for otherwise we would have an utterly empty concept. Examples of such defining characteristics are, as we have already seen, self-overcoming, honesty, and dignity. The other way in which the "nature" of the Superman is made determinate is in terms of relative goals, which are related to the specific circumstances that obtain in the present. That is to say, Nietzsche's "critique" of the contemporary situation posits certain more or less immediate goals which lie along the path to the Superman, but they are nonetheless relative goals, for when they are achieved they too must be surpassed. An example of this is Nietzsche's notion of the "democratization" of Europe which he sees as a temporary goal along the path to the Superman. Democratization is not in itself a goal, but rather a stage to be realized and then overcome in man's struggle for self-overcoming. Total self-overcoming is, for Nietzsche, a contradiction in terms. Man will always have the task of overcoming himself, but as he proceeds higher and higher along this path, his immediate goal will no longer be visible to us from where we now stand. Thus the dialectical contents of the new philosophies cannot be determined in advance, but the dynamics of self-overcoming will continue to provide the conceptual framework. From this we can see that the doctrines of Nietzsche's philosophy are not designed to legislate particular values that are then to be absolutized. On the contrary, specific values must be determined situationally and these situations cannot be predicted.

The deeper one attempts to penetrate into Nietzsche's thought the clearer it becomes that Nietzsche's whole project was in many ways a radical experiment beyond tradition. Nietzsche himself describes his work as a "philosophy for the future." In order to grasp fully Nietzsche's philosophical "revolution," an interpretation is needed which explicates his doctrines in terms of his dialectical mode of communication. Nietzsche's aim in communication was the involvement of the whole person not simply the intellect. Nietzsche rejects traditional dualisms and his notion of communication is an illustration of his attempt to overcome the dichotomy of reason and emotion. In spite of Heidegger's arguments to the contrary, Nietzsche also rejects the dualism of subject and object. His conception of life in some ways anticipates Heidegger's notion of Being-in-the-World, although Heidegger's notion is more fully developed in a systematic fashion. Furthermore, Nietzsche goes beyond tradition in the penetration of his psychological insights and creates a new focus on the motivations for human behavior, especially in its relation to value problems.

All the evidence points to a belief on Nietzsche's part that he is presenting a new and fundamental insight into the human condition and while this insight may not be precisely new, certainly Nietzsche presents it with much greater force than any philosopher prior to his time. To grasp the essential nature of this insight depends upon recognizing the essential dualism in the essence of the human being which is the motive force for the dialectical development of the whole of Nietzsche's philosophy.

CHAPTER V

AN ALTERNATIVE INTERPRETATION:
A FUNDAMENTAL DUALISM IN
NIETZSCHE'S THOUGHT

In the preceding chapters we have tried to show, by means of an examination of the interpretations of Jaspers and Heidegger, the negative consequences of attempting an interpretation of Nietzsche without having first taken into account the essential dualism in Nietzsche's theory of man which constitutes the core of his philosophy. In fact, it is precisely because Jaspers and Heidegger have basically ignored this dualism that they can arrive at two *radically different* interpretations. Certain aspects of these interpretations are so starkly in opposition, that one sometimes wonders if they are both talking about the same philosopher. One of the best illustrations of this opposition is to be found in a comparison between Heidegger's derivation of truth from *homoiosis* and Jaspers' explication of truth as contradiction in the form of vicious circularity. Heidegger seizes on the metaphysical or cosmological pole of the dualism, and Jaspers on the pole of philosophical anthropology. For Heidegger, all of Nietzsche's philosophy can be subsumed under metaphysics and, for Jaspers, what cannot be subsumed under philosophical anthropology is either aberrant, or more or less irrelevant.

It is interesting that both Heidegger and Jaspers implicitly recognize this dualism, as we saw in the course of our analysis; but because of the initial biases which condition their interpretations, neither of them goes on to explore its ramifications. In their own way, each of their interpretations points to the need for a recognition of this fundamental dualism. This shows up in terms of the consequences of ignoring or denying this dialectical interplay between the cosmological and the anthropological perspectives. Consider, for example, Jaspers' emphasis on philosophical anthropology. From his discussions it is clear that, even though he often does not agree with Nietzsche, Jaspers has great respect for Nietzsche's powers of insight and his ability to push the analysis of a problem to its most primordial foundations. Yet, at the same time, his interpretation necessitates accepting the idea that Nietzsche's metaphysical insights are naive to the point of self-refutation. This is a difficult view to accept, and in terms of the thesis of the dualism it is not necessary to accept it. However, one might ask in defense of Jaspers, if Jaspers is so naive as not to see this dualism in Nietzsche's thought. And, of course, the answer is that Jaspers is not naive. We have already pointed out that he does recognize the dualism, but he does not develop it. The reasons for this are to be found in Jaspers' own philosophical position and his rejection of Nietzsche's non-traditional notion of TRANSCENDENCE.

Heidegger's "resolution" of the dualism in terms of metaphysics is equally unsatisfactory. His "metaphysicalization" of Nietzsche leaves one in a quandary regarding large and significant sections of Nietzsche's thought. This is in part due to an over-reaction on Heidegger's part against the previous interpretations of Nietzsche as a life-philosopher, a value philosopher, or a philosopher-poet. Certainly there is just cause for Heidegger's reaction, but the extremism of his reaction tends to cast the whole dimension of philosophical anthropology into limbo. As a result, Heidegger's interpretation is not only one-sided, but is misleading as well. Let us, therefore, take a retrospective look at Nietzsche's philosophy in terms of the thesis of the dualism presented by the opposition of the perspectives of cosmology and philosophical anthropology in an attempt to discover the significance and the ramifications of this thesis for interpreting Nietzsche.

NIETZSCHE'S METAPHYSICS AND EPISTEMOLOGY

In the metaphysics and epistemology of Nietzsche, there are two problems which lead to the thesis of a fundamental dualism – the problem of truth and the problem of Eternal Recurrence. Nietzsche's statement that all truths are fictions (perspectives of *anthropos*) leads either to vicious circularity or else to a distinction between levels. That is to say, either the statement itself is a fiction, in which case we have a paradox, or else the statement is a meta-truth which does not apply to itself. We have already examined some of the arguments against accepting it as a paradox and have seen some of the advantages of accepting it as a meta-truth or TRUTH. On reflection, we can see that the acceptance of the paradox is absolutely disastrous with regard to Nietzsche's metaphysics, for then his fundamental doctrines of Being as Becoming, the Will to Power as Becoming, the doctrine of Transvaluation as the means to the Superman – all of this and much more would be reduced to fictions and would create more paradoxes. If, however, we accept the notion of a TRUTH that is not fiction, then we are faced with the question as to how this difference in levels is possible, for the level of TRUTH has to be one which is not within the perspectives of life. The answer must be that there is a possibility inherent in the human being for adopting a perspective which is opposed to the perspectives of life. This is the cosmological perspective which we have described as TRANSCENDENCE because of its opposition to the perspectives of life. There is nothing new or radically mystical about this perspective; it has been with us since man first began to philosophize. The French biologist Rostand states the vision of this perspective in an especially powerful way.

The human species will disappear. Little by little the small star which is our sun will lose its lightening and warming force. Then, of all this human and superhuman civilization, these discoveries, philosophies, ideals, religions, nothing will subsist. In this minuscule corner of the universe, the pale adventure of the protoplasm will be eliminated forever – the adventure which perhaps is finished already in other worlds and may be renewed in another world, which is everywhere supported by the same illusions, creating the same tortures, everywhere equally absurd and vain, everywhere promised final failure and infinite darkness from the start.[1]

This is the perspective opposed to life and it is contained in the essential nature of man. Its mere acceptance results in radical nihilism which, for Nietzsche, must be overcome. The nullity revealed by the thought of death becomes a double reflection and gives a new significance to life and leads to Nietzsche's notion of the "eternalization" of the moment. For Nietzsche, the cosmological perspective must not result in a stagnation and resignation, but rather should establish a dialogue with life which reveals not only its transitoriness, but its beauty and meaning as well. In *The Joyful Wisdom* Nietzsche observes (in a section called "The Thought of Death") that men do not want to think of death. Nietzsche regards this as good and states his wish that men would devote their attentions to life.

It gives me a melancholy happiness to live in the midst of this confusion of streets, of necessities, of voices: how much enjoyment, impatience and desire, how much thirsty life and drunkenness of life comes to light here every moment! And yet it will soon be so still for all these shouting, lively, life-loving people! How everyone's shadow, his gloomy travelling-companion stands behind him! It is always as in the last moment before the departure of an emigrant-ship:

---

[1] Rostand quoted in Wilfrid Desan, *The Tragic Finale* (New York, 1960), p. 2.

people have more than ever to say to one another, the hour presses, the ocean with its lonely silence waits impatiently behind all the noise – so greedy, so certain of its prey! And all, all, suppose that the past has been nothing or a small matter, that the near future is everything: hence this haste, this crying, this self-deafening and self-overreaching! Everyone wants to be foremost in this future, – and yet death and the stillness of death are the only things certain and common to all in this future! How strange that this sole thing that is certain and common to all, exercises almost no influence on men, and that they are the *furthest* from regarding themselves as the brotherhood of death! It makes me happy to see that men do not want to think at all of the idea of death! I would fain do something to make the idea of life even a hundred times *more worthy of their attention*.[2]

This passage is especially important in two ways. First of all, it emphasizes Nietzsche's central focus on life and its celebration. Secondly, it underscores the finality of the vision of the cosmological perspective that "death and the stillness of death are the only things certain and common to all in this future!" This is consistent with Nietzsche's view that ultimately life is tragic, that woven into the fabric of life is the terrifying aspect of death, but this too must be finally affirmed. This view is one that Nietzsche held throughout his active life and in 1888 he wrote the following:

The *profundity of the tragic artist* lies in this, that his aesthetic instinct surveys the more remote consequences, that he does not halt shortsightedly at what is closest at hand, that he affirms the *large-scale economy* which justifies the *terrifying*, the *evil*, the *questionable* – and more than merely justifies them.[3]

It is at this point that we arrive at the full significance of Nietzsche's thesis that art is higher than truth. In knowledge and action man is always limited by the perspectives of his existence. His highest creative act is not the pursuit of truth, but the attempt to create himself as a work of art. This for Nietzsche is the source of redemption – not a redemption "beyond" life, but a redemption *within* life itself. In 1886 he wrote,

Art as the *redemption of the man of knowledge* – of those who see the terrifying and questionable character of existence, who want to see it, the men of tragic knowledge.

Art as the *redemption of the man of action* – of those who not only see the terrifying and questionable character of existence but live it, want to live it, the tragic-warlike man, the hero.[4]

For Nietzsche, the rejection of all traditional forms of transcendence is a necessity, for only through this rejection is it possible for man to

---

[2] Nietzsche, *The Joyful Wisdom*, pp. 215–16.
[3] Nietzsche, *The Will to Power*, p. 451.
[4] *Ibid.*, p. 452.

appropriate life for himself and create himself as the highest expression of the Will to Power. From all of this, it seems justified to argue that there is rooted in Nietzsche's theory of man the irreconcilable dualism between the cosmological perspective and the perspectives of philosophical anthropology.

This leaves us with the problem of accounting for the metaphysical or literal version of the doctrine of Eternal Recurrence. As we have seen, neither Jaspers' interpretation nor Heidegger's can convincingly account for this aspect of Nietzsche's philosophy. It is important here to remember that Nietzsche himself is ambivalent about this doctrine and even goes so far as to say that it may not be true – "Let others wrestle with it." In terms of the thesis of the irreconcilable dualism in the nature of man, an explanation comes immediately to the fore, namely, that the metaphysical doctrine of Eternal Recurrence is the attempt to reconcile the two poles of the dualism. However, the only possibility for such a "reconciliation" is a doctrine of transcendence. Jaspers is quite right in pointing out that Nietzsche's thought does at times push out in this direction. To the very end, however, Nietzsche continues to reject the traditional forms of transcendence. The impulse toward transcendence, toward the absolute, is far from mysterious. Nietzsche accounts for it in his discussion of the perspectives of philosophical anthropology. Man has the urgent need to discover some absolute foundation which justifies and gives permanence to his existence. He has the desperate desire to see himself as somehow central to the issues of the cosmos. For Nietzsche, philosophy is no mere intellectual game; it is the most intense involvement with existence itself. Thus, it is not only not surprising that Nietzsche himself experienced this impulse toward the absolute, it is a revelation of the depths of his experience of the human condition. Nietzsche recognizes this impulse in himself and calls it the "longing for eternity." "All joy wants deep profound eternity." This is the source of Nietzsche's desire to reconcile the irreconcilable. From the standpoint of ontology only, excluding any theological dimensions, the metaphysical doctrine of Eternal Recurrence demands a doctrine of Being as transcendence which would not only introduce paradoxes into Nietzsche's metaphysics, but would raise questions about the "scientific" nature of his presuppositions as well.

There are five advantages to interpreting Nietzsche in terms of this thesis of an irreconcilable dualism grounded in his theory of man. (1) This thesis eliminates unnecessary paradoxes in Nietzsche's philosophy as a whole and presents a more coherent view of the relationships between the various doctrines. (2) This interpretive approach explains Nietzsche's self-admitted ambivalence toward the doctrine of Eternal Recurrence. (3) It also accounts for the origin of the metaphysical version of Eternal Recurrence in such a way as to remain consistent with Nietzsche's rejection of the traditional doctrines of transcendence. (4) This thesis transforms the meaning of the anthropological version of Eternal Recurrence in such a way as to make it of even greater significance. (5) The thesis of a dualism, both poles of which are grounded in the essence of man himself, provides the basis for the notion of a dialectic which grasps the essentially dynamic character of Nietzsche's philosophizing. In fact, it is only in terms of such a notion of dialectic that the full meaning of the Transvaluation of all values can be grasped.

NIETZSCHE'S PHILOSOPHICAL ANTHROPOLOGY

With regard to Nietzsche's philosophical anthropology, there are two major interpretive problems – Transvaluation and Eternal Recurrence as a doctrine of the "eternalization" of the moment. In both Jaspers' and Heidegger's interpretations it is difficult to understand the workings of Transvaluation. If, however, we accept the thesis of the dualism, then the general outlines of the dialectic of Transvaluation become visible. The confrontation with the TRUTH revealed by the cosmological perspective creates a new significance for life through the transformation of the meaning of time. T. S. Eliot expresses this insight regarding time in the first of his *Four Quartets*.

If all time is eternally present
All time is unredeemable.
What might have been is an abstraction
Remaining a perpetual possibility
Only in a world of speculation.[5]

Nietzsche's demand is that one not live in a "world of speculation." The past takes on its significance because we appropriate it and affirm it; we *Will* it to have been thus. If "all time is unredeemable" then we must create in the present in the fullest and highest manner of which we are capable. However, Nietzsche's celebration of the present, the "eternalization" of the moment, is not a doctrine of hedonism.

---

[5] T. S. Eliot, *Four Quartets* (New York, 1943), p. 3.

There is a radical distinction between the ecstatic affirmation of existence and the pursuit of pleasure. The pursuit of pleasure is directed outside of oneself in that its satisfaction depends on externals which define one's situation. Nietzsche's conception of affirmation, however, comes from the inner depths of the individual himself. For Nietzsche, pleasure can never be the goal of existence; the goal is self-overcoming and the attempt to realize one's possibilities in the richest way. This goal is determined by the dialectical opposition of the perspectives of cosmology and life. The highest *art* of living is to create for oneself as many moments as possible that one would be *willing* to live again and again. This is the anthropological significance of Eternal Recurrence. To live a life dominated by this vision would be to demand continuously the very best of which one is capable. To Nietzsche this "aesthetic" of existence is the only possible "justification" for life.

In terms of the dialectic demanded by the dualism of perspectives the dynamic character of the doctrine of the Superman receives a new emphasis. Man, as the "not-yet fixated animal," will, as long as his species survives, be in the process of self-definition. There will always be something in man which must be overcome. Nietzsche fully realized that human advancement is an erratic thing. He even points out that in spite of man's cleverness and inventiveness, he has not yet sufficiently matured to "humanize" his technological creations. He also realized that every age will have its "sacred" beliefs, its "new" absolutes to restrict and suppress creativity. In every age it will be a fundamental TRUTH that "the Superman has not yet arrived."

The doctrines of Eternal Recurrence (anthropologically considered) and Transvaluation are Nietzsche's answer to radical nihilism. It is an answer of tragic strength. Nietzsche had little sympathy for those who indulge in self-pity. For Nietzsche, those who do not have the strength to face the TRUTH of their existence, just pass away and are forgotten, for they are the despisers of life, the poisoners who want to keep man enslaved through doctrines of a better life "beyond." This is the meaning of Nietzsche's conceptions of "breeding" and "annihilation;" namely, the overcoming of the despisers of life and the creation of conditions which will demand the strength to create values in the face of one's own finitude. Consider the figure of Oedipus had he bemoaned his fate. His fellow citizens would soon have come to regard him as irritating and troublesome. Only by accepting his fate with dignity could he maintain his tragic dimension and keep it from degenerating into something merely pathetic. For Nietzsche, only through *amor fati* is it possible for man to retain his dignity and create for himself a tragic, but noble existence. Nietzsche firmly believes that if man cannot do this, then he deserves to succumb. If mankind can preserve itself only as the "last men," then it is better that such a species does not survive.

For Nietzsche, doctrines of transcendence are flights from the TRUTH which is revealed to us by the cosmological perspective and are, thereby, flights from life as well. The thesis of the dualism helps us to understand Nietzsche's criticism of doctrines of transcendence as a form of *hybris*. Nietzsche argues that notions of transcendence are designed to give man a special place in the cosmos as though creation had taken place for his benefit. At the same time such doctrines rob man of his dignity and freedom by legislating his act. This claim to special significance within the cosmos Nietzsche unreservedly brands as *hybris*. His own conception of the Superman, he believes, escapes the charge, for in the dialectic of Transvaluation there is always the opposing cosmological perspective to balance man's view of himself and crush his conceit and arrogance. For Nietzsche, man's only possible claim to dignity is grounded in the possibility of self-creating and self-overcoming in the face of his recognition of his own finitude – an insight which is revealed to him through the cosmological perspective.

THE QUESTION OF TELOS

At first glance it may seem odd to attempt to apply the notion of telos to the thinking of Nietzsche, Heidegger, and Jaspers. However, the term will serve our purposes here if we understand it primarily in the sense of a "direction" of thought without presupposing a closed philosophical system. In Jaspers' philosophy it is not difficult to discern the telos. Jaspers' thinking moves quite explicitly toward transcendence through *Existenz* which is itself graspable only in relation to transcendence. Thus, very roughly, we might say that the telos of Jaspers' thought is the authentic self-apprehension of *Existenz* by means of a dual understanding: an understanding of *Existenz* in relation to its world and an understanding of *Existenz* itself as an aspect of transcendence which stands related to the world. No matter how ambiguous one may regard the central concepts in Jaspers' philosophy, it is clear that Jaspers himself conceives of them as moving in a very definite direction.

With regard to Nietzsche and Heidegger the situation is much more complex. For both thinkers, as we move toward their later thought, the major problem becomes that of Time. Nietzsche wrestles with the problem of Time in two apparently opposed ways. Time as Eternal Recurrence understood from the standpoint of cosmology stands opposed to the perspectives of philosophical anthropology especially as presented in the doctrine of *amor fati*. We have already discussed how Nietzsche himself was pulled first toward one pole and then toward the other. We further noted that this opposition, which is rooted in the very constitution of man himself, is the fundamental motive force for dialectic within Nietzsche's thought. We can now see that the crucial turning point of this dialectic is the concept of Time. The passion for the eternal must confront the recognition of finitude and this confrontation produces what Nietzsche regards as the greatest torment of human existence and yet, at the same time, the greatest joy. For Nietzsche this dialectic cannot be overcome and the attempt to escape from it by accepting only one pole and ignoring the other results in disaster. To succumb to the passion for the eternal means that one must create absolutes – illusions which can only be maintained at immense spiritual cost and which are, in Nietzsche's view, ultimately life-negating. On the other hand, to succumb to the recognition of one's own finitude and annihilation results in Hamlet's condition (as Nietzsche interprets it in *The Birth of Tragedy*) where the grasping of cosmological TRUTH reduces him to inaction, since all action seems equally absurd and futile. Nietzsche regards both of these extremes as Nihilism. A fixation at either of these poles is life-destroying and denies the possibility of the dialectical movement which Nietzsche believes can be achieved through art. In art, the Dionysian TRUTH of annihilation is fused with the Apollonian deception of permanent form to create something higher than either – *myth!* Thus the attempt at a Dionysian-Apollonian synthesis through art is at the same time the attempt at a metaphysical synthesis of Heraclitus and Parmenides. *Amor fati* becomes Nietzsche's last great attempt at the fusion of two poles which he knows to be ultimately irreconcilable. There is a profound metaphysical irony in the concept of *amor fati*, because its most profound meaning must ultimately be to will one's own annihilation by creating "eternal" moments. That Nietzsche realized the final impossibility of such a fusion – an ecstatic despair – is clear, for he says that there never has been and never shall be a Superman precisely because the dialectic itself can never be overcome; only man at a particular stage can be overcome. In order to communicate this vision,

Nietzsche turns to myth – the myth of the Superman who in the end is transformed into Dionysus and even at this level of myth, the dialectic is still operative. Nietzsche presents the opposition of Dionysus and the "Crucified."

Dionysus versus the "Crucified": there you have the antithesis. It is *not* a difference in regard to their martyrdom – it is a difference in the meaning of it. Life itself, its eternal fruitfulness and recurrence, creates torment, destruction, the will to annihilation. In the other case, suffering – the "Crucified as the innocent one" – counts as an objection to this life, as a formula for its condemnation. – One will see that the problem is that of the meaning of suffering: whether a Christian meaning or a tragic meaning. In the former case, it is supposed to be the path to a holy existence; in the latter case, being is counted as *holy enough* to justify even a monstrous amount of suffering. The tragic man affirms even the harshest suffering: he is sufficiently strong, rich, and capable of deifying to do so. The Christian denies even the happiest lot on earth: he is sufficiently weak, poor, disinherited to suffer from life in whatever form he meets it. The god on the cross is a curse on life, a signpost to seek redemption from life; Dionysus cut to pieces is a *promise* of life: it will be eternally reborn and return again from destruction.[6]

This passage was written in 1888 and it is significant that at this late period Nietzsche returns with such intensity to the theme of myth and the manner in which he executes this "recurrence" is even more significant. In the passage above, in reference to the Dionysian, he speaks of being "capable of deifying." After our lengthy discussions concerning Nietzsche's attacks on transcendence, this phrase might seem to suggest a reversal in Nietzsche's position. There is, however, no such reversal. We can perhaps best understand Nietzsche's return by reminding ourselves of some of his earliest remarks on myth in *The Birth of Tragedy*. In discussing the myth of the capture of Silenus by King Midas, Nietzsche presents, through the wisdom of Silenus, a statement of the cosmological perspective.

Oh, wretched ephemeral race, children of chance and misery, why do you compel me to tell you what it would be most expedient for you not to hear? What is best of all is utterly beyond your reach: not to be born, not to *be*, to be *nothing*. But the second best for you is – to die soon.[7]

This, of course, is the terrible Dionysian TRUTH that the dualism in man's very constitution permits him to encounter. But this cosmological TRUTH produced its dialectical reaction *within* the perspectives of philosophical anthropology and by this means all of the suffering, "the overwhelming dismay in the face of the titanic power of nature, the Moira enthroned inexorably over all knowledge," the terror of

---

[6] Nietzsche, *The Will to Power*, pp. 542–43.
[7] Nietzsche, *The Birth of Tragedy*, p. 42.

transitoriness; "all this was again and again overcome by the Greeks with the aid of the Olympian *middle world* of art; or at any rate it was veiled and withdrawn from sight." [8] Thus the Olympian gods evolved out of an existential necessity and they justified the life of man by living it themselves. This, Nietzsche argues, reversed the wisdom of Silenus and the wisdom of the hero, the tragic man, is transformed to read "to die soon is the worst of all for them, the next worst – to die at all." [9] Here already we see the "longing for the eternal" and the seeds for the myth of Eternal Recurrence. The question now arises as to why we should speak of Eternal Recurrence as a myth. In a later section of the same book Nietzsche defines myth as "a concentrated image of the world that, as a condensation of phenomena, cannot dispense with miracles." [10] He then adds:

> The images of the myth have to be the unnoticed omnipresent demonic guardians, under whose care the young soul grows to maturity and whose signs help the man to interpret his life and struggles. Even the state knows no more powerful unwritten laws than the mythical foundation that guarantees its connection with religion and its growth from mythical notions.[11]

We are now in a position to draw some important conclusions. It should now be clear that the capacity for "deifying" which Nietzsche speaks of, is inseparably bound up with myth and its creations are produced to serve life; that is, they are affirmations of existence and they transform the Dionysian terror into Apollonian beauty. Thus the deifying function of myth, as Nietzsche conceives it, remains authentic only insofar as its creations are anthropomorphic and life-enriching. When myth moves to realms "beyond" the perspectives of philosophical anthropology and posits a transcendence, then it betrays life. Furthermore, the Superman as a goal (or telos) toward whom the longing of our arrows is fixed is perfectly consistent with Nietzsche's conception of myth, for the Superman is never finally realizable since no matter how far man progresses, there always remain aspects of the self to be yet overcome. Nietzsche's gradual transformation of the Superman into the figure of Dionysus underscores even more emphatically the ceaseless dialectic of self-overcoming.

The myth of Eternal Recurrence becomes the guiding force in the movement of the dialectic toward the telos of the Superman or the

---

[8] *Ibid.*, p. 42.
[9] *Ibid.*, p. 43.
[10] *Ibid.*, p. 135.
[11] *Ibid.*, p. 135.

Dionysian man. Modern man, too, must live in the "middle world of art" and transform himself into the highest work of art by attempting to transform his very existence into the ritual of the myth. But for modern man this middle world cannot be the world of the Olympians. At this point it becomes clear that Nietzsche is not advocating a Romantic flight into the past, a return to the old Hellas. Nietzsche aims toward the future, towards the transformation of man himself and the conditions of his existence, so that man can produce something that can truly be called "Culture." This process cannot ignore science and technology, but must rather humanize them. This is the aim of Nietzsche's "Great Politics" – a Culture in which science and technology are given a *human* telos by means of the myths of Eternal Recurrence and the figure of the Dionysus-Superman. Such a task creates the necessity for the doctrine of the Transvaluation of all values, thus bringing all the major doctrines of Nietzsche's philosophy into harmony through the use of myth, since the Will to Power is the force that must affect the Transvaluation to open the path for the movement toward the Dionysus-Superman.

The recognition of the urgency of such a re-orientation of human culture is something which Heidegger and Nietzsche share. Nietzsche does not view the problem in terms of optimism or pessimism, but rather in terms of a radical Either/Or. Either man transforms himself and creates a new meaning for himself or else he does not deserve to survive as a species. Heidegger's view regarding the urgency of reversing man's spiritual degeneration is strikingly similar to Nietzsche's.

The spiritual decline of the earth is so far advanced that the nations are in danger of losing the last bit of spiritual energy that makes it possible to see the decline (taken in relation to the history of "being") and to appraise it as such. This simple observation has nothing to do with *Kultur-pessimismus*, and of course it has nothing to do with any sort of optimism either; for the darkening of the world, the flight of the gods, the destruction of the earth, the transformation of men into a mass, the hatred and suspicion of everything free and creative, have assumed such proportions throughout the earth that such childish categories as pessimism and optimism have long since become absurd.[12]

One is also reminded here of Nietzsche's passage on "the last men" in *Thus Spake Zarathustra*. Not only are the diagnoses similar, but the suggestions as to the directions in which man must move in order to overcome this decline seem to be parallel. Heidegger here speaks of the

---

[12] Heidegger, *Introduction to Metaphysics*, p. 38.

"flight of the gods" and elsewhere adds that we live in an age when the old gods have taken flight and the new gods have not yet arrived. Thus, Heidegger too turns unmistakably toward myth and when he turns to the themes of man's poetically dwelling upon the earth in essays on Hölderlin and man's striving to move into the openness of Being in his work on Rilke, we begin to get a clearer indication of the direction of Heidegger's project for the "overcoming of metaphysics." This mytho-poetic concern takes on even more definite form when Heidegger develops his notion of the Quadrate or "foursome" (*das Geviert*) in the essay *Bauen Wohnen Denken* (*Working, Dwelling, Thinking*). This "foursome" is: earth, gods, sky, and mortals. It is at this point that we can consider the suggestion made in the previous chapter regarding the possibility of an alternative interpretation of Heidegger's work that would make Nietzsche's charge of transcendence inapplicable. This is especially important in light of the fact that a number of Heidegger's more recent interpreters view his position as a "philosophy of immanence" rather than transcendence. The grounds for this interpretation become evident when we consider Heidegger's insistence that Being is not a principle or a "ground" for the world, that Being is the "nearest to man yet the farthest," that the possibility for bringing Being out of "hiddenness" into the "open" is omnipresent, and that the Being-question is something which man himself can "exist" in his "dwelling" upon the earth. We might then hazard the following suggestion; namely, that Heidegger, like Nietzsche, driven to the very limits of language and representational conceptualization moves toward mytho-poetic thinking in order to communicate the "overcoming" or the transcendence-immanence dichotomy. Thus, it might be argued, that every attempt to do a static analysis of the mytho-poetic "constructs," which are designed to convey this "overcoming" necessarily reveal components which suggest transcendence and others which suggest immanence. This would mean that only within the flow of the mytho-poetic thinking itself could the proper synthesis take place which would authentically communicate the essential insights.

Such a view is, however, unsatisfactory for three reasons. (1) The above position implicitly lays claim to an immunity from criticism in the manner previously presented in the passage by J. Glenn Gray. (2) There is a difficulty with regard to the unquestionably unique and sometimes eccentric development of Heidegger's mytho-poetic thinking which leads one to inquire into how many of Heidegger's *Holzwege* are indeed "paths which don't lead anywhere." An attempt to imitate

Heidegger's kind of poetizing-thinking is an invitation to the disaster of unintelligibility. Heidegger's attempts to communicate in this manner are provocative partly due to their being grounded in the work of great poets such as Rilke and Hölderlin, but perhaps even more importantly are due to the extraordinary mind of Heidegger himself, the uniqueness and isolation of which leave an unmistakable imprint on all that he produces. In his poetizing-thinking Heidegger has isolated himself more and more from the traditional modes of philosophical thought and, while this, in itself, is not an objection to his project, he has not provided much help in gaining access to the realm of these later investigations. Furthermore, Heidegger has seemingly made little effort to provide a "gathering-together" of the various facets of his explorations in the realm of THOUGHT. His probings into Rilke and Hölderlin, his "return" to the Greeks, the endless "linguistic" circumambulations suggest a Dante without a Virgil. (3) As we observed before, in Heidegger's most recent writings there is a further development which leads to the notion of the "overcoming of overcoming" or, alternately stated, a further transformation of his THOUGHT which isolates it even more fully from the previous connections with traditional philosophy. There is a significant sense in which his latest works point to an "abandonment" or final radical separation from Western metaphysics and an attempt to return to fundamental ontology through poetizing-thinking. There is a growing affinity between Heidegger's later works and certain modes of Oriental thought. Richardson, for example, points out a parallel between Heidegger's notion of the Quadrate or "foursome" and a similar notion in the works of Laotse.[13] There is, however, an even more important parallel here, for the thought of Taoism is non-dialectical in character and Heidegger seems to be moving in that direction. Heidegger's use of mytho-poetic thinking is certainly different from Nietzsche's concern with myth, for Heidegger does not invest it with the dialectical significance of cultural transformation. Heidegger, like the Taoist, moves more and more into an inner realm of THOUGHT which takes precedence over all of the social, political and cultural considerations. *Thus, Heidegger's last "overcoming" is ultimately an attempt to overcome dialectic itself! The final consequence of this is that Heidegger's THOUGHT has no telos!* Heidegger's "nonassertive assertion" that "the appropriating event events by appropriating" seems extremely remote as a response to his recognition of the

---

[13] Richardson, Heidegger: *Through Phenomenology to Thought*, p. 571.

urgency of the need for significant response in order to reverse the spiritual decline which he himself diagnosed so eloquently earlier.

It should now be apparent that even though there are some significant parallels between the philosophies of Jaspers, Heidegger and Nietzsche the paths which they finally take are radically divergent. Which of these three paths, if any, will prove to be most valuable in contributing to the humanizing of future culture cannot be determined in advance. What is clear is that any one of the three could provide a meaningful new direction for the evolution of the human spirit.

SOME CONCLUDING REMARKS

It is not the function of interpretation to render its subject immune from criticism and, in any case, Nietzsche needs no apologist. However, it is the responsibility of interpretation to explicate its subject in such a way as to bring out its fullest significance. There is much that can be criticized in Nietzsche and many perspectives from which such an enterprise can be undertaken. However, an age which has heaped so much blame on Nietzsche and has perversely distorted so many of his ideas owes him a fair hearing. The thesis of the fundamental dualism in Nietzsche's thought is here presented as an insight which has that aim in mind. The insights we have gained in our analyses present the outline for an interpretation of Nietzsche which is an attempt to understand his philosophy in his own terms. No interpretation can be completely unbiased, but obvious biases and distortions must be eliminated. In fact, an interpretation which does not critically examine its own standpoint is always in danger of reading its own presuppositions into its subject.

There is no fear that anyone will have "the last word" about Nietzsche. For Nietzsche, philosophy itself is process and it becomes dogmatic only at the cost of undermining itself. The dialogue that is genuine philosophy pushes man to the limits of his self-understanding. This is the dialogue between cosmology and anthropology. Man can attain a cosmic perspective "beyond" and opposed to life – a perspective which reveals to him that Becoming has no absolute values or goals. The metaphysics of the Will to Power is neutral value-wise; the cosmos neither values nor dis-values man. However, man as a specific individualized manifestation of the Will to Power must exist in terms of evaluation and so there arises an unbridgeable gap between his cosmic perspective and his "existential" perspectives – a gap that Nietzsche himself was at times tempted to try to bridge. It was perhaps this very temptation which Nietzsche was thinking about when he had Zarathustra say:

How lovely it is that there are words and sounds! Are not words and sounds rainbows and illusive bridges between things which are eternally apart?

To every soul there belongs another world; for every soul, every other soul, is an afterworld. Precisely between what is most similar, illusion lies most beautifully; for the smallest cleft is the hardest to bridge.[14]

[14] Nietzsche, *Zarathustra*, p. 329.

BIBLIOGRAPHY

NIETZSCHE'S WORKS

Nietzsche, Friedrich Wilhelm. *Beyond Good and Evil: Prelude to a Philosophy of the Future*. Translated by Walter Kaufmann. New York: Random House, Inc., 1966.

— *The Birth of Tragedy and The Case of Wagner*. Translated by Walter Kaufmann. New York: Random House, Inc., 1967.

— *The Complete Works of Friedrich Nietzsche*. Vol. I: *The Birth of Tragedy*. Translated by William A. Haussmann. Vol. II: *Early Greek Philosophy and Other Essays*. Translated by M. A. Mügge. Vol. III: *The Future of Our Educational Institutions*. Translated by J. M. Kennedy. Vol. IV: *Thoughts Out of Season, Part I*. Translated by A. M. Ludovici. Vol. V: *Thoughts Out of Season, Part II*. Translated by Adrian Collins. Vol. VI: *Human, All Too Human, Part I*. Translated by Helen Zimmern. Vol. VII: *Human, All Too Human, Part II*. Translated by Paul V. Cohn. Vol. VIII: *The Case of Wagner*. Translated by A. M. Ludovici. Vol. IX: *The Dawn of Day*. Translated by J. M. Kennedy. Vol. X: *The Joyful Wisdom*. Translated by Thomas Common. Vol. XI: *Thus Spake Zarathustra*. Translated by Thomas Common. Vol. XII: *Beyond Good and Evil*. Translated by Helen Zimmern. Vol. XIII: *The Genealogy of Morals*. Translated by Horace B. Samuel. Vol. XIV: *The Will to Power, Part I*. Translated by A. M. Ludovici. Vol. XV: *The Will to Power, Part II*. Translated by A. M. Ludovici. Vol. XVI: *The Twilight of the Idols*. Translated by A. M. Ludovici. Vol. XVII: *Ecce Homo and Poetry*. Translated by A. M. Ludovici. Vol. XVIII: *Index to Works*. Compiled by Robert Guppy. Edited by Oscar Levy. New York: Russell and Russell, Inc., 1964.

— *On the Genealogy of Morals and Ecce Homo*. Translated by Walter Kaufmann. New York: Random House, Inc., 1967.

— *Philosophy in the Tragic Age of the Greeks*. Translated by Marianne Cowan. Chicago: Henry Regnery Company, 1962.

— *The Philosophy of Nietzsche. Thus Spake Zarathustra*. Transeated by Thomas Common. *Beyond Good and Evil*. Translated by Helen Zimmlrn. *The Genealogy of Morals*. Translated by Horace B. Samuel. *Ecce Homo*. Translated by Clifton P. Fadiman. *The Birth of Tragedy from the Spirit of Music*. Translated by Clifton P. Fadiman. Edited by Willard Huntington Wright. New York: Random House, Inc., 1954.

— *The Portable Nietzsche. Letter to His Sister. Fragment of a Critique of Schopenhauer. On Ethics. Note* (1870–71). From *Homer's Contest. Notes* (1873). From *On Truth and Lie in an Extra-Moral Sense. Notes about Wagner. Notes* (1874). *Notes* (1875). From *Human, All-Too-Human*. From *Mixed Opinions and Maxims*. From *The Wanderer and His Shadow. Letter to Overbeck. Notes* (1880–

81). From *The Dawn. Postcard to Overbeck.* From *The Gay Science. Draft of a Letter to Paul Ree. Thus Spoke Zarathustra. Note* (1884). *Letter to Overbeck. Letter to His Sister. Letter to Overbeck. Notes.* From *a Draft for a Preface.* From *Beyond Good and Evil.* From *The Gay Science:* Book V. From *Toward a Genealogy of Morals. Letter to Overbeck. Notes* (1887). *Letter to His Sister. Notes* (1888). From *The Wagner Case. Twilight of the Idols. The Antichrist.* From *Ecce Homo. Nietzsche contra Wagner. Letter to Gast. Letter to Jacob Burckhardt. Letter to Overbeck.* Selected and translated, with an introduction, prefaces, and notes, by Walter Kaufmann. New York: The Viking Press, Inc., 1967.

— *Schopenhauer as Educator.* Translated by James W. Hillesheim and Malcolm R. Simpson. Chicago: Henry Regnery Company, 1965.

— *The Use and Abuse of History.* Translated by Adrian Collins. Indianapolis: The Bobbs-Merrill Company, Inc., 1957.

— *Vorspiel einer Philosophie der Zukunft: Aus dem Nachlass.* Edited by Karl Löwith. Frankfurt am Main: Fischer Bücherei, 1959.

— *Werke in drei Bänden.* Vol. I: *Die Geburt der Tragödie. Unzeitgemässe Betrachtungen. Menschliches, Allzumenschliches. Morgenröte.* Vol. II: *Die fröhliche Wissenschaft. Also sprach Zarathustra. Jenseits von Gut und Böse. Zur Genealogie der Moral. Der Fall Wagner. Götzen-Dämmerung. Nietzsche contra Wagner. Ecce homo. Der Antichrist. Dionysos-Dithyramben.* Vol. III: *Autobiographisches aus den Jahren 1856–1859. Homer und die klassische Philologie. Über die Zukunft unserer Bildungs-Anstalten. Fünf Vorreden zu fünf ungeschriebenen Büchern. Ein Neujahrswort an den Herausgeber der Wochenschrift "Im neuen Reich." Mahnruf an die Deutschen. Über Wahrheit und Lüge im aussermoralischen Sinn. Wir Philologen. Wissenschaft und Weisheit im Kampfe. Die Philosophie im tragischen Zeitalter der Griechen. Aus dem Nachlass der Achtzigerjahre. Briefe.* Edited by Karl Schlechta. Munich: Carl Hanser Verlag, 1954.

— *The Will to Power.* Translated by Walter Kaufmann and R. J. Hollingdale. New York: Random House, Inc., 1967.

WORKS ON NIETZSCHE

Danto, Arthur C. *Nietzsche as Philosopher.* New York: Macmillan Company, 1965.

Gould, George M. "Nietzsche," in *Biographic Clinics.* 4 vols.; Philadelphia: P. Blakiston's Son and Co., 1904, II, 285–322.

Hamburger, Michael. *From Exorcism to Prophecy: The Premisses of Modern German Literature.* London: Longmans, Green and Co., Ltd., 1965.

Heidegger, Martin. *Nietzsche.* 2 vols. Pfüllingen: Verlag Günther Neske, 1961.

— "Nietzsches Wort 'Gott ist tot'," in *Holzwege.* Frankfurt am Main: Vittorio Kostermann, 1957, pp. 193–247.

— "Who Is Nietzsche's Zarathustra?," in *The Review of Metaphysics,* Vol. XX, no. 3. Translated by Bernard Magnus. New York: Harper and Row Publishers, March 1967, pp. 411–431.

Huneker, James. "Phases of Nietzsche," in *Egoists: A Book of Supermen.* New York: Charles Scribner's Sons, 1910, pp. 236–68.

Jaspers, Karl. *Nietzsche: An Introduction to the Understanding of His Philosophical Activity.* Translated by Charles F. Wallraff and Frederick J. Schmitz. Tucson: The University of Arizona Press, 1966.

— *Nietzsche and Christianity.* Translated by E. B. Ashton. Chicago: Henry Regnery Company, 1967.

Kaufmann, Walter. *Nietzsche: Philosopher, Psychologist, Antichrist*. New York: The World Publishing Company, 1966.

— "Jaspers' Relation to Nietzsche," in *The Philosophy of Karl Jaspers*. "The Library of Living Philosophers," New York: Tudor Publishing Company, 1957, pp. 407–36.

Love, Frederick R. *Young Nietzsche and the Wagnerian Experience*. "Studies in the Germanic Languages and Literatures," Vol. 39. Chapel Hill: University of North Carolina Press, 1963.

Salter, William Mackintire. *Nietzsche the Thinker: A Study*. New York: Henry Holt and Company, 1917.

Santayana, George. "Nietzsche and Schopenhauer," in *Egotism in German Philosophy*. New York: Charles Scribner's Sons, n.d., pp. 114–22.

Werkmeister, William Henry. "Nietzsche's Transvaluation of Values," in *Theories of Ethics*. Lincoln, Nebraska: Johnsen Publishing Company, 1961, pp. 168–241.

OTHER SOURCES

Descartes, René. "Discourse on Method," in *Discourse on Method, Optics, Geometry and Meteorology*. Translated by Paul J. Olscamp. Indianapolis: The Bobbs-Merrill Company, Inc., 1965, pp. 3–62.

Diemer, Alwin. *Edmund Husserl: Versuch einer systematischen Darstellung seiner Phänomenologie*. Meisenheim am Glan: Verlag Anton Hain K.G., 1956.

Earle, William. "Introduction," in Karl Jaspers' *Reason and Existenz*. New York: The Noonday Press, 1960, pp. 9–15.

— "Ontological Autobiography," in *Phenomenology in America*. Edited by James M. Edie. Chicago: Quadrangle Books, Inc., 1967, pp. 69–79.

Eliade, Mircea. *The Sacred and the Profane*. Translated by Willard R. Trask. New York: Harper and Row Publishers, 1961.

Eliot, T. S. *Four Quartets*. New York: Harcourt, Brace and World, Inc., 1943.

Freud, Sigmund. "Thoughts for the Times on War and Death," in *On Creativity and the Unconscious: Papers on the Psychology of Art, Literature, Love, Religion*. Translated under the supervision of Joan Riviere. New York: Harper and Row Publishers, 1965, pp. 206–35.

— "On the History of the Psycho-analytic Movement," in *The Complete Psychological Works of Sigmund Freud*. Translated and edited by James Strachey London: The Hogarth Press, 1957, XIV, 7–66.

Gray, J. Glenn. "Splendor of the Simple," in *On Understanding Violence Philosophically and Other Essays*. New York: Harper and Row, 1970.

Heidegger, Martin. *Being and Time*. Translated by John Macquarrie and Edward Robinson. London: SCM Press Ltd., 1962.

— *Introduction to Metaphysics*. Translated by Ralph Manheim. New Haven: Yale University Press, 1959.

— "The Origin of the Work of Art," in *Philosophies of Art and Beauty: Selected Readings in Aesthetics from Plato to Heidegger*. Edited by Albert Hofstadter and Richard Kuhns. New York: Random House, Inc., 1964, pp. 649–701.

— "Plato's Doctrine of Truth," in *Philosophy in the Twentieth Century*. Translated by John Barlow. 4 vols.; New York: Random House, Inc., 1962, III, 251–70.

— *What Is Called Thinking?* Translated by Fred D. Wieck and J. Glenn Gray. New York: Harper and Row Publishers, 1968.

— "Zeit und Sein," in *L'Endurance de la pensée. Poursaluer Jean Beaufret.* Edited by René Char. Paris: Édition Plon, 1968.

Jaspers, Karl. *The Great Philosophers.* 3 vols. Edited by Hannah Arendt. Translated by Ralph Manheim. New York: Harcourt, Brace, and World, Inc., 1966.

— *Reason and Existenz.* Translated by William Earle. New York: The Noonday Press, 1960.

Jung, Carl Gustav. *Two Essays on Analytical Psychology.* Vol. VII of *The Collected Works of C. G. Jung.* Translated by R. F. C. Hull. New York: The Bollingen Foundation, Pantheon Books, Inc., 1953.

Kierkegaard, Søren. *Either/Or.* 2 vols. Translated by Walter Lowrie. Garden City: Doubleday and Company, Inc., 1959.

Kisiel, Theodore. "The Language of the Event: The Event of Language," in *Heidegger and the Path of Thinking.* Edited by John Sallis. Pittsburgh: Duquesne University Press, 1970.

Macomber, William B. *The Anatomy of Disillusion: Martin Heidegger's Notion of Truth.* Evanston: Northwestern University Press, 1967.

Moulton, James Hope. *Early Religious Poetry of Persia.* Cambridge: Cambridge University Press, 1911.

Newman, Ernest. *The Life of Richard Wagner.* 4 vols. New York: Alfred A. Knopf, 1946.

Reinhardt, Kurt. *The Existentialist Revolt.* New York: Frederick Ungar Publishing Company, 1960.

Richardson, William J. *Heidegger: Through Phenomenology to Thought.* Preface by Martin Heidegger. The Hague: Martinus Nijhoff, 1963.

Rostand, Maurice. "Introductory Quotation," in Wilfrid Desan's *The Tragic Finale: An Essay on the Philosophy of Jean-Paul Sartre.* New York: Harper and Brothers, 1960, p. 3.

Vaihinger, Hans. *The Philosophy of 'As if'.* Translated by C. K. Ogden. New York: Harcourt, Brace and Company, Inc., 1924.

Werkmeister, William Henry. *Man and His Values.* Lincoln, Nebraska: University of Nebraska Press, 1967.

INDEX OF NAMES